NEA:
Trojan Horse
in
American
Education

Books by Samuel L. Blumenfeld

For Ordering Information See Last Pages Of Book

NEA: TROJAN HORSE IN AMERICAN EDUCATION

Samuel L. Blumenfeld

THE PARADIGM COMPANY

Boise, Idaho

Grateful acknowledgment is made for permission to reprint excerpts from *The Transformation of the School* by Lawrence A. Cremin. Copyright © 1961 by Lawrence A. Cremin. Reprinted by permission of Alfred A. Knopf, Inc.

FIRST PRINTING   —   10,000, SEPTEMBER,1984
SECOND PRINTING —   10,000, DECEMBER, 1984
THIRD PRINTING   —   15,000, APRIL, 1985
FOURTH PRINTING —   20,000, JUNE, 1985
FIFTH PRINTING   —   5,000, OCTOBER, 1989
SIXTH PRINTING   —   5,000, NOVEMBER, 1990

For information:
The Paradigm Company
Box 45161
Boise, Idaho 83711
(208) 322-4440

Library of Congress Cataloging in Publication Data

Blumenfeld, Samuel L.
    NEA, Trojan horse in American education

    Includes Index
    1. National Education Association of the United
States—History.   2. National Education Association of the United
States—Political activity.   3. Public schools—United
States—History.   I. Title.   II. Title: N.E.A., Trojan horse in American
education.
L13.N49B58   1984   370'.6'073   84-16546

ISBN 0-941995-07-0

This book is dedicated to

PAT ROBERTSON

for giving America the hope of redemption

SUSAN STAUB

for fighting forced unionism in education

MARVA COLLINS

for demonstrating the true meaning of Teacher

REV. EVERETT SILEVEN

imprisoned in Nebraska

for defending religious freedom

Contents

Preface to the 1990 Printing

It is six years since the first publication of *NEA: Trojan Horse in American Education.* The book was written to make Americans aware of the growing political power of the organized teachers of America, a power that has stood in the way of true educational reform and made it difficult, if not impossible, for conservatives to gain control of Congress and the state legislatures. And while the book did inform many Americans of things they needed to know, particularly about the union's monopolistic tendencies and its humanist, radical-leftist social ideology, it had no visible impact on the fortunes of the NEA.

In fact, during the Reagan years the NEA made enormous gains in union membership, teacher salaries and benefits, and political influence. In 1982 the average public school teacher salary was $19,274. In 1990 it was up to $33,300. In 1982 per pupil expenditure was $2,726. In 1990 the national average was over $5,600. Total expenditure for public education rose from $134.5 billion in 1984 to $231 billion in 1990, an increase of $97 billion in six years!

As for political influence, the NEA's clout was demonstrated by the high win rate of NEA-backed candidates at all levels, except the Presidency. In short, never have America's public school teachers been as prosperous and politically powerful as they are today. And never has American public education been in worse shape.

"Nationwide, nearly a million students graduate each year unable to read and write, and 1 in 4 never graduates at all," reported *U.S. News & World Report* of May 18, 1987. And in October of that year, David Kearns, chairman of the Xerox Corporation, denounced the public schools as "a failed monopoly," producing workers "with a 50 percent defect rate." Businesses must hire workers "who can't read, write or count," he said—then spend $25 billion a year to train them. (*USA Today*, 10/27/89).

On May 3, 1989, Secretary of Education, Dr. Lauro Cavazos, released his department's sixth annual report card on American schools. He reported that the high-school dropout rate was rising, that the education reform movement "had lost its momentum," that test scores were still far below their 1960s peak, that we were still "wallowing in a tide of mediocrity," and that we were "spending more and getting less for our dollar."

"We're standing still," said Dr. Cavazos. "The situation scares me and I hope it scares you....We must do better or perish as the nation we know today." What a grim assessment by the nation's highest educational official! And the response of the NEA was as predictable as the seasons: "We need more money."

The startling contrast between a teachers' union enjoying unprecedented prosperity and success, and the public schools their members teach in, producing functional illiterates by the millions is enough to bewilder the average American. But anyone who has read this book knows why the education reform movement, which began in 1983 with the *A Nation at Risk* report, has been a resounding failure: the organized teachers are far more interested in political power than in education.

And there is no indication that the NEA intends to alter its priorities in the foreseeable future, thus making it highly unlikely that the teachers of America will be able to deliver the academic excellence the nation has been clamoring for.

If we have learned anything from the last five years, it is that the leaders of the organized education establishment refuse to learn anything from their critics, have nothing but disdain for the parents who place their children in their hands, show contempt for the taxpayers who support them, and exhibit a cold institutionalized sadism toward the children they supposedly teach.

The sorry truth is that for many children the public school has become a place where minds are destroyed and the future laid waste.

Public education cannot be reformed in the manner that parents and businessmen want it reformed because they cannot force the educators to want what they want. The educators want something else. They use convoluted jargon and professionalese to describe what they want, and because the public cannot understand them, the educators get what they want and the money to pay for it.

The purpose of this book is to help the reader understand what it is the educators want, why they want it, and how they have worked to get it. Once that is understood, the reader will know what to do about taxes and education. Only an informed public will be able to save America from its self-appointed "educators." Indeed, as Dr. Cavazos has warned, we must do better or perish as the nation we know.

S.L.B.
October 1990

Acknowledgments

This book could not have been written without the help of the many people who, over the months, sent the author a ton of material which greatly facilitated his research. Among them are Geraldine Rodgers of Lyndhurst, New Jersey; Henry P. Leighton of Cumberland, North Carolina; Kathryn Diehl of Lima, Ohio; Maureen Heaton of Santa Rosa, California; Jack Maguire of Belmont, Massachusetts; Barry Klein of Houston, Texas; Hughs Farmer of Henderson, Kentucky; Elizabeth Zutt of Evansville, Indiana; Bettina Rubicam, president of the Reading Reform Foundation; Susan Staub, director of Concerned Educators Against Forced Unionism; and Amy Bragg of the National Conservative Foundation. Their help was invaluable and is greatly appreciated.

Also helpful with their encouragement and support were Pat Robertson of the Christian Broadcasting Network; Ralph Smeed and Jonathan Smith of the Center for the Study of Market Alternatives in Caldwell, Idaho; Robert Sweet of the Office of Policy Development, The White House; and Maurice Clements, Joe Hautzinger, and C.L. "Butch" Otter. My major debt, however, is to Peter Watt, manager at Paradigm, who kept this project on track and dutifully guided it to its successful completion.

I am also grateful to Alan Hodge for his thoughtful reading of the first draft and to Richard Dingman for his helpful suggestions. There are others whom I cannot thank publicly, but they know that I am grateful for their help beyond measure.

And finally, lest the reader think otherwise, I wish to make it clear that the purpose of this book is not to disparage the thousands of dedicated teachers who must perform sometimes superhuman tasks. I shall always be grateful to those teachers in the public schools of New York, from 1931 to 1943, whose influences determined the course of my life: Miss Sullivan and Miss Murray, my first and second grade teachers, who taught me to read at P.S. 170; Miss Bender at P.S. 62 who kindled my love of classical music; Mrs. Strongin at Knowlton Junior High School, who stimulated my interest in French; and Mr. Greene at Stuyvesant High School, who encouraged me to become a writer. I learned from them how important teachers can be in the life of a student. I shall never forget them.

—Samuel L. Blumenfeld
Boston, May 31, 1984

Introduction: Why This Book?

Over the past decade Americans have become slowly aware that something is happening in their political life which has never happened before. Public school teachers, once loved and respected for their devotion to their profession, have become militantly politicized and are now the most active and powerful advocates of the political and social agendas of the radical left. The National Education Association, which represents 1.7 million teachers, has decided that its members are no longer satisfied with merely being public servants. They want to become political masters.

Sam Lambert, executive secretary of the NEA, predicted in 1967: "NEA will become a political power second to no other special interest group. . . . NEA will organize this profession from top to bottom into logical operational units that can move swiftly and effectively and with power unmatched by any other organized group in the nation."[1]

The NEA's obsession with power ought to alarm and concern all Americans, for the teachers have the organizational means to control the political destiny of this nation: 4,000 to 6,000 NEA members in each of the nation's 435 Congressional districts; 12,000 local NEA units permitting control of every school district in the country; and 50 powerful state associations that are quickly becoming the controlling power bloc in state politics.

What would Americans think if any other group of public employees—be they policemen, tax collectors, or the military—decided to organize themselves nationally in order to achieve political dominance? We'd consider it an unmitigated threat to our freedom whether the group was of the left or the right.

It happened in France. Everyone thought that Marxism was dying in France, that the intellectuals were discovering the virtues of capitalism, when all of a sudden the socialists took power. It was the teachers who did it. A reviewer of Katherine Auspitz's *The Radical Bourgeoisie* explained how it happened:

"The secret to understanding the Mitterrand government is to begin with the recognition that school teachers are the largest occupational bloc of socialist deputies. Mitterrand's wife is the daughter of teachers. Mitterrand supported measures to unify parochial and public schools of France before he was elected.

"It was just 100 years ago that laws were passed establishing free, compulsory, secular schooling for French children of both sexes. Universal schooling, more than nationalization or any other single measure, represents the policy response of left-center governments to the problem of breaking with corporate authority—whether of church, state or modern corporations. All else is secondary."[2]

In April 1984 the socialist government of France moved to take control of the nation's 10,000 private schools, most of them Catholic. The private schools had made the fatal mistake of accepting government subsidies. Now they're paying the price.

Is it happening here? In Nebraska the state now regulates church schools which accept no support from the government. The regulations were enacted by a legislature controlled by the Nebraska State Education Association. Resistance to these regulations has been met with school closures and the imprisonment of church ministers and parents in violation of their Constitutional rights.

Has the radical left decided that the best way to achieve power in America is through the organized political action of public school teachers? Are American teachers being trained and manipulated by the NEA to bring socialism to America? If they are, then the NEA is little more than the socialist Trojan horse within our political walls.

The purpose of this book is to make Americans aware that our public school teachers are no longer the benign, neutral servants of our communities. They are being used by clever political activists to bring the radical left to power. The radicals may not succeed in this election or the next, but their ability to control and influence the minds of our youth has given them the confidence that someday they will succeed.

The NEA's dominant position in the Democratic party has already made that party virtually a captive of the far left. And there are many liberal politicians who like what the teachers are doing because it serves their political ambitions.

Meanwhile, the public schools are falling apart and academic standards are at their lowest. At least a million students emerge from high school each year as functional illiterates thanks to the educational malpractice rampant in American public schools. The students may not be learning much, but they are getting heavy doses of propaganda from their politicized teachers.

It is an old truism that those who control the schools control the future. The NEA controls the schools and is determined to control our future. No group of so-called public servants should have that much power, the kind of power that can undermine the very foundation of American freedom. For the NEA not only wants monopoly power over education but power to make the taxpayer serve the NEA.

It is time for Americans to realize what the NEA is doing. The American taxpayer must decide if this is what he wants for those hard-earned dollars. We are being told by the NEA that Americans will have to pay higher taxes if they want better education. We challenge that assertion, for the record of the last twenty years is clear: never has more money been spent on public education and never have the results been worse. Doubling school expenditures would probably give us even worse results.

If we really want educational excellence in this country, why don't we rely on those schools that are already providing it *without* burdening the taxpayer: the private, non-governmental schools? Private schools succeed for one very simple reason: they go out of business if they don't. That's obviously not the case with government schools. The worse they do, the more money they get! It's a no-win situation for the American taxpayer. For the American child, it's academic disaster.

If America wants educational excellence, it will have to get rid of politicized teachers, educator lobbyists, educational malpractice and failure and a crushing tax burden. It can do this by taking a long hard look at centralized, bureaucratized public education and deciding that the country can do very well without it.

You the voter, you the taxpayer will have to decide if you want to go where the NEA wants to take you. If you don't, then you will have to act now, for the teachers are already very well organized and have managed to put in their pockets a large number of your elected representatives in Congress and your state legislatures. The NEA wants to control you because you pay their salaries. And the only way they can control you is to control the political-legislative machinery that will force you to do their bidding.

That's the challenge and the threat that the NEA poses today.

A note about the plan of this book. When I started writing, I realized that in order to tell the story of the NEA I would also have to tell the story of public education, for it is impossible to understand the one without the other. The NEA, in fact, is nothing more than a reflection of the ideological currents that have shaped our public schools from the beginning to the present. The result is a book larger in scope than its title suggests, one that will permit the reader to see clearly beyond the myths we have all been led to believe about our hallowed public schools.

The plain, unvarnished truth is that public education is a shoddy, fraudulent piece of goods sold to the public at an astronomical price. It's time the American consumer knew the extent of the fraud which is victimizing millions of children each year. A consumer can sue a private company for shoddy goods and misrepresentation. Indeed, Vietnam veterans have even sued the manufacturers of agent orange and won. But a student whose life has been ruined by educational malpractice in a public school has no recourse to the law. The educators are accountable to no one but themselves.

It's time the fraud was stopped. It's time for the American people to rise up and throw off a tyranny that can only get worse if nothing is done. There is a time to stand up and be counted. That time is now.

PART ONE

Delving Into the Past to Understand the Present

1. How We Got Public Education

The National Education Association was founded in 1857 by individuals who had worked hard to promote the public school movement in the United States. Thus, in order to understand the philosophical base of the NEA it is necessary to understand how and why Americans decided to put education in the hands of government.

Contrary to popular belief, the Constitution of the United States makes no mention of education. In fact, public education as we know it today did not begin to exist in this country until the 1840s. The idea of a state-owned and -controlled education system did not even originate in America. It was imported from Prussia, where an authoritarian monarchy used centralized, government-owned and -controlled schools and compulsory attendance for its own political and social purposes.

Why Americans decided to adopt the Prussian system instead of keeping education free of government interference is one of the most fascinating stories of our early history. It illustrates the power of educators when they get hold of an idea and tenaciously promote it—for better or for worse.

Believe it or not, the reasons why Americans turned over

education to the government, despite considerable opposition, had nothing to do with economics or academics. In fact, the historical evidence indicates that prior to the introduction of public education and compulsory school attendance, Americans were probably the most literate people in the world. It is even probable that the decline in literary taste in this country began with the growth and spread of public education with its watered down literary standards.

And certainly the problem was not economic, for the poor could always get an education if they wanted it. In some towns there were more charity and free schools, supported by private philanthropy and school funds, than poor pupils to go round. In Pennsylvania, for example, the state paid the tuition of any child whose parents could not afford to send him to a private school.

Despite the existence of slavery in the South, the first fifty years of the United States was as close to a libertarian society as has ever existed. For education, it meant complete freedom and diversity. There were no accrediting agencies, no regulatory boards, no state textbook selection committees, no teacher certification requirements. Parents had the freedom to choose whatever kind of school or education they wanted for their children. Home tutoring was common and there were private schools of every sort and size: church schools, academies for college preparation, seminaries, dames' schools for primary education, charity schools for the poor, tutors, and common schools.

The common schools were the original public schools and were to be found in New England and adjoining areas to which New Englanders had migrated. They were first created in the very early days of the Puritan commonwealth as a means of insuring the transference of the Calvinist Puritan religion from one generation to the next. The Reformation had replaced Papal authority with Biblical authority, and the latter required a high degree of Biblical literacy. In addition, the Puritan leaders had been impressed with the public schools created by Luther and the German princes as a means of inculcating religious doctrine and maintaining social order in the Protestant states. Also, Harvard College had been founded in 1636, with the aid of a government grant, as a seminary for educating the commonwealth's future leaders, and it was found that a system of lower feeder schools was necessary to help find and develop local talent and to prepare such youngsters for higher studies at Harvard and future careers as magistrates and clergymen.

Thus the common schools of New England, supported by the local communities came into existence. The law required the creation of common schools in the smaller towns plus grammar schools in the larger towns, where Latin and Greek were to be taught. Latin and Greek were required, as well as Hebrew in the colleges, because these were the original languages of the Bible and of theological literature. However, all of the schools were strictly local schools, financed locally, and controlled by local committees who set their own standards, chose their own teachers, selected their own textbooks. There was no central authority dictating how the schools were to be run, just as there was no central authority dictating how the local church was to be run. Ministers were elected by their parishoners, and both schoolmasters and clergymen were paid by the towns. But the school laws did not preclude the creation of private schools by private individuals.

Thus, the Bible commonwealth was a network of communities—small republics—linked by a common Calvinist ideology, with a Governor and representative legislature overseeing the whole, exercising a civil authority limited by the higher laws of God. The churches ran the towns, and church members ran the legislature. Thus, while the ideology was orthodox, the political form was quite democratic. The community conferred authority only on those it elected.

Was this a theocracy? Scholars have never quite been able to decide one way or another, for there was enough of a separation between the civil authority and the clergy to make the colony much less of a theocracy than it has gained a reputation for being. There was no religious hierarchy, and the Governor was purely a civil figure. But one thing we do know is that of all the English colonies, Massachusetts was the least tolerant of publicly expressed heretical teachings. The common schools, in fact, were created as religious instruments for teaching the catechism of the established orthodox Calvinist sect. The catechism was synonomous with literacy; and since a Bible commonwealth required a literate community for its preservation, religious and secular literacy went hand in hand. However, were it not for religious reasons, it is doubtful that the Massachusetts legislature would have enacted its school laws, for none of the other colonies enacted such laws. This did not mean that the people in the other colonies were less devout or had less religious content in their education. The other colonies, populated by a variety of sects, simply maintained a greater separation between church and civil authority.

The Bible commonwealth did not last long. The growth of the colony, the development of trade, the influx of other religious sects, the increased general prosperity and the emergence of religious liberalism tended to weaken the hold of the austere Puritan orthodoxy. Enforcement of the school laws grew lax, and private schools sprung up to teach the more practical commercial subjects. By 1720, for example, Boston had far more private schools than public ones, and by the close of the American Revolution, many towns had no common schools at all.

However, in drafting its new state constitution in 1780, Massachusetts decided to reinstate the old school laws, primarily to maintain the continuity of its educational institutions. John Adams framed the article which both confirmed the special legal status of Harvard and emphasized the commonwealth's continued interest in public education. The strongest support for the article came from the Harvard-Boston establishment which wanted to maintain the link between government and school. Harvard had been created with the help of a government grant and had been the recipient of many such grants over the years. In addition, members of the government had been on the Harvard Board of Overseers since 1642. The new constitution merely maintained the continuity of that relationship.

Connecticut, which had modeled its colonial laws on those of Massachusetts, followed suit and maintained the continuity of its common schools. New Hampshire did similarly. In New York State, the legislature in 1795 appropriated a large sum of money for the purpose of encouraging and maintaining schools in its cities and towns. The money was derived from the Land Ordinances passed by the Continental Congress in 1785 and 1787 which set aside a section of land in each Congressional township for the purpose of creating a state fund for education. Many towns took advantage of this school fund and established common schools. But these schools were only partially financed by the state fund. The counties were required to raise matching funds, and tuition was also paid by parents. In addition, wherever state governments showed an interest in promoting schools, private schools were also eligible for subsidies.

At the start of the new nation, Boston was the only American city to have a public school system, but it was hardly a system in today's sense of the word. Primary education was still left to the private dames' schools, and literacy was a requisite for entering the public grammar school at the age of seven. There was, of course, no compulsory attendance law. The pride of the system was the elitist Latin School which prepared students for Harvard. Most of the children who attended it came from the upper ranks of Boston society. Thus, the public school was not conceived in the post-Revolutionary period as a means of lifting the lowly masses from illiteracy. It was simply an institutional holdover from earlier days. At the same time private schools were flourishing, and most parents preferred them to the public ones.

For the next twenty years public and private schools coexisted in Massachusetts, with the more efficient private sector expanding slowly at the expense of the public sector. Outside of Boston, the growing middle and professional classes were abandoning the dilapidated public schools for the new private academies. Only in Boston did the public schools hold their own, and it was in Boston, in 1818, that the first move to expand the public sector at the expense of the private was made. This was a complete reversal of the general trend away from the public school generated by free-market forces. The promoters of the move wanted the city to establish a system of public primary schools and phase out the private dames' schools. The reasons given were that there were too many delinquent children roaming the streets and too many poor parents who could not afford to send their children to the dames' schools, thus depriving them of the literacy necessary for entering the public grammar schools.

To find out if this were indeed the case, the school committee appointed a subcommittee to make a city-wide survey of the schooling situation. The survey, the first of its kind ever to be made in this country, revealed some very interesting facts. About 2,360 pupils attended the eight public schools, but more than 4,000 pupils attended the 150 or so private schools. The survey also revealed that 283 children between the ages of four and seven, and 243 children over seven, attended no school at all.[3] In short, over 90 per cent of the city's children attended school, despite the fact that there were no compulsory attendance laws and the primary schools were private. And it was obvious that even if primary education were made public, some parents would still keep their children at home, since there were already in existence eight charity primary schools for poor children. The committee thus recommended against establishing public primary schools since the vast majority of parents were willing to pay for private instruction and the charity schools were available for those who could not afford to pay anything.

The promoters of the public primary schools waged a vigorous campaign in the press. The fact that over 90 per cent of the children were in school was to them no cause for rejoicing. They focussed on the several hundred who were not. "What are those children doing?" they asked. "Who has charge of them? Where do they live? Why are they not in school?" They warned that unless these children were rescued from neglect, they would surely become the criminals of tomorrow, and their cost to society would be far greater than the cost of public primary schools.

What is curious about this campaign is that the promoters never suggested that perhaps the city might subsidize the tuition of children whose parents could not afford to send them to the dames' schools, thereby saving the taxpayers the cost of an entire public primary system. What they insisted on was an expansion of the public school system to include the primary grades, and they would not settle for anything less. Their persistence paid off, and primary education was finally made public. Three of the campaign's most active promoters, in fact, were appointed members of the new primary school committee.

Who were the promoters of this campaign? Why did they wage it with such fervor and determination? And why did they not seek a solution to the problem through private philanthropy or public subsidy, solutions far less costly to the taxpayer? At a time when the public, through its market choices, clearly showed that it favored the private approach to education, why did the promoters insist on an expansion of the public system? To answer these questions, one must know something about what was going on in the minds of Americans during this period.

The first fifty years of American history are generally passed over lightly by scholars on their way from the Revolution to the Civil War. We know some general facts about the period: the framing of the Constitution, the Louisiana Purchase, the War of 1812, the Battle of New Orleans, the Jacksonian era. But we are seldom made aware of the incredible intellectual and philosophical changes that were taking place in that transition period from pre-industrial to industrial society. The emphasis in the history books is always on political and military events interlaced with material progress: the invention of the steamboat, the railroad, the cotton gin.

What also took place during that period was an intellectual event of great importance—probably the most important in American history: the takeover of Harvard by the Unitarians in 1805 and the expulsion of the Calvinists. That takeover not only made Harvard the citadel of religious and moral liberalism, but also the citadel of anti-Calvinism. Once the significance of that event is understood, the intellectual history of America suddenly begins to make much more sense, for no event has had a greater long-range influence on American intellectual, cultural, and political life than this one.

The issues at stake were fundamental: the nature of God and the nature of man. The liberals, brought up in the moral, benevolent atmosphere of a free, prosperous, ever-expanding society, could no longer accept the Calvinist world-view which placed the Bible at the center of spiritual and moral understanding. The liberals found the Calvinist doctrines of innate depravity, predestination, election, and reprobation particularly repugnant. Calvin's was a God-centered world-view in which a man's life was determined by his personal relationship to an all-powerful, objectively real God who had expressed His will in the Old and New Testaments. The Ten Commandments were the essence of God's law. They provided protection to life and property and codified commitment to God and family. They were the restraints that would save men from becoming the victims of their own innate depravity.

The Unitarians rejected all of this. They could not believe in the existence of an unfair, unjust God who elects a few and rejects others; a God who favors some and condemns the rest. Calvin was the first to admit that these doctrines seem unjust and repugnant but he answered that God has placed a limit on what man is permitted to know and that man therefore has no choice but to accept God's will as revealed in the Scriptures and by the cold facts of life. Those facts include the existence of evil, the sufferings of the innocent, the triumph of tyrants, the general difficulties of the human condition in a world ruled by an omnipotent God who, despite all of this, is still a benevolent God because he created man to begin with.

The Unitarians accepted the notion that God created man, but they also insisted that man was given the freedom to make of his life whatever he can. It is man himself who decides, through his life on earth, whether he goes to heaven or hell. He is not innately depraved. He is, in fact, rational and perfectible. As for the existence of evil, they believed that it was caused by ignorance, poverty, social injustice, and other environmental and social factors. Education, the Unitarians decided, is the only way to solve the problem of evil. Education would eliminate ignorance, which would eliminate poverty, which would eliminate social injustice, which would eliminate crime. They believed that moral progress is as attainable as material progress once the principles of improvement are discovered. In this scheme of things there was no place for a triune God or a divine Christ through whom salvation was attainable.

It was therefore only natural that the Unitarians would shift their practice of religion from the worship of a harmless, benevolent God of limited powers to the creation of institutions on earth to improve the character of man. The one institution that the Unitarians decided could be used to carry out this formidable task was the public school. Their first organized effort was the campaign in 1818 to create public primary schools in Boston.

Why only public schools and not private or charity schools? Because private schools were run and controlled by individuals who might have entirely different views concerning the nature of man. Besides, private owners were forced by economic reality to concentrate on teaching skills rather than forming character. As for the church schools, they were too sectarian, and the charity schools were usually run by Calvinists. Only the public schools, controlled in Boston by the affluent Unitarian establishment, could become that secular instrument of salvation.

But why did the first organized effort take place in 1818? Because, at around that time, a man in Scotland had proudly broadcast to the civilized world that he had discovered the basic principle of moral improvement. His name was Robert Owen, and we know of him today as the father of socialism. Owen was a self-made manufacturer who became a social messiah when he "discovered" what he considered to be the basic truth about human character: that a man's character is made for him by society through upbringing, education, and environment and not by himself as the religionists taught. Children in a cannibal society grow up to be adult cannibals. Children in a selfish, competitive society grow up to be selfish and competitive. No one was innately depraved or evil. An infant is a glob of plastic that can be molded to have whatever character society wishes him to have. Owen started publishing his ideas in 1813, and in 1816 to prove that he was right, established his famous Institution for the Formation of Character at New Lanark. Through a secular, scientific curriculum coupled with the notion that each pupil must strive to make his fellow pupils happy, Owen hoped to turn out little rational cooperative human beings, devoid of selfishness, supersition, and all of the other traits found in capitalist man.

All of these ideas were music to the ears of the Boston Unitarians who wanted confirmation that man is indeed perfectible through the process of education. But Owen had stressed that the earlier you start training the child the better chance you have to mold his character, which is why the Unitarians launched their campaign to create public primary schools. This was only the first step, for in 1816 Owen had published an essay outlining a plan for a *national* system of education in England whereby the character of a whole nation could be molded to the good of all. He wrote:

At present, there are not any individuals in the kingdom who have been trained to instruct the rising generation, as it is for the interest and happiness of all that it should be instructed. The training of those who are to form the future man becomes a consideration of the utmost magnitude: for, on due reflection, it will appear that instruction to the young must be, of necessity, the only foundation upon which the superstructure of society can be raised. Let this instruction continue to be left, as heretofore, to chance, and often to the most inefficient members of the community, and society must still experience the endless miseries which arise from such weak and puerile conduct. On the contrary, let the instruction of the young be well devised and well executed, and no subsequent proceedings in the state can be materially injurious. For it may truly be said to be a wonder-working power; one that merits the deepest attention of the legislature; with ease it may be used to train man into a daemon of mischief to himself and all around him, or into an agent of unlimited benevolence.[4]

Thus, socialism began as an educational movement to reform the character of man into "future man". Today we call him Soviet man. Leaving education "to chance" meant leaving it private, and that is why in 1818 the Unitarians insisted on creating public primary schools rather than subsidizing pupils to attend private ones. It was also the beginning of the organized movement that was to culminate in the creation of our compulsory public education system.

From the very beginning, the Unitarians and socialists were the prime movers and leaders of this long-range sustained effort. Between 1823 and 1825, James G. Carter, a Harvard Unitarian, published a series of essays deploring the general trend away from the common schools and advocating the expansion of public education and the creation of state-supported teachers' seminaries. Owen had stressed the need for such seminaries and in his book called them "the most powerful instrument for good that has ever yet been placed in the hands of man."[5] The Harvard-Unitarian elite gave Carter's proposals its strongest endorsement and widest circulation.

In 1825, Robert Owen came to America to establish his

communist colony at New Harmony, Indiana. The experiment received a great deal of newspaper publicity and attracted a large number of followers. It was called "an experiment in social reform through cooperation and rational education." But in less than two years it failed. The problem, Owen decided, was that people raised and educated under the old system were incapable of adapting themselves to the communist way of life no matter how much they professed to believe in it. Therefore, the Owenites decided that rational education would have to precede the creation of a socialist society, and they subsequently launched a strong campaign to promote a national system of secular education. Owen's son, Robert Dale Owen, and Frances Wright set up headquarters in New York, helped organize the Workingmen's Party as a front for Owenite ideas, published a radical weekly paper called *The Free Enquirer,* and lectured widely on socialism and national education. Their antireligious views turned so many people away from Owenism, however, that they were forced to adopt covert techniques to further their ends. One of the men attracted to their cause was Orestes Brownson, a writer and editor, whose remarkable religious odyssey took him from Calvinism to Universalism to Socialism to Unitarianism and finally to Catholicism. Years later, describing his short experience with the Owenites, Brownson wrote:

> But the more immediate work was to get our system of schools adopted. To this end it was proposed to organize the whole Union secretly, very much on the plan of the Carbonari of Europe, of whom at that time I knew nothing. The members of this secret society were to avail themselves of all the means in their power, each in his own locality, to form public opinion in favor of education by the state at the public expense, and to get such men elected to the legislatures as would be likely to favor our purposes. How far the secret organization extended, I do not know; but I do know that a considerable portion of the State of New York was organized, for I was myself one of the agents for organizing it.[6]

So now we know that as early as 1829, the socialists had adopted covert techniques to further their ends in the United

States, techniques which they continued to use for decades.

It was also in 1829 that Josiah Holbrook launched the Lyceum movement to organize the educators of America into a powerful lobby for public education. Was Holbrook a covert Owenite? Circumstantial evidence seems to indicate that he was. And if the socialists decided to further their cause by working through the instrument of public education, we can then understand why the system has had such a pro-socialist bias for as long as any of us can remember. Indeed, public education was to become the socialists' *primary* instrument for promoting socialism.

In promoting socialism one also promoted the state, for the secular state was to be the primary political instrument for exercising man's rational power. When Frances Wright, the Owenite feminist, lectured in the United States for a national system of education, she left no doubt that the state was to be the ultimate beneficiary of such a system. She said in 1829:

> That one measure, by which alone childhood may find sure protection; by which alone youth may be made wise, industrious, moral, and happy; by which alone the citizens of this land may be made, in very deed, *free and equal*. That measure—you know it. It is national, rational, republican education; free for all at the expense of all; conducted under the guardianship of the state, at the expense of the state, for the honor, the happiness, the virtue, the salvation of the state.[7]

But while Josiah Holbrook, with active help from the Unitarians, was organizing the educators through the Lyceum movement, and the Owenites were agitating for a national system of education, the American people were going in the opposite direction. The free market favored private education, and new private academies were springing up all over the country, particularly in Massachusetts where the town-supported common schools were being abandoned by the middle class.

Thus, had free-market forces been permitted to operate in the educational field without ideological opposition, the common schools would have either disappeared or been reduced to their most rudimentary function as dispensers of free elementary education to a dwindling constituency. In the long run, it would have been more economical for the towns to pay for the tuition of poor children to attend private schools, than to maintain free schools. So the problem was never one of economics; it was, from the very beginning, philosophical.

If both the socialists and the Unitarians embraced educational statism as the future way to human moral progress, it was for two reasons: first, they rejected the Biblical, Calvinist view of man; and second, they rejected the Biblical view of history. Man, as sinful and depraved, was replaced by Man who was rational, benevolent, and innately good. But the American form of limited government with its elaborate checks and balances had been created on the basis of the Calvinist distrust of human nature. The Calvinists didn't believe that power corrupts man, but that man corrupts power. Man is a sinner by nature and therefore cannot be trusted with power. Only a true fear of God, they believed, can hold sinful man in check.

As the orthodox faith waned in the nineteenth century and faith in rational man grew, Western culture began to accept a reverse philosophy of human nature. To explain why man does the evil things he does, they turned from theology to psychology. The first pseudo-scientific attempt to explain the origin of criminal behavior was Phrenology, and its teachings had considerable impact on the thinking of many 19th century educators, including Horace Mann.

As for the Biblical view of history, the Romantic movement projected a new heroic image of man as conquerer and innovator, and mankind was viewed in a universal sense as one big progressive family. Thus was born the myth of moral progress: the idea that man was getting morally better and better.

The prime modern promoter of this idea was the German philosopher Georg Friedrich Hegel (1770–1831) who formulated the dialectical process of human moral progress, a process liberated from the strictures of the Old and New Testaments. He replaced the objectively real God of the Bible with a subjective Pantheism in which man was revealed as the highest manifestation of God in the universe. Rational, heroic, perfectible man was thus elevated to godlike status, and his secular state was expected to dispense a justice and equality not to be found in the Scriptures. Liberated, unrestrained rational man would create, not unlimited evil as the Calvinists believed, but unlimited good.

It was only natural, therefore, that the Harvard-Unitarian elite would look toward Prussia for their statist models. And they found exactly what they were looking for in the Prussian state system of compulsory education, with its truant officers, graded classes, and uniform curriculum. That system had been set up in 1819, and Robert Owen claims in his autobiography that the Prussian system was built on his ideas. Of course, Luther had advocated public schools at the time of the Reformation. But the Prussian system was a model of centralized control, and it had the one feature that Owen considered indispensable for a successful state system: state training schools for teachers. It was acknowledged by the Prussians that you really could not control education until you controlled the teachers and their indoctrination. In other words, teachers were to be the front-line troops for statism.

Members of the Harvard-Unitarian elite had acquired a taste for German education while studying in Germany, but Americans had no interest in adopting such a system for themselves. In 1833, however, a French professor of philosophy, Victor Cousin, published a lengthy report on the Prussian system for his own government, which was subsequently translated into English and published in the United States. It was exactly what the public school movement needed, and it was distributed among American educators who began to arrive at a consensus that the Prussian system was the way to go.

The fact that Cousin had written the report added to its prestige, for Cousin was the main transmission belt of Hegelianism to the Harvard elite. His series of lectures on Hegel's history of philosophy was widely read among the Harvard Unitarians, many of whom became Transcendentalists.

Thus, by the time Horace Mann entered the scene in 1837 as the first Secretary of the newly created Massachusetts Board of Education, the groundwork had been thoroughly done by the Owenites, Unitarians, and Hegelians. Mann, a talented lawyer legislator, was chosen by the Harvard-Unitarian elite to bring educational statism to Massachusetts because he had demonstrated that when it came to legislation, he could give the liberals whatever they wanted. They had enormous confidence in him and he never disappointed them.

If any single person can claim credit for changing America's social, academic, and ultimately political direction from a libertarian to a statist one, the credit must go to Horace Mann, for it was Mann who was able to overcome the considerable opposition to statism, while others could not. The key to Mann's success was in his peculiar sense of mission, combined with his practical political experience as a legislator, and the strong financial, cultural, and social backing of the Harvard-Unitarian elite.

He hated Calvinism with a passion and fought Calvinist opposition with a ferocity that disturbed some, but delighted most, of his Unitarian backers. But he succeeded mainly because he knew how to divide the opposition. By the mid-1830s, even some Trinitarian Protestants were being swayed by German religious liberalism. Also, Protestant leaders like Calvin Stowe and Lyman Beecher, who were based in Ohio, saw in the Prussian educational system a model they could use in their own efforts to maintain the Protestant character of American culture in the face of massive Catholic immigration.

In any case, the backbone of the opposition to educational statism was made up primarily of orthodox Calvinists who feared the long-range antireligious effects of secular public education and favored the decentralized common-school system as it existed before the Board of Education came into being. One of them summed it up in these words in the *Christian Witness* in 1844:

> We do not need this central, all-absorbing power; it is anti-republican in all its bearings, well-adapted perhaps, to Prussia, and other European despotisms, but not wanted here.[8]

Despite considerable and continued opposition, all attempts to stop the growth of educational statism failed. Thus, from its very inception educational statism was the prime promoter of statism itself in America. To Mann, the symbol of the triumph of statism was in the creation of the first State normal school. The normal school was the state-financed and -controlled teachers' college. No sooner had Mann been appointed Secretary of the Board of Education by Gov. Edward Everett than he got to work setting up the first normal school in Lexington. It was done through the financial help of a prominent Unitarian industrialist, whose funds were matched by the state legislature. It was established in 1838 as an experiment. Opposition to the idea of state-controlled teacher training remained strong, until 1845 when the opposition was finally overcome.

In March 1845, the Massachusetts Legislature voted to appropriate $5,000 in matching funds to the $5,000 raised by Mann's Harvard-Unitarian friends to build two additional normal schools. In describing the dedication ceremony at one of the schools, Mann wrote this in the *Common School Journal* (October 1, 1846):

> What constituted the crowning circumstance of the whole was, that the Legislature, in making the grant, changed the title or designation of the schools. In all previous reports, laws, and resolves, they had been called "Normal Schools." But by the resolves for the erection of the new houses, it was provided that these schools should thereafter be known and designated as *State* Normal Schools,—the State thus giving to them a paternal name, as the sign of adoption, and the pledge of its affection.

To Mann, who believed the normal school to be "a new

instrumentality in the advancement of the race," the linking of state power to teacher education was indeed a crowning circumstance, creating what James G. Carter had described in 1825 as a powerful "engine to sway the public sentiment, the public morals, and the public religion, more powerful than any other in the possession of government."[9] Carter was perfectly right, for once a nation's teachers' colleges become the main vehicle through which the philosophy of statism is advanced, that philosophy will very soon infect every other aspect of society.

The simple truth that experience has taught us is that the most potent and significant expression of statism is a State educational system. Without it, statism is impossible. With it, the State can, and has, become everything.

2. In the Beginning

The NEA was founded in 1857 at a meeting in Philadelphia called by the presidents of ten state teachers associations. One of the organizers, Thomas W. Valentine, president of the New York Teachers Association, told the gathering:

> Twelve years ago, in the Empire State, the first state association of teachers in this country was formed. . . . Previous to this organization teachers everywhere were almost entirely unacquainted with each other. But what a mighty change a few years have wrought! Besides many minor organizations, there are now not less than twenty-three state teachers associations, each doing good work in its own sphere of labor, and today I trust we shall proceed to raise the capstone which shall bind all together in one solid, substantial structure.
> . . .
> What we want is an association that shall embrace all the teachers of our whole country, which shall hold its meeting at such central points as shall accommodate all sections and combine all interests. And we need this not merely to promote the interests of our own profession, but to gather up and arrange the educational statistics of our country, so that the people may know what is really being done for public education, and what yet remains to be done. I trust the time will come when our government will have its educational de-

partment just as it now has one for agriculture, for the interior, for the navy, etc.[1]

Thus, the teachers were setting out to do what local state control of public education made impossible: create the basis of a *national* system of education. While the educators held up as their ideal the Prussian system which was national and centralized, such centralization was impossible in this country. But by organizing themselves nationally, the teachers could at least gain some of the professional benefits of a national system. Thus it should come as no surprise that the call for a federal department of education was made at the very first organizational meeting. The Prussians had a Ministry of Education, so why shouldn't Americans have one as well?

Initially, the organization was called the National Teachers Association, and its stated aim was "to elevate the character and advance the interests of the profession of teaching, and to promote the cause of public education in the United States." Membership was limited to "any gentleman who is regularly occupied in teaching in a public or private elementary school, college, or university, or who is regularly employed as a private tutor, as the editor of an educational journal, or as a superintendent of schools." In 1866 membership was expanded to include women. (In 1984 membership was open "to all persons actively engaged in the profession of teaching or in other educational work or to persons interested in advancing the cause of public education who shall agree to subscribe to the goals and objectives of the Association.")

In 1870 the name of the organization was changed to National Educational Association and the doors of membership were thrown wide open to include "any person in any way connected with the work of education." This immediately enhanced the commercial benefits of the organization, for now book publishers, salesmen and suppliers could also join. The public schools had become an expanding national market. The annual meetings, with their commercial exhibits, enabled all of these people to make the necessary connections.

More importantly, the NEA became the forum in which all of the vital educational issues of the time were aired: public versus private education; secularism versus religion; the role of government in education; teacher training and philosophies of education; curriculum content; discipline; school financing—problems which are still with us today and just as insoluble now as they were then.

Many of these problems were caused by the government's very intrusion into education. The educators found themselves defending and promoting an institution that had to have a recognizable public mission to justify its claim on public funds. Even in the early days of public education, a consensus view justifying the new and developing system was never really achieved for one very simple reason: it could not satisfy the needs and values of all the citizens. In fact, it never has and never will.

The two major issues that faced educators in those early days were those of government schools versus private schools and religious versus secular education. The American people had to make choices in each of these issues. But the choices were never made all at once. They seemed to evolve in small incremental steps, always with the tacit and sometimes explicit understanding that if the people didn't like what they were getting, they could always go back to what they had before.

The argument in favor of private education was perhaps best expressed by Edward Hitchcock in 1845 when describing the virtues of the private academy:

> My chief objects are, to bring prominently before you the principle, that systems of education ought to be wisely suited to the character and condition of the people among whom they are introduced; and then to proceed to show that the system of American academies is well adapted to the character, habits and wants of this country. . . .
>
> The essential features of this [Academy] system are, first, that it affords an opportunity for youth of both sexes, from every class in the

community, to enjoy an elevated course of instruction, on almost every elementary branch of science or literature, to which they may choose to attend, and for a longer or shorter period, as they shall wish. Secondly, it enables those youths, who aim at the liberal professions, or a literary life, to pursue a prescribed course of classical studies, preparatory to an admission to higher seminaries.

Now I maintain, in the first place, that such a system is well suited to the character of the government in this country.

In most European countries, the education of the people is almost entirely under the control of the government, and is used as an engine of tremendous power for the support of the government; even in a country where the schools are so admirable as in Prussia. Excellent facilities for instruction are, indeed, provided in many of those schools. But the course of study is rigidly prescribed; and the youth who refuses to follow that course, will be sure to fail of receiving the patronage of the government; and to fail of this, is to fail of every lucrative and honorable, I had almost said useful, situation. Now this may be best for men living under arbitrary, or aristocratic forms of government. But in this country the government presumes that every parent is intelligent and judicious enough to judge what sort of an education it is best to give his children; and, therefore, it leaves the community to establish such seminaries as it pleases; extending to them only its protection and occasional pecuniary aid.[2]

Hitchcock not only understood the political implications of government-controlled schooling, but also the need for religion in education which the secular public school could not provide. He said:

. . . The true policy of every literary institution is, to secure the favor of God, by honoring Him, and it may be sure of all the prosperity that will be best for it. And confident am I, that those seminaries will be most prosperous, that are most decided and consistent in their efforts to promote the spiritual welfare of their pupils. Let the trustees and instructors boldly declare their desire and intention to make vigorous efforts for the conversion and salvation of their pupils. . . . The few among us who are decidedly hostile to religion, can, if they please, attempt to found literary institutions where religion is excluded.[3]

Others objected to the public schools because of the taxes required to support them. When an act establishing free schools throughout the state of New York was passed on March 26, 1849, a group of citizens petitioned the legislature to repeal it. "We consider said law," they wrote, "to be worse than the enactments of Great Britain, which caused the American Revolution, for they were enforced by a despotic foreign power, but this School Law is enforced upon us unjustly, by our neighbors, whom we heretofore considered and treated as friends. . . . We are alarmed at the rapid increase of taxation, and rely upon the wisdom of the Legislature for the arrest of its progress; and fondly indulge the hope that we shall not be compelled to endure the humiliating transition from the elevated position of Free Men, to the deplorable condition of free slaves."[4]

The law was not repealed, even though it did mean a substantial increase in taxes. Indeed, by 1885, one educator could write:

> The fundamental principle that "the property of the State must be taxed to educate the children of the State," now finds general acceptance in all parts of our Union. The sentiment that the "perpetuity of the republic requires intelligence and virtue in the masses," is very generally received. And since the free discussion of certain questions of common interest which have arisen since the war—especially the public interest occasioned by the problem of *seven* million ignorant colored people enfranchised by constitutional amendment—the problem of the education of the masses has assumed new and more vital interest. It has brought before the American people and before the American Congress the great question of national aid to education.[5]

By 1905, 22 percent of all public expenditures in the United States would be going to pay for public education.[6]

The founders of the NEA were firmly committed to the idea of government-owned and -controlled schools. Most of them had either taught in private academies or had actually owned academies that failed. They knew how difficult it was to run a private school and make ends meet. All of them eventually found their way into the growing public system, for the local governments went to the private schools to recruit their first superintendents and principals. The educators immediately recognized that the public system not only offered them financial security but the prestige and power of a government position. Relieved of the financial responsibility of running a school they were able to devote their energies to the more theoretical aspects of educational philosophy. Meanwhile, they attacked the private schools at every possible occasion.

At the Cincinnati convention of 1858, Zalman Richards, one of the founders of the new association, spoke scornfully of the great number of private schools that were founded upon nothing but "flaming circulars and pretentious advertisements" and housed in any kind of room or building "that would keep the children *in* and the world *out.*" The profession is degraded, he said, by the existence of such so-called schools.

Yet it was these small private schools, often conducted in the home of an educator-proprietor at no expense to the taxpayer, which turned out literate, well-behaved young citizens who went on to college or into commerce or the professions. The interesting rooms and houses of private schools would give way to the public school house, with its cold institutional architecture. The latter would soon take its place beside the town hall, firehouse, court house and prison as a state institution representing the state's business.

But if the public school systems in America fell far short of their Prussian models in centralized control, it was because America was still a very rural country with one-room schoolhouses predominating. In these small towns, the schools were run by homogeneous communities sharing the same religious beliefs.

But it was in the large cities and more populated areas, where many different religious sects or denominations resided, that the religious issue raised serious problems. Protestant educators and leaders saw the issue in terms of sectarian versus non-sectarian religious instruction. They assumed that *some* religious instruction was not only desirable but necessary in the public schools, but agreed that it ought not to include the doctrines of any particular sect or denomination. Atheist educators saw the issue in terms of religion versus secularism—the supernatural versus science—but few atheists were willing to define the issue publicly in such openly anti-religious terms. Yet, in their arguments against religious instruction, non-sectarian usually meant "secular." But America was still largely a religious country, and public education would have never gotten off the ground if religion were to be excluded from it entirely.

Orthodox Protestants were particularly wary of what non-sectarian secular education would do to the religious faith of American children. Liberal Protestants insisted that the public schools could inculcate the basic principles of Christianity without violating the doctrine of separation of church and state. Simple Bible reading would accomplish that. If the various sects could only agree on a set of basic Christian precepts that could be taught in the public schools, then all would be well.

But the orthodox disagreed. To them, non-sectarian education was indeed secular education. One of them wrote in May 1844:

> The idea of a religion to be *permitted* to be taught in our schools, in which all are at present agreed, is a mockery. There is really no such thing except it be what is termed natural religion. There is not a point in the *Christian* scheme, deemed important, and of a *doctrinal* character, that is not disputed, or disallowed by some. As to the "precepts," perhaps, there may be a pretty general agreement, and that this is one *great* branch of the Christian scheme we allow. But is this all—all that the sons of the Puritans are willing to have taught in their public schools?[7]

In July 1848, the General Association of Massachusetts, representing the Protestant denominations in the state, held a conference to discuss the issue. There was such deep disagreement between orthodox and liberals on the subject that the delegates decided to appoint a committee "to investigate the relations between the system of common school education and the religious interest of the young." On the basis of the committee's report, the Association would then decide what course to take.

The committee filed its report in 1849, and the liberal view prevailed. It said:

> The benefits of this system, in offering instruction to all, are so many and so great that its religious deficiences,—*especially since they can be otherwise supplied,* do not seem to be a sufficient reason for abandoning it, and adopting in place of it, a system of denominational parochial schools.
>
> If, however, we were to recommend any system to take its place, it would be that of private schools formed by the union of Evangelical Christians of different denominations in which all the fundamental doctrines of Christianity could be taught.
>
> It is however a great evil to withdraw from the established system of common schools, the interest and influence of the religious part of the community. On the whole, it seems to be the wisest course, at least for the present, to do all in our power to perfect so far as it can be done, not only its intellectual, but also its moral and religious character.
>
> *If after a full and faithful experiment, it should at last be seen that fidelity to the religious interests of our children forbids a further patronage of the system,* we can unite with the Evangelical Christians in the estabishment of private schools, in which more full doctrinal religious instruction may be possible.
>
> *But, until we are forced to this result, it seems to us desirable that the religious community do all in their power to give an opportunity for a full and fair experiment of the existing system, including not only the common schools, but also the Normal Schools and the Board of Education.*[8]

Thus, a compromise had been reached between orthodox and liberals. They would participate in the public education system on an experimental basis. They reserved the right to withdraw from it if the system turned out to be a danger to religious faith.

There was another reason why the Protestant religionists decided to join the secularists in promoting the public school movement. They shared a common concern with, if not fear of, the massive Catholic immigration to the United States during that period. In fact, the chairman of the General Association of Massachusetts was Edward Beecher, son of Rev. Lyman Beecher of the Lane Theological Seminary, Cincinnati, Ohio, who had written a book in 1835, entitled *A Plea for the West,* alerting Protestants to a "Popish" conspiracy to take over the Mississippi Valley. Lyman Beecher's associate, Calvin Stowe, was one of the many educators who traveled to Prussia and wrote a glowing report on the Prussian education system which he urged the people of Ohio to emulate in order to stem the Roman tide. He argued that Protestants had to put aside sectarian differences and unite to defend Protestant republican America against the "Romish designs."

Catholics, too, had to make a choice about the common schools. Should they attend them or not? Painfully aware of the growing nativist prejudice against Catholics, they tried to get Catholic teachers to teach Catholic children in common schools. But the Protestant and secular authorities would not agree to this injection of sectarianism in the system. The Catholics then tried to get public funding for their own schools since they too paid taxes. But the secularists argued that if Catholic schools were publicly funded, then all sectarian schools would want the same funding. Such a policy would negate the entire purpose of the free non-sectarian common school which all children could attend and which the anti-religionists wanted.

The Catholic hierarchy finally decided that it had no choice but to create a parochial school system of its own if Catholics were to preserve the faith of Catholic children. One Catholic spokesman expressed his views of the common schools quite candidly in the late 1850s:

> So far as Catholics are concerned, the system of Common Schools in this country is a monstrous engine of injustice and tyranny. Practically, it operates a gigantic scheme for proselytism. By numerous

secret appliances, and even sometimes by open or imperfectly disguised machinery, the faith of our children is gradually undermined, and they are trained up to be ashamed of, and to abandon the religion of their fathers. It was bad enough, if this was all done with the money of others; but when it is accomplished, at least in part, *by our own money,* it is really atrocious. It is not to be concealed or denied, that the so-called literature of this country, the taste for which is fostered by our Common Schools, and which is constantly brought to bear on the training of our children, is not of a character to form their tender minds to wholesome moral principles, much less to solid Christian piety. In general, so far as it professes to be *religious,* it is anti-Catholic, and so far as it is secular, it is pagan.[9]

During that period there were anti-Catholic riots in Philadelphia, New York and Boston, instigated by a growing nativist paranoia. But Catholics remained steadfast in their convictions. Bishop John Hughes of New York, ever outspoken in defense of Catholic rights, even goaded the nativists when in 1850 he sermonized:

> Protestantism pretends to have discovered a great secret. Protestantism startles our Eastern borders occasionally on the intention of the Pope with regard to the Valley of the Mississippi, and dreams he has made a wonderful discovery. Not at all. Everyone should know it. Everybody should know that we have for our mission to convert the world, including the inhabitants of the United States, the people of the cities, the people of the country, the officers of the Navy and the Marines, commanders of the Army, and Legislatures, and Senate, the Cabinet, the President and all.[10]

Such language only drove more Protestants into the public schools in order to create a united front against the Catholics. Rev. Edward Beecher's book, *The Papal Conspiracy Exposed,* published in 1855, convinced many Protestant evangelicals to throw in their lot with the secularists even though they shared the Catholics' fear of secularism. They undoubtedly agreed with what Bishop Hughes told New York City officials in 1840:

> To make an infidel what is it necessary to do? Cage him up in a room, give him a secular education from the age of five years to

twenty-one, and I ask you what he will come out, if not an infidel? . . .
Now I ask you whether it was the intention of the Legislature of New
York, or of the people of the State, that the public schools should be
made precisely such as the infidels want? . . . They say their instruction is not sectarianism; but it is; and of what kind? The sectarianism
of infidelity in its every feature.[11]

Orthodox Protestants were indeed faced with the same
problem facing the Catholics: should they form sectarian
parochial school systems of their own, or join the secularists
and risk the loss of religious faith among their children? The
Lutherans already had a parochial system of their own, and
the Episcopalians and Presbyterians endeavored to create
their own school systems. But by 1870, support for the Protestant parochial schools was all but gone. Protestant denominations continued to support individual private schools and colleges, but no parochial system of any Protestant denomination survived beyond 1870, except the Lutheran system
of the Missouri Synod. One would have to wait a hundred years before Protestants in any large numbers would become sufficiently alarmed by secularism to assert a renewed
responsibility to educate their own children in church
schools.

It should be noted that the academic world of America
during the period of the consolidation of public education was
dominated by Harvard University, the seat of Unitarianism
and religious liberalism. It waged a ceaseless campaign to
promote a secular view of the world.

Members of the NEA represented those in the education
field most dedicated to the growth and development of public
education. The atheists, socialists, Unitarians, and Hegelians
among them could support secular public schooling without
reservations. Protestant believers had to give up all sectarian
considerations in order to participate. They were required to
compromise, whereas the others were not. Also the Catholic
issue had settled the matter of public funding: only the secular
public schools would be the beneficiaries of public funds, making secularism the only educational philosophy financed by

government. This would give secularism an enormous advantage over every other "ism" in our society.

A truly neutral government would have agreed to fund *all* schools, religious or otherwise. But by insisting that only *one* kind of school have exclusive right to public funds, the American people had inadvertantly created an official religion: secularism—which, for all practical purposes, is another definition of atheism.

3. Consolidation of the System

It stands to reason that those who rose highest in the public school establishment and the NEA were those most strongly committed to secularism and statism—for these were the two conceptual pillars on which the system was being built.

Secularism required on the part of the religionists giving up the notion that true education is impossible without religion. It also required accepting the notion that secularism is spiritually neutral. Having Sunday School to fall back on was of some consolation to the Protestants but not the Catholics. Statism required a surrender of parental rights and freedoms in favor of the supposed greater rights of the community or state.

The educators found plenty of philosophical backing for both secularism and statism and these arguments were voiced at many NEA conventions. They had to be voiced because the public, never happy over ever-increasing taxes, had to be constantly reassured that public education was not only necessary for our civilization but indispensable to the survival of the country.

The philosophy the secular educators fell back on to justify the existence and constant expansion of public education was

Hegelianism, the same philosophy on which the Prussian education system was based. This was a philosophy developed by Georg Friedrich Hegel (1770–1831) in Germany during the early part of the 19th century. Today, writers tend to belabor Hegel's complexity, and there are probably as many interpretations of Hegel as there are interpreters. But whatever his overall complexity may be, his basic ideas were simple enough to be fully understood by those who intended to restructure the world according to their meaning.

Hegel denied that God is a personality or entity apart from the universe he created—such as Jehovah of the Bible or Jesus Christ who was his divine presence on earth—a God with whom one could form a covenant. To Hegel that was all mythology. His view was that God is everything that exists, all inclusive, and that everything in the universe is a part of God. This concept is known as "pantheism."

Hegel said that the Universe is nothing more than God's mind, or spirit, or energy, in the process of achieving its own perfection or self-realization. The process, as human beings saw it and lived it, was history, and the dynamic method whereby perfection was being achieved is the dialectic. The dialectic is an evolutionary process in which the present state of things, with all of its inner contradictions, is known as the "thesis" which is then challenged by an "antithesis" which then, after a prolonged struggle between the two, emerges as a "synthesis." This synthesis then becomes the new "thesis" which in turn is challenged by the inevitable antithesis which, after the necessary struggle, becomes the new synthesis. The process is supposed to go on ad infinitum until perfection or self-realization is reached. Thus, Hegel saw history as an evolutionary process of dialectical idealism heading toward perfection.

To Hegel, man's mind is a microcosm of the divine mind. Nature, or the material world, is the outer form of this divine spirit. Man, as part of nature, is made in the image of God, and his mind is the highest manifestation of the God spirit in nature, for, as one American educator put it, man "*is* Divinity awaking out of the sleep of infinitely self-expanded being. And as the expansion is infinite, so the concentration of Return is infinite, assuring to the individual soul an infinite destiny, consisting of endless progress in self-realization, one essential phase of which must be an ever-deepening consciousness of its own Godlikeness."[1]

This was heady stuff for the Harvard intellectuals whose Puritan ancestors believed in the depraved, fallen nature of man and his need for salvation through Christ. They preferred Hegel's vision of a pantheist universe, in which God was reduced to a state of harmless energy, and Man elevated to the position of God. It was a wonderfully sinless universe in which mankind was free to create heaven on earth. Christ was indeed divine, but only in the sense that all men are divine. If Christianity was to be practiced in harmony with Hegelianism, it would not be a covenant religion with salvation through grace (orthodoxy), but a philosophical religion preaching ethics and good works (liberalism).

But then along came Karl Marx and the materialists who said that the dialectical conflict was indeed the historical process whereby the world was evolving but that the divine energy idea was a lot of bunk. Soulless matter in motion was all there was, and Man was just another form of matter. The struggle between capitalism and socialism, between the proletariat and the bourgeoisie, was the dialectical struggle taking place during this phase of human history. Communist revolutionaries were capable of speeding up the process by taking an active part in intensifying the dialectical conflict between the classes. It was Marx's dialectical materialism which gave the atheist revolutionaries the philosophical base to justify their inhuman behavior.

How did Hegel's philosophy elevate the status of the state? It was quite simple. If in a pantheist universe there was no objectively real God handing down His law to His creatures, then the only law that could exist is man's law. In fact, in a pantheist universe, man's law becomes indistinguishable from God's law, for man's mind is supposedly the highest manifestation of the universal divine spirit. Indeed, in such a universe one can go further and assert that man's law *is* God's law, and that his State *is* supreme for there is no other law above it.

This doctrine had profoundly dangerous implications for America. The American form of government had been created by Calvinists and other Christians who believed that God's law was superior to man's law, and that the state, or government, is "instituted among Men, driving their just Powers from the Consent of the Governed" for the purpose of securing men's inherent, God-given rights and protecting them from tyrants who would deprive them of these rights. This necessitated a government of limited powers, limited by divine laws higher than its own. On the other hand, the Hegelians, by asserting that there was no law but man's law, had elevated the State to a virtual divine status.

Hegelianism began to infect American intellectuals in the 1830s. Calvinists were particularly alarmed at its spread among Harvard's Unitarian elite. The deification of man was seen as the most ominous sign of the new philosophy. The *Princeton Review* wrote in 1840:

> The most offensive aspect of this whole system is, that in deifying men, it deifies the worst passions of our nature. "This," says a writer in Hengstenberg's Journal, "is the true, positive blasphemy of God,—this veiled blasphemy,—this diabolism of the deceitful angel of light,—this speaking of reckless words, with which the man of sin sets himself in the temple of God, showing himself that he is God. The atheist cannot blaspheme with such power as this; his blasphemy is negative; he simply says, There is no God. It is only out of Pantheism that a blasphemy can proceed, so wild, of such inspired mockery, so devoutly godless, so desperate in its love of the world; a blasphemy at once so seductive, and so offensive, that it may well call for the destruction of the world."

In terms of education, however, Hegelianism seemed far less radical and dangerous than its theology. Indeed it was quite conservative, for the Hegelians placed great emphasis on the development of the mind. Man's mind is what distinguished him from the animals and made him the highest manifestation of the universal divine spirit in nature. Therefore, it was the duty of a Hegelian to create the kind of state-controlled secular educational system that emphasized man's intellectual development.

Ironically, after 1880 some of the sharpest criticism of progressive child-centered education came from Hegelian educators, one of whom wrote:

> Hegel is in full accord with what in one or another form is the world-old doctrine that, as the child of nature, man is evil; that is, that his immediate inclinations pertain to his animal nature, and that only through training and discipline can he be brought into the state of positive moral life. . . .
>
> . . . Hegel should have little patience with the sentimental sympathy for mere childhood as such and which would at all cost please the child—eliminating law by substituting the child's caprice in place of law, and thus encouraging a mere self-seeking interest on the part of the child, which interest Hegel pronounces "the root of all evil." On the contrary, the child "must learn to obey precisely because his will is not yet rational" or matured as will. . . .
>
> The child, instead of being humored and excused in respect to his irregularities, must be brought to prize order and punctuality. . . . This is to be accomplished through the steady pressure of a wise, consistent, albeit kindly, *authority*. To endeavor always to *persuade* the child that the thing required of him is something that will prove pleasing to him, is to pervert his mind and confirm him in the belief that he ought to do nothing except what will give him pleasure in the doing.[2]

The most prominent Hegelian educator in America was William Torrey Harris who became president of the NEA in 1875 and was appointed United States Commissioner of Education in 1889 by President Harrison. Born in Connecticut in 1835, Harris was educated at private academies and graduated from Yale in 1857. It was at Yale that A. Bronson Alcott, a Transcendentalist, got Harris interested in philosophy. In 1858 Harris began his career in the public schools of

St. Louis, Missouri, first as assistant teacher, then teacher, principal, assistant superintendent, and finally superintendent. In the 1860s he became an enthusiastic believer in Hegel's philosophy and founded the Philosophical Society of St. Louis and the *Journal of Speculative Philosophy*. In 1873 he became president of the National Association of School Superintendents. He was also a life director of the NEA and spoke more often—145 times—at NEA conventions than any other educator.

In 1880 he resigned his position in St. Louis and settled in Concord, Massachusetts, as a member of the School of Philosophy. He was U.S. Commissioner of Education from 1889 to 1906. As commissioner he set the standards of public education according to Hegel's philosophy. Punctuality, discipline, grammar, study of the classics—all the trappings of so-called "traditional" education—were emphasized. Much of this traditional curriculum was agreeable to religionists, but its results were not what they expected. To a fundamental Christian, education that fosters secular intellectual development encourages intellectual pride and arrogance and the belief that man can be as God—the sin of pride. But within a religious context, intellectual development can lead to a greater understanding of God's sovereignty and a reverence for His creation.

The statist agenda of the public educators was well aired at annual NEA conventions. In 1865, Samuel S. Greene of Rhode Island called for a National System of Education. In 1866, Zalmon Richards reiterated the need for a U.S. Department of Education. In 1869, Charles Brooks, Unitarian minister from Massachusetts and a tireless advocate of the Prussian system, called for a National System of Free Schools. In 1873 and '74, calls for a National University—a sort of intellectual West Point—came from William T. Harris, Harvard president Charles W. Eliot, and Andrew D. White. Speeches advocating National Aid to Public Education of some kind or another could be heard at virtually every NEA convention from 1869 onward. The statist philosophy was promoted in such speeches as "The Duties of an American State in Respect to Higher Education" (1866), "Education and the Building of the State" (1881), "The State and School; the Foundation Principle of Education by the State" (1882), "Supervision of Private Schools by the State or Municipal Authorities" (1893), "Democracy and Education" (1898), "The Duty of the State in Education" (1899), etc. The educators were far ahead of the general public in their advocacy of government-owned and -controlled schooling for the benefit, not of the individual, but of the state.

Meanwhile, the state system continued to grow in two directions—downward to include more younger children and upward to include older children. In 1873 there were 42 public kindergartens in the U.S. By 1902 there were 3,244. In 1860 there were only 69 public high schools in the U.S. By 1900 about 700,000 young Americans were attending public high schools. Many private academies, unable to compete with these free schools, disappeared.

Statist arguments were used to expand the public system to include high schools. At the St. Louis NEA meeting in 1871, Newton Bateman, the Illinois state superintendent of public instruction, used these remarkable words to justify the state's interest in public high schools:

> The amount of latent and dormant power; of wealth-discovering and wealth-producing energy; of beauty-loving and beauty-inspiring taste and skill, that lie concealed and slumbering in the brains and hearts and hands of the keen, shrewd, capable, but untutored millions of our youth, is beyond computation. Now over all this unreclaimed but magnificent intellectual and moral territory, over all of these minds and souls and bodies, with their untold possibilities of good, the State has, in my opinion, a sort of *right of eminent domain* and not only may, but should exercise it in the interest of her own prosperity and dignity.[3]

What Bateman was saying, in effect, is that the State may compel any of its citizens' children to submit to training by the

State for the benefit of the State. He was echoing those German philosophers who believed that "the happiness of the individual should be included in and made subservient to the general good."[4] Such collectivist philosophy was in total contradiction to the principles of individual freedom on which this nation had been founded. The American form of government was created to protect individual rights, not abrogate them. Yet, apparently public educators were more than willing to abandon these principles in order to justify the expansion of a system of public education in which they had strong economic and professional interests.

In 1906 the NEA reached its fiftieth birthday. To celebrate the occasion, it published a volume of anniversary papers. One of the distinguished educators invited to contribute to the volume was Friedrich Paulsen of the University of Berlin, whose paper was entitled "The Past and the Future of German Education." The Prussian system had served as the ideal model for American public educators, and they were interested in how the German system was evolving. Paulsen wrote:

> In looking back over the entire field, we observe that two general principles stand out quite prominently: on one hand, the constant tendency to secularize institutions of learning and to place them under the management of the state, and on the other hand, the continuous dissemination of systematic school training over ever-widening circles of the community, or, if I may use the term the "democratization" of education.
>
> The first of these tendencies, which we might call progressive declericalization, manifests itself first of all in external secularization, that is, the passing of the control of education from the church to the state. . . . The cause of this movement evidently lies in the general deterioration of the church, and in the advancement of the state as the ruling power in modern life. . . .
>
> The Universities were the first to discard the old system, the process taking place definitely and generally during the eighteenth century; prior to that time, at least the faculty of philosophy,

in addition to the theological faculty, was effectively controlled by the ecclesiastical system of instruction. At the present day, even theology has become a science that measures truth by means of immanent standards, at least that is the case in the evangelical church. . . .

The state will not surrender the right to regulate education after having once attained this right. . . . Besides, we cannot deny that education is too intimately associated with the enlarged purposes and tasks of the state for the latter to countenance a return from the new political to the old ecclesiastical order. Every modern civilized nation conceives as its mission the preservation and elevation of its people. From the political and economic, the intellectual and moral standpoints, indeed, a nation is nothing more than the organization of the people with this end in view. . . .

It is safe to say that the recent successes of the German people have done much to convince other nations how important a national system of education and training is for the entire population, for the efficient self-development of the people from the military and economic standpoints as well.[5]

Little did Professor Paulsen know that the whole Hegelian scheme of secular nation-states in Europe, supposedly dedicated to the "preservation and elevation" of their peoples, would in eight short years explode into the bloodiest war until then in history, resulting in the deaths of millions. And nineteen years later, it would produce the monstrous regime of Adolf Hitler with its pagan symbolism, demented racism, and unprecedented barbarism. We now know that it was the Hegelian professors and scientists in German universities who prepared the way to paganism. Indeed, the critics of 1840 were chillingly prophetic when they warned that Hegelianism was "so devoutly godless . . . that it may call for the destruction of the world."

4. The Impact of Evolution

In its early years the National Educational Association was little more than a forum for the men who were shaping and running America's growing public school systems. The association itself was operated out of the home of its unpaid secretary who did all the letter writing and arranged the yearly gatherings. In fact, it wasn't until 1893 that the NEA elected its first paid secretary. He was Irwin Shepard, president of the Normal School at Winona, Minnesota. Shepard resigned his Normal School presidency and set up NEA headquarters in his home in Winona where he ran the affairs of the association until 1912 at an annual salary of $4,000.

At the first organizational meeting in 1857, the attendees elected a president, twelve vice presidents representing twelve different states, a secretary, treasurer and two counselors, all of whom became the board of directors. From then on, a relatively small group of activists, usually state superintendents, played muscial chairs as officers of the association.

Membership did not reach over 400 until 1884, when then president, Thomas W. Bicknell, launched a vigorous publicity campaign to get teachers and superintendents to attend the upcoming NEA convention at Madison, Wisconsin. Over 2,400 people attended, making it the largest NEA meeting since the association's inception. But membership fell the following year to 625. After 1886, however, membership remained over the 1,000 mark, fluctuating from year to year. In 1887 it was 9,115; in 1896 it was down to 1,579. After that, the NEA continued to grow, albeit slowly. In 1918 membership reached the 10,000 mark. Four years later, in 1922, the number of members had increased ten-fold to 118,032. In 1931 membership reached a new high of 220,149 only to decline during the Depression to a low of 165,448 in 1936. It wasn't until 1943 that the NEA regained the membership it had lost during the economic slump. By 1945 it was up to 331,605. In 1953 it reached the half-million mark, and in 1956, the one hundredth anniversary of the NEA, membership stood at its highest, 659,190.

The changing membership reflected the association's changing functions. As a forum, the association was of small benefit to the classroom teacher. Its major economic benefit was to superintendents, principals, publishers and school suppliers. In 1906, for example, 48 publishing representatives, including the presidents of Silver Burdett, D. Appleton & Company, and Funk & Wagnalls, were listed as members in New York state. Representatives from Universal Publishing, D. C. Heath, American Book Company, Milton Bradley, Prang, Longmans Green, Ginn & Company were also listed.

In 1906 the association was incorporated by an act of Congress as the National Education Association. In 1917 it decided to locate its headquarters in Washington, D.C. where it could begin to exert a more direct influence on the lawmakers of America. By then it had become a much more powerful force than merely a forum. Much of that was due to the profound transformations taking place within the profession.

However, before examining these transformations, it is useful to know something about how the NEA conducted its business. Because NEA membership was open to virtually everyone connected with education, it drew many people with different interests in the profession. And so it was decided in 1870 to create within the NEA different departments that would serve as forums for different interest groups. Each department would have its own president, vice president and secretary, but all would be under the NEA umbrella.

What it meant in actuality was the absorption of several already existing organizations into the NEA as departments and the creation of two entirely new ones. Thus, the American Normal School Association, founded in 1858, became the NEA's Department of Normal Schools, and the National Association of School Superintendents, founded in 1865, became the Department of School Superintendence. The two entirely new entities were the Department of Elementary Education for primary teachers and the Department of Higher Education for the college biggies. As President Hagar put it at the close of the 1870 convention:

> We shall thus gather all classes of educators from the lowest to the highest, colaborers in one broad field, and that field our country.

New departments were added as the need arose. In 1875, a Department of Industrial Education was created which was renamed the Department of Manual Training in 1899. Then came departments for Art Education (1883), Kindergarten Instruction (1884), Music Instruction (1884), Secondary Education (1886), Business Education (1892), and Child-Study (1894). The latter department would spearhead the Progressive Movement. Additional departments were created for Physical Education (1895), Natural Science Instruction (1895), School Administration (1895), Libraries (1896), Education of the Deaf, Blind and Feebleminded (1897) which in 1902 became known as Special Education; Indian Education (1899), and Technical Education (1905). In all, by 1905 a total of 18 departments had been created, plus a very special entity called the National Council of Education.

In 1879, Thomas W. Bicknell, founder of the *National Journal of Education,* called for the creation of a special body of top educational leaders and experts within the NEA to "discuss questions involving the principles and philosophy of education, and sustaining an advisory relation to state and national systems of education." A committee was formed to prepare a plan for such an organization. What emerged in 1880 was the National Council of Education, a sort of exclusive body of top leaders who were in key positions of power and influence within the educational establishment.

Some of the better known educators involved as members, speakers or honorary members were W. T. Harris, John Dewey, Nicholas Murray Butler, G. Stanley Hall, Josiah Royce, Charles W. Eliot, and James Earl Russell. It was in the forum of the National Council where the struggle between Hegelian and Progressive views began to take shape. The proceedings of the meetings reveal the ideas that were setting the stage for the profound changes that would take place within American education from the 1890s onward.

Actually, the struggle was between a new faith in science and a waning faith in Christianity and Hegelianism. An absolute faith in science became the driving force behind the progressives. To them the Bible and its pessimistic view of man's nature was folklore, and Hegel's universal mind-spirit was unprovable philosophical speculation. Science, on the other hand, relied on empirical evidence only—what could be seen, touched, and measured. Subject man to scientific investigation, and the laboratory would reveal the secrets of human nature and enable educators to create the kinds of schools and curricula which would produce, if not perfect men, at least the kinds of men and women the educators considered desirable.

The most important idea that would influence the educators was that of evolution—the notion that man, through a process of natural selection, had evolved to his present state from a common animal ancestry. Evolution was as sharp a break with the Biblical view of creation as anyone could make, and it was quickly picked up by those anxious to disprove the validity of orthodox religion. Evolution also shifted interest away from Hegel. Hegel had dealt with moral and social evolution by way of the dialectic which was somehow connected with that evolving universal world spirit. To Hegel, man's mind was directly linked to the great infinite mind and was a microcosm of it. But according to Darwin, a naturalist, man was linked downward to the lower animals and shared his ancestry with the apes. There was no mystical pantheistic spirit involved in the physical process of evolution. It was all "matter in motion," and it fit in very well with the dialectical materialism of the atheist Marxists who were now able to link man's physical evolution with his social evolution. And it was all, according to them, an inevitable historical process.

Darwin's book, *Origin of Species,* was published in 1859. But its influence on American educators was not felt until the 1880s when, through laboratory work in German universities, the field of psychology caught up with those of physiology and biology.

For years, German influence on American educators was quite strong. It had started in the early 1800s when the Harvard Unitarians sent their most promising young professors not to Oxford or Cambridge but to Gottingen and Berlin to sop up German religious liberalism and scholarship. Then, Hegel's transcendental philosophy intoxicated the New England intellectuals, and the much-vaunted Prussian school system became the model that Horace Mann, Calvin Stowe, and others flocked to inspect, write about, and reconstruct in America. The state of Michigan adopted the Prussian plan lock, stock and barrel, creating at its head the University of Michigan.

By the mid-1800s the cultural and intellectual traffic between the United States and Germany was quite intense. In the 1880s more than 2,000 Americans were enrolled in German universities. By the end of the century two generations of American students came home from Europe believing in German scientific solutions to American problems.

The most prominent American scholar to study in Germany was William James. While still a medical student at Harvard, James visited the University of Berlin in 1867 where he attended lectures by Helmholz on physiology. Helmholz and his assistant, Wilhelm Wundt, were applying scientific methods to the study of the nervous systems of frogs, dogs, and other animals in their laboratory through vivisection. Since it was generally accepted that man and the lower animals had a common ancestry, such study was a prelude to the scientific study of man himself.

The following year another young American traveled to Europe to soak up German science and philosophy. He was G. Stanley Hall who spent 1868–69 at the University of Berlin studying theology and physiology. While James had come from a sophisticated, religiously liberal family and could take German philosophy in his stride, Hall, a product of an orthodox New England farm family, totally succumbed to German influences.

"Germany almost remade me," he later wrote. "I came home feeling that I had also attained maturity in my religious consciousness, where most suffer such dwarfing arrest. I had felt the charm of pantheism, which has inspired and exerted so much of its subtle influence, especially through the medium of poetry, in those whose creed abhors it; of agnosticism, more or less common but so strangled by religious affirmations; of even materialism, for I had read Buchner and Moleschott; had wrestled with Karl Marx and half accepted what I understood of him; thought Comte and the Positivists had pretty much made out their case and that the theological if not the metaphysical stage of thought should be transcended. But the only whole-hearted scheme of things which I had accepted with ardor and abandon was that of an evolution which applied no whit less to the soul than the body of man. This was bedrock. Darwin, Haeckel, and especially Herbert Spencer seemed then to me to represent the most advanced stage of human thought."[1]

Hall returned to the United States in 1871 in full revolt against his Puritan upbringing. "I fairly loathed and hated so much that I saw about me that I now realize," he wrote years later, "more clearly than ever how possible it would have been for me to have drifted into some, perhaps almost any, camp of radicals and to have come into such open rupture with the scheme of things as they were that I should have been stigmatized as dangerous, at least for any academic career, where the motto was Safety First. And as this was the only way left open, the alternative being the dread one of going back to the farm, it was most fortunate that these deeply stirred instincts of revolt were never openly expressed and my rank heresies and socialistic leanings unknown."[2]

In 1872, Hall took a teaching position at Antioch College, Yellow Springs, Ohio, a "western outpost of Unitarianism" where Horace Mann spent the last fourteen years of his life. "From Antioch," writes Hall, "I several times made excursions to St. Louis to spend Saturday evening with the Hegelian, William T. Harris, who had won national fame by his educational reconstruction of the St. Louis schools, which was widely copied." A member of that St. Louis group was Thomas Davidson who would in 1883 found the Fabian Society in London. The Fabians would socialize Britain through their slow method of permeation.

Hall was determined to return to Germany for further study in psychology. He had read Wundt's new book on psychology and wanted to study with the master himself. But before doing so he spent the year 1875 teaching English at Harvard. During that period Hall and James became intimate friends, sharing a strong interest in experimental psychology. Hall spent the next two years at the University of Leipzig. He was the first American to work in Wundt's new laboratory devoted to experimental psychology. He also worked in Prof. Ludwig's physiology lab, where experiments were conducted on living tissue, using rats, rabbits, guinea pigs, dogs, pigeons, etc. Hall then spent a year at the University of Berlin working with Prof. Helmholtz, the first scientist to accurately measure the rate of the transmission of a stimulus along nerves by using the sciatic nerve in the frog.

Hall then returned to Harvard where he was the first to receive a Ph.D. in psychology, after which he was invited by Johns Hopkins University to lecture for a year and then set up, in 1882, America's first psychology lab. His department became the nation's leader in experimental psychology.

One of Hall's first students was John Dewey who spent three years sopping up Hall's fervor for evolution and German philosophy. Dewey had come from the same sort of rural New England background as did Hall, and both men rebelled against the same religious orthodoxy. Max Eastman writes: "Unless you understand how exciting it is to fall in love with Hegel—and what hard work—there was very little Dewey could tell you about those three years at Johns Hopkins."[3]

Hall originated the idea of subjecting psychic processes to the same exact, objective, and experimental methods that muscular and nerve tissue were subjected to in experimental physiology. It was Freudianism which later came closest to fulfilling that function in psychology. Hall was also instrumental in focusing interest and research in a new area of psychological investigation, that of child-study. The work he and others did in this field would provide the "scientific" basis for the progressive education movement.

But Hall's strongest influence was in spreading the gospel of evolution. He writes: "As soon as I first heard it in my youth I think I must have been almost hypnotized by the word 'evolution,' which was music to my ear and seemed to fit my mouth better than any other."[4] Hall conceived the whole world, material and spiritual, as an organic unity in which supernaturalism played no part. Man had a "soul," but only in a pantheistic sense. Jesus was a great man and teacher, but not God. Thus, to Hall, man's salvation· was to be found in science, psychology and education. His vision was truly that of the secular humanist when he wrote:

> Nature and Man—there is nothing else outside, above, or beyond these in the universe. . . . Only now is man beginning to realize that he is truly supreme in all the universe we know and that there is nothing above or beyond him. . . . Man sees his destiny, which is to rule the world within and without by the power that comes from knowledge. . . . Science is both his organ of apprehension and his tool by which he

must make his sovereignty complete, come fully into his kingdom, and make his reign supreme. Thus, again, we see that research is his highest function.[5]

Hall's influence among educators can be measured by the fact that he was one of the most frequent and popular speakers at NEA conventions from 1885 to 1900 or so and was instrumental in helping to create the NEA's Child-Study Department. Also, his many students went on to create departments of experimental psychology in many other universities.

In 1889 Hall became president of the newly created Clark University in Worcester, Massachusetts. It was established as a graduate school with a heavy emphasis on psychology, and it quickly became the headquarters of the child-study movement. While many of Hall's students went on to positions of influence elsewhere, Clark University, because of financial problems, nowhere attained the influence and power in American education comparable to that of Teachers College at Columbia University in New York.

Teachers College, first known as College for the Training of Teachers, was founded in 1889 by Nicholas Murray Butler, then associate professor of philosophy, and Frederick Barnard, president of Columbia University, at the very same time that Clark was established. The goal of Butler and Barnard was to create a college that would stress professionalism in teaching. The profession had never enjoyed the prestige of other professions such as law or medicine. The new college would change all that.

In 1892 its name was changed to Teachers College and in 1893 it became the pedagogy department of Columbia. The college floundered until 1897 when James Earl Russell, at the age of 33, became dean-elect. Russell had spent the years 1893–95 at Leipzig getting a Ph.D. from Prof. Wundt. His enthusiasm for the New Psychology was unbounded. From then on, it was merely a matter of time before the Wundtian new psychology would become the dominating force in American pedagogy.

5. Turning Children Into Animals

It was James Earl Russell's vision and drive that turned Teachers College into the "West Point of progressive education." He made it the largest and most influential school of education in the world by bringing to its faculty other dedicated practitioners of the New Psychology. In this he was helped by the indefatigable James McKeen Cattell who, in 1891, had established Columbia University's department of psychology. Cattell had received his Ph.D. from Prof. Wundt in 1886 after spending two years working in the professor's laboratory at Leipzig. It was there that Cattell had performed his experiments on reading that would revolutionize the teaching of reading in America and thereby create the reading problem we have today. What went wrong? Educators adopted the notion that half-baked, untried educational "science" could substitute for a thousand years of hard-learned teaching experience.

Probably the single most influential psychologist to join the faculty of Teachers College was not G. Stanley Hall's prize pupil, John Dewey, but Edward L. Thorndike, who had gotten his master's degree at Harvard in 1897 working under William James. According to Lawrence Cremin's *Transformation of the School:*

> It was at Harvard that Thorndike undertook his first work with animal learning, a course of experimentation destined profoundly to influence the American school. He began investigating instinctive and intelligent behavior in chickens, a line of research so novel that he was refused space to experiment at the University and had to undertake his research in the basement of the James house in Cambridge. . . . A fellowship from Columbia brought Thorndike to New York to study with James McKeen Cattell. . . . He continued the experiments he had begun at Harvard, and in 1898 produced a dissertation on *Animal Intelligence* which stands as a landmark in the history of psychology.
>
> What was the nature of the experiments? Basically, they involved an animal in a problem box, a situation in which a specific behavior, like pressing down a lever, was rewarded with escape from the box and a bit of food. The animal was placed in the box, and after a period of random activity, it pressed the lever and received the reward. In subsequent trials the period between the animal's being introduced into the situation and the pressing of the lever decreased, to a point at which introduction into the box occasioned a lunge at the lever and the conclusion of the experiment.
>
> Thorndike called the process by which the animals tended to repeat ever more efficiently and economically behaviors which were rewarded *learning,* and out of his experiment came a new theory of learning and a new "law" founded on that theory. The theory maintained that learning involves the wedding of a specific response to a specific stimulus through a physiological bond in the neural system, so that the stimulus regularly calls forth the response. In Thorndike's words, the *bond* between S and R is "stamped in" by being continually rewarded. And from this follows what Thorndike called the "law of effect"—namely, that a satisfactory outcome of any response tends to "stamp in" its connection with a given situation, and conversely, that an unsatisfactory outcome tends to stamp out the bond or connection. Whereas previous theories had emphasized practice, or repetition, Thorndike gave equal weight to outcomes—to success or failure, reward or punishment, satisfaction or annoyance to the learner.

... Thorndike's experiment inaugurated the laboratory study of animal learning, assuming that a demonstration of the conditions of animal behavior under laboratory conditions, could help solve the general problems of psychology. The assumption, of course, represents a synthesis of scientific method and evolutionary doctrine, since in the absence of the latter animal learning would hardly have been considered a suitable topic for a psychologist. Equally important, perhaps, Thorndike's new law implied a new theory of mind. Building on the idea of the reflex arc, which connected the brain and neural tissue with the total behavior of the organism, he ended the search for mind by eliminating it as a separate entity. Mind appeared in the total response of the organism to its environment.

As Thorndike later pointed out in his classic three-volume work *Educational Psychology,* this conception does more than render psychology a science by making it the study of observable, measurable human behavior. In one fell swoop, it discards the Biblical view that man's nature is essentially sinful and hence untrustworthy; the Rousseauan view that man's nature is essentially good and hence always right; and the Lockean view that man's nature is ultimately plastic and hence completely modifiable. Human nature, Thorndike maintained, is simply a mass of "original tendencies" that can be exploited for good or bad, depending on what learning takes place.[1]

Thorndike was thoroughly convinced that his discoveries in animal learning could provide a scientific basis for the teaching profession. "The best way with children," he wrote, "may often be, in the pompous words of an animal trainer, 'to arrange everything in connection with the trick so that the animal will be compelled by the laws of his own nature to perform it.' "

Cremin writes:

Ultimately, Thorndike's goal was a comprehensive science of pedagogy on which all education could be based. His faith in quantified methods was unbounded, and he was quoted ad nauseam to the effect that everything that exists exists in quantity and can be measured. . . . He deeply believed that with the training of a sufficient number of educational experts, many of the gnawing controversies that had plagued educators since the beginning of time would disappear.[2]

The profound effects Thorndike's theories had on American education cannot be overestimated. They were, as were Pavlov's experiments in the 1920s, a natural development of Wundtian psychology. Wundt had said: "If we try to answer the general question of the genetic relation of man to the animals on the ground of a comparison of their psychical attributes, it must be admitted . . . that it is possible that human consciousness has developed from a lower form of animal consciousness."

But perhaps the best summing up of Thorndike's view will be found in his own words in the final paragraph of his book, *Animal Intelligence,* published in 1911:

> Nowhere more truly than in his mental capacities is man a part of nature. His instincts, that is, his inborn tendencies to feel and act in certain ways, show throughout marks of kinship with the lower animals, especially with our nearest relatives physically, the monkeys. His sense-powers show no new creation. His intellect we have seen to be a simple though extended variation from the general animal sort. This again is presaged by the similar variation in the case of the monkeys. Amongst the minds of animals that of man leads, not as a demigod from another planet, but as a king from the same race.[3]

Thus, the theory of evolution, applied to the mind, was used by Thorndike and other psychologists as a basis for building a new theory of learning by conditioning. Children were to be considered as animals—for, after all, man was nothing more than the "king" of the animals, as Thorndike put it—and the classroom was to be transformed into a laboratory providing the optimum environment in which learning by reflex conditioning could take place. It was this view of man and learning which provided the theoretical basis for progressive education. A new type of classroom, a new type of teacher, and new classroom materials and books would have to be developed to duplicate the conditions of the psych lab.

Thus, the idea that evolution is merely a theory taught in the biology classroom is erroneous. Evolution is at the very basis of modern public education where the child is taught that he is an animal linked by evolution to the monkeys. His school materials have been designed to teach him as an animal, using Thorndike's stimuli-reponse techniques which are now universally used throughout American education. So we ought not to be surprised when students act like animals and call their public school a "zoo." The message has gotten through to them, and they are behaving in a manner faithful to the concepts of the men at Teachers College who conceived their education.

In contrast, children in a Christian school are taught that they are human beings created in God's image and accountable to their Creator. These children are expected to act like human beings, and they do. Their link is not downward through evolution to the monkeys, but upward, through the Bible, to their Creator.

While Thorndike developed and formulated the psychological basis for progressive education, John Dewey formulated its social aims. Dewey joined the faculty at Columbia in 1904 as a professor of philosophy. In 1884 he had gone from Johns Hopkins to the University of Michigan and, in 1894, to the University of Chicago as head of the department of philosophy, psychology and education. It was there, in 1896, that Dewey created the famous Laboratory School which was to be for his department what a lab is for a biology or chemistry department.

Dewey had wanted to test certain philosophical and psychological ideas in practical application with real live children, and a laboratory school was the best place in which to do it. As with so many liberal intellectuals who had abandoned Christianity, Dewey's philosophy had evolved from Hegelian idealism to socialist materialism. The purpose of the school was to show experimentally how education could be reformed to create little socialists instead of little capitalists who, in the long run, would change the American economic system.

"The school's ultimate social ideal was the transformation of society through a new, socially minded individualism."[4]

According to Dewey, the traditional school encouraged competitive individualism. "[E]ach child sits in his place in a fixed row of desks and faces, not his companions as an active, guided social group, but his teacher as an instructor and disciplinarian. He studies largely by himself and for himself and is, during much of the time, in direct competition with his mates."[5]

The classroom had to be transformed to encourage social contact. "The physical set-up of the classrooms of the Laboratory School with their movable chairs helped to make each period a social occasion. In all classes teacher and children started off the day's work with a face-to-face discussion of cooperative plans for individual and group activity."[6]

It was clear to Dewey that reform in the classroom had to precede reform in society at large. Thus, the battle was between cooperation and competition, the group and the individual, socialism and capitalism. Dewey hoped to find a means of reconciling the needs of the individual with the needs of the collective. If collectivism had become his religion, it was because Humanity had replaced God as the focus of his loyalty. He made that clear when he wrote in *A Common Faith:*

> The ideal ends to which we attach our faith are not shadowy and wavering. They assume concrete form in our understanding of our relations to one another and the values contained in these relations. We, who now live, are part of a humanity that extends into the remote past, a humanity that has interacted with nature. The things in civilization we most prize are not ourselves. They exist by grace of the doings and sufferings of the continuous human community in which we are a link. Ours is the responsibility of conserving, transmitting, rectifying and expanding the heritage of values we have received that

those who come after us may receive it more solid and secure, more widely accessible and more generously shared than we have received it. Here are all the elements for a religious faith that shall not be confined to sect, class, or race.[7]

It was thus Dewey who began to fashion a new materialist religion in which humanity was venerated instead of God. This is basically the religion of Secular Humanism, and this is what has become the official religion of the United States, for it is the only religion permitted in its public schools and totally supported by government funds. The Constitution of the United States forbids the government from establishing a national religion. But we have one, whether the people know it or not.

None of this would have happened had not the teaching profession gained a new prestige and status. Prior to the progressive revolution, colleges and universities had left teacher training up to the Normal Schools, and prior to that the private academies produced the teachers of America. It was not thought that teachers needed a college or university education. With the advent of public education, the Normal Schools took over teacher training. But at the turn of the century, when teacher training was converted into a science by the Wundtian psychologists, the universities began to build graduate schools of education along with departments of psychology and experimental psychology labs. Behavioral psychology had elevated the teaching profession to a new exalted position, and education had given psychology a whole new field in which to practice its skills. In addition, John Dewey gave education a social mission of exalted revolutionary proportions: the transformation of American society from capitalism to socialism.

The marriage between behavioral psychology and education, a union made in Leipzig and consummated at Teachers College, has worked to the benefit of both parties, for both are now the recipient of massive public financing and have waxed fat and prosperous because of it. Each depends on the other for its prestige and academic standing, and that is one of the reasons why public education cannot be reformed. The marriage made in Leipzig has been institutionalized in every college and university in America, and you cannot reform education without first divorcing it from behavioral psychology.

PART TWO

Creating an Education Establishment

6. The Education Mafia

When Dewey came to Columbia in 1904, at the invitation of James McKeen Cattell, the university and its Teachers College became the undisputed training center for the new scientifically based "progressive" education. Its graduates fanned out across America to become deans and professors at other teachers colleges and superintendents of entire public school systems. Their loyalty to their mentors was demonstrated by how well they implemented their teachings in the schools of America. Among the alumni were Elwood P. Cubberly, George D. Strayer, George H. Betts, Edward C. Elliott, Walter A. Jessup, William H. Kilpatrick, Bruce R. Payne, David S. Snedden, Lotus D. Coffman.

Cubberly became dean of the School of Education at Stanford; Strayer, professor at Teachers College and president of the NEA in 1918–19; Betts, professor of education at Northwestern; Elliott, president of Purdue; Jessup, president of the University of Iowa and president of the Carnegie Foundation for the Advancement of Teaching; Kilpatrick, professor at Teachers College and a founder of Bennington College; Payne, president of George Peabody College in Nashville; Snedden,

Massachusetts State Commissioner of Education; Coffman, dean of the College of Education at the University of Minnesota, and later the university's president.

These were just a few of the men who created a network of control and influence that was to change the face of public education in America. David Tyack, in his revealing book, *Managers of Virtue,* describes the tremendous power the network was able to wield:

> Networks resist definition. The word itself is a metaphor for a connecting web with much open space. As we use the term here, we mean an informal association of individuals who occupied influential positions (usually in university education departments or schools, as policy analysts or researchers in foundations, and as key superintendents), who shared common purposes (to solve social and economic problems by educational means through "scientific" diagnosis and prescription), who had common interests in furthering their own careers, and who had come to know one another mostly through face-to-face interactions and through their similar writing and research. They controlled important resources: money, the creation of reputations, the placement of students and friends, the training of subordinates and future leaders, and influences over professional associations and public legislative and administrative bodies.[1]

The education mafia became known as the "Educational Trust" and they held annual meetings under an umbrella called the Cleveland Conference, named thus because the first conference had been held in Cleveland in 1915. This exclusive club began with 19 members, including those graduates of Columbia and Teachers College named at the beginning of the chapter. Among the others were James R. Angell, a colleague of Dewey's at the University of Chicago who became its president and later president of Yale. Angell had gotten his M.A. under William James at Harvard, his Ph.D. at Leipzig and was the first president of the American Psychological Association and later became a trustee of the Rockefeller Foundation; Leonard Ayres, director of the Russell Sage Foundation; Abraham Flexner, director of the Rockefeller Institute; Paul

Hanus, who set up Harvard's Graduate School of Education with the help of Rockefeller's General Education Board; Frank E. Spaulding, another Leipzig Ph.D. who organized Yale's Department of Education, was its chairman and later also a member of the General Education Board; Paul Monroe, director of Columbia's school of education and later founder and president of the World Federation of Education Associations; and Edward L. Thorndike.

The guiding spirit of the education mafia was Charles Judd who got his Ph.D. in 1896 from Prof. Wundt at Leipzig and became head of the Department of Education at the University of Chicago in 1909. He represented, *par excellence,* the Wundtian psychologist determined to reform American education according to scientific, evolutionary principles. According to Tyack:

> He had a vision that both the structure of the schools and the curriculum needed radical revision, but that change would take place "in the haphazard fashion that has characterized our school history unless some group gets together and undertakes, in a cooperative way, to coordinate reforms."[2]

Judd urged the members of the Cleveland Conference to jump into the breach and undertake "the positive and aggressive task of . . . a detailed reorganization of the materials of instruction in schools of all grades. . . . It is intended that we make the undertaking as broad and democratic as possible by furnishing the energy for organizing a general movement at the same time we stimulate each other to make direct contributions wherever possible."

Tyack comments: "There was, of course, some incongruity in the notion of a small, self-appointed group of experts proposing a 'democratic' revision of studies from the top down." Of course, the experts didn't bother to consult the parents of America. This radical revision was to be effected after the professionals got rid of local lay control of the public schools through a process of centralization.

Was the Cleveland Conference a conspiracy? It had no constitution, no minutes, no officers, no bylaws, and no "public life" whereby its deliberations could be scrutinized. It was, in short, very much a private, if not secret, organization, determining the future of *public,* taxpayer-supported education. And we can assume that there were many secret meetings and conversations among the small inner circle to determine, among other things, who to place where.

The education mafia was efficiently run by godfathers stationed in key universities: Cubberly at Stanford who was known as "Dad" by his graduate students, Judd at the University of Chicago, Strayer at Teachers College, New York. Tyack writes:

> But it is one of the best known secrets in the fraternity of male administrators, a frequent topic of the higher gossip at meetings though hardly ever discussed in print, that there were "placement barons," usually professors of educational administration in universities such as Teachers College, Harvard, University of Chicago, or Stanford who had an inside track in placing their graduates in important positions. One educator commented after spending a weekend with Cubberly in Palo Alto that "Cubberly had an educational Tammany Hall that made the Strayer-Engelhardt Tammany Hall in New York look very weak."[3]

But a placement baron could only be a power broker if the school board recognized his authority. And that is why the education mafia promoted "reform" of local school governance that wrested control of the public schools from elected politicians and put it in the hands of appointed professional educators. The reform movement had actually started in New York in 1896 under the leadership of Nicholas Murray Butler, then a professor at Columbia, and financed by the socially prominent. The movement spread across America. The results gave the godfathers enormous leverage and power in local communities. Tyack writes:

> In Detroit, for example, local reformers who had fought for a new

city charter and abolished the old ward-elected board of education turned for their superintendent to "the new school of professionally trained educators" and elected Charles Chadsey, trained at Teachers College and a protégé of George Strayer.[4]

And what happened if you disobeyed your godfather? According to Tyack:

> One principal recalled "Strayer's Law" for dealing with disloyal subordinates: "Give 'em the ax."[5]

The radical revision of the public school curriculum could only be implemented if the superintendents, principals and professors, who were placed in strategic positions of power by their mentors, pushed for the reforms the godfathers wanted, regardless of what parents or traditional teachers desired. That, for example, is how the progressives were able to replace phonics with look-say instruction in virtually all of the primary schools of America in a few short years. The two most prominent creators of look-say instruction materials were William Scott Gray, who worked under Judd, the mastermind of the Cleveland Conference, and Arthur I. Gates, who worked under Thorndike at Teachers College. Getting the books into the schools was easy, for according to Tyack: "The network of obligations linked local superintendents more to their sponsors than to their local patrons and clients."

So if you were a parent and wondered why your Johnny wasn't learning to read and found your local school superintendent unresponsive to parental concerns, the answer is that his career depended not on pleasing parents but on pleasing his sponsor. After all, if that's the way the godfathers said that reading ought to be taught, what superintendent would be so foolhardy as to contradict them?

The progressive network shared a number of basic beliefs that would form the philosophical foundation of the new curriculum: an absolute faith in science and the theory of evolution; a belief that children could be taught very much like animals in accordance with the new behavioral psychology; a conviction that there was no place for religion in education and that traditional values were an obstacle to social progress which had to be removed.

It stands to reason that most of the progressives, by definition, were political liberals and that many, like Dewey, considered socialism morally superior to capitalism. And it was Dewey's ideas, expressed in *School and Society,* which shaped much of the social content of the new curriculum. In the years to come the progressives would make skillful use of the NEA to get America to accept their educational agenda for the future.

7. The Progressives Take Over the NEA

It was only natural that the progressives would eventually take control of the NEA. And that was not difficult to do, for it wasn't until 1898 that the NEA even had its first full-time paid secretary. Although by 1900 there were about a half million public school teachers in America, the NEA's membership in that year was only 2,332, representing, for all practical purposes, the active elite of the profession, along with textbook publishers, education editors and foundation directors. This small cadre of leaders kept in touch through correspondence and met annually at the NEA's convention or at the gathering of its elite inner body, the National Council of Education.

There were, of course, philosophical disagreements among the elite. William T. Harris, the Hegelian, emphasized the need for discipline and the training of the mind and the maintenance of civilization through study of the classical languages; Charles W. Eliot, president of Harvard, reflected William James' pragmatism and preferred to replace the classical languages of antiquity with modern languages, mathematics and science; and Nicholas Murray Butler, the youngest of the three, represented the new professionalism of the educator-psychologist being honed at Teachers College, Columbia.

The most important act of the old guard elite was the formation in 1892 of the Committee of Ten on Secondary School Studies with Charles W. Eliot as its chairman. The committee had been formed to establish uniform curriculum guidelines and standards for the nation's secondary schools. Until then the role of secondary education was seen as college preparatory. But with the growth of public high schools and the increasing number of secondary students not going on to college, there was a need to decide what subjects to teach, the order of teaching them, and the amount of time to devote to each one of them.

Nine committees, comprised of university professors and secondary teachers, deliberated over nine subject areas: Latin, Greek, English, Modern Languages, Mathematics, Sciences, Natural History, History and Government, and Geography. When the deliberations were completed and reviewed, the Committee of Ten recommended that the secondary schools offer four basic programs: (1) Classical, including Latin, Greek, English, German and French, Mathematics, Science, Geography; (2) Latin Scientific, eliminating Greek and emphasizing science; (3) Modern Languages, replacing Latin and Greek with two modern languages; (4) English, offering only one foreign language—ancient or modern—and stressing English and the other subjects.

The major shift was from the classical curriculum to a more modern program of studies. One of the programs eliminated the classical languages altogether and another made them optional. Clearly a compromise had been reached between Harris and Eliot, but the trend was unmistakable. The classicists warned that discarding Latin and Greek would only serve to undermine the cultural foundations of our civilization. But Nicholas Murray Butler persuaded the public otherwise. He wrote in the *Atlantic Monthly* of March 1894 that if the recommendations were followed, the future "graduate of a secondary school will have had four years of strong and effective mental training, no matter which of the four school programmes he has followed, and the college can safely admit him to its courses." Then he added:

> And finally, what is the effect of this prolonged and earnest investigation upon that ideal of a liberal education that has so long been held in esteem among us? It will not have escaped notice that only one of the committee's four programmes makes a place for the study of Greek, while one excludes Greek and Latin. . . . Between a diminution of the time given to classical study and a relapse into quasi barbarism there is no necessary relation of cause and effect. May not the American say, as did Paulsen of his countrymen, that "idealism generally, if we will use this word of so many meanings, is a thing which is not implanted from without, but grows from within, and that, in particular, the idealism in the character of the German people has deeper roots than the Greek and Latin lessons of our gymnasia."

The tragedy, which neither Butler nor Prof. Paulsen of the University of Berlin could have foreseen, is that Germany did indeed fall into barbarism. Whether the German education system was or was not to blame we have yet to find out. But the German example has taught us that a civilized nation, served by great universities and steeped in science and psychology, can virtually overnight lapse into sickening barbarism.

Despite the shift from the classics to a more modern curriculum, which represented a victory for Charles W. Eliot and Nicholas Murray Butler, the emphasis was still on mental training. As William T. Harris put it: "The school gives the youth the tools of thought. . . . He studies the structure of language in grammar, and this reveals the structure of intellect."[1]

The Committee of Ten not only set the course of American education for the next twenty-five years or so, but it also represented an important milestone in NEA history. It marked the end of the NEA's limited function as a discussion club and the beginning of its expanded role as a formulator of national education policy. America did not have, nor want, a European-style "ministry of education" that could reform the nation's schools by decree. And so it was decided by the educators that the NEA would have to perform that function. Nicholas Murray Butler articulated the problem when he wrote in 1894:

> In this country . . . where no central educational administration exists, and where bureaucracy is not popular, educational reforms can be brought about only by persuasion and cooperation, for no official and no institution is empowered to dictate to us. The press, the platform, the teachers' meeting, must be availed of to put forward new ideas, and women in large numbers must be reasoned with and convinced in order to secure their acceptance.[2]

In other words, the educators would have to learn to manipulate the press, con the public, and influence the teachers. The NEA would eventually learn to do all of these and much more.

The Committee of Ten's views on education reflected those of an older generation of educators who had not been bitten by the Leipzig bug. But by 1915 most of the members of the committee were either dead or in retirement. Harris had died in 1909 and Eliot had retired from the presidency of Harvard in the same year. A younger generation—imbued with Wundtian psychology and Deweyism—had taken over, and the first major product of the new progressive outlook was the report of the NEA's Commission on the Reorganization of Secondary Education issued in 1918.

The Commission had been created in 1913 to redefine the functions of the American high school whose student population had grown from 202,963 in 1890 to 1,645,171 in 1918. The reforms recommended by the Commission were called *Cardinal Principles of Secondary Education,* and they reflected the full influence of the new psychology as well as Dewey's new educational agenda for a socialist society. The shift in emphasis from intellectual development to social development was revolutionary.

Dewey strongly opposed the traditional system which encouraged the development of the independent mind ready to compete in capitalist society. "The mere absorbing of facts and truths," he wrote in *School and Society,* "is so exclusively individual an affair that it tends very naturally to pass into selfishness."[3] And to Dewey selfishness was synonomous with capitalism. If education was to lead the next generation to socialism, it would have to be much less intellectual and much more social. Dewey wrote in *My Pedagogic Creed:*

> I believe that the social life of the child is the basis of concentration, or correlation, in all his training or growth. . . . I believe, therefore, that the true center of correlation on the school subjects is not science, nor literature, nor history, nor geography, but the child's social activities. I believe, therefore, in the so-called expressive or constructive activities as the center of correlation. I believe that this gives the standard for the place of cooking, sewing, manual training, etc., in the school.[4]

It is obvious that the Commission had taken Dewey's ideas very much to heart in concocting their Cardinal Principles as the main objectives of education. The Cardinal Principles were: (1) Health, (2) Command of Fundamental Processes, (3) Worthy home-membership, (4) Vocation, (5) Citizenship, (6) Worthy use of leisure time, and (7) Ethical Character. The report stated:

> No curriculum in the secondary school can be regarded as satisfactory unless it gives due attention to each of the objectives of education outlined herein.
>
> Health, as an objective, makes imperative an adequate time assignment for physical training and requires science courses properly focused upon personal and community hygiene, the principles of sanitation, and their applications. Command of fundamental processes necessitates thorough courses in the English language as a means of taking in and giving forth ideas. Worthy home-membership calls for the redirection of much of the work in literature, art, and the social

studies. For girls it necessitates adequate courses in household arts. Citizenship demands that the social studies be given a prominent place. Vocation as an objective requires that many pupils devote much of their time to specific preparation for a definite trade or occupation, and that some pursue studies that serve as a basis for advanced work in higher institutions. The worthy use of leisure calls for courses in literature, art, music, and science so taught as to develop appreciation. It necessitates also a margin of free electives to be chosen on the basis of personal avocational interests.[5]

It took a while for the Cardinal Principles, combined with Thorndike's animal training, to transform American education into the confusing, chaotic mess we have today. The rejection of strenuous mental training (cognitive skills) in favor of social and motor skills (the affective domain) would eventually undermine the entire education system, despite the valiant resistance of many excellent teachers who held back the revolution for twenty years or so. The progressives simply waited for these old-fashioned teachers to retire. The new ones coming out of the teachers' colleges, trained in the new educational psychology, would obey their superintendents and principals who had been put into place by the godfathers.

The Cardinal Principles had indeed emphasized the importance of the new psychology and how it should be applied in reforming public education. The implication was that because previous generations lacked the insights of "educational psychology," their methods were backward, unscientific, inadequate or misguided. In addition, the Cardinal Principles put forth its own collectivist view of democracy with this curious definition:

> The purpose of democracy is so to organize society that each member may develop his personality primarily through activities designed for the well-being of his fellow members and of society as a whole.

In other words, the purpose of government is the development of a socially-oriented personality. The report adds:

Consequently, education in a democracy, both within and without the school, should develop in each individual the knowledge, interests, ideals, habits, and powers whereby he will find his place and use that place to shape both himself and society toward ever nobler ends.

So the purpose of education is to help you find your "place" in society, and you are to use that "place" to further "shape" yourself, whatever that means, and shape society "toward ever nobler ends." That was the kind of intellectual inanity that was to form the philosophical foundation of the American education system.

Who were the educators who put the Cardinal Principles together? Tyack writes:

> Among members-at-large of the committee that wrote the influential report called *The Cardinal Principles of Secondary Education* (1918) were three education professors (one a university professor who had recently been an education professor), the United States commissioner of education, a normal school principal, a YMCA secretary, and three state and local adminstrators. Men like Judd were important behind-the-scenes influences on the work of the curriculum committees.[6]

Actually, the driving force behind the commission was its chairman, Clarence Darwin Kingsley, State Superintendent of High Schools in Massachusetts, who had gotten his Master's degree at Teachers College in 1904 and his job in 1912 through David Snedden, Massachusetts Commissioner of Education, a 1907 Ph.D. from Teachers College. Snedden became a member of the semi-secret Cleveland Conference in 1915 and in 1916 became a professor of education at Teachers College. The radical reform and reorganization advocated by the Cardinal Principles was exactly what the Cleveland Conference mafia wanted.

It was in 1913 that Kingsley put together his NEA Commission on the Reorganization of Secondary Education. Kingsley had been chairman of the NEA's Committee of Nine on the Articulation of High School and College in 1910. The Commission on the Reorganization of Secondary Education did not complete its work until 1923. It is said that after their publication in 1918, generations of prospective teachers memorized the Cardinal Principles and wrote them down on tests.

Among the members of the committee recruited by Kingsley was Thomas H. Briggs, a professor of education at Teachers College who had collaborated with another Columbia Ph.D., Lotus Coffman, in writing a textbook on reading which was published in 1908. Coffman became dean of the college of education at the University of Minnesota in 1915 and president of the University in 1920. Another member was William Heard Kilpatrick who had studied under Dewey at both Chicago and Columbia and whom Dewey called "the best I ever had."[7] Kilpatrick, as a professor at Teachers College, became famous, according to Cremin, for "reconciling Thorndike's connectionism with the Deweyan view of education."[8] Kilpatrick became one of the key theorists and developers of progressive education, actively advancing the cause well into the 1950s.

Another interesting member was Otis W. Caldwell, professor of education at Teachers College and director of the experimental Lincoln School, founded in 1917 with the help of Rockefeller money as a laboratory in which to test the new science of education. John D. Rockefeller, Jr., sent four of his five sons to the school. Jules Abel, in his book on the Rockefellers published in 1967, revealed what the Lincoln School did for the boys' literacy:

> Laurence gives startling confirmation as to "Why Johnnie Can't Read." He says that the Lincoln School did not teach him to read and write as he wishes he now could. Nelson, today, admits that reading for him is a "slow and tortuous process" that he does not enjoy doing but compels himself to do it. This is significant evidence in the debate that has raged about modern educational techniques.[9]

Another interesting member of the committee was Henry Neumann of the Ethical Culture School of New York. Mr. Neumann had undoubtedly been called in to provide some input on the matter of the committee's seventh Cardinal Principle, Ethical Character. Since the new science of education excluded religion of any kind from public education, something else had to be found to perform its moral function. The Ethical Culture movement had been founded in 1876 by Felix Adler who saw the need to provide nontheistic religion for people who no longer could accept the traditional views. It is religious humanism with the goal of inspiring people "with the ideal that the ethical perfection of human society is the ultimate aim."[10] This goal dovetailed nicely with Dewey's. Since religious humanism is now the only religion permitted in the public schools and is the only religion publicly funded by the government, this makes it the government's own establishment of religion, something strictly forbidden by the United States Constitution. Of course it doesn't seem that way, because religious humanism is propagated through social studies textbooks and not any church services. "While Ethical Culture is recognized as a religion," say the Ethical Culturists, "there is no prayer, communion or confession, no theology or set of doctrines, no scripture."[11]

Thus, the Cardinal Principles launched a new era for American education based on a philosophy that fostered socialism, animal training, and atheism. Should the results we see today surprise anyone? The Cardinal Principles also confirmed the NEA as the formulator of national education policy.

8. NEA: Ministry of Education or Labor Union?

In 1917, with the appointment of Dr. James W. Crabtree as secretary, the NEA decided to set up its permanent headquarters in Washington, D.C. The decision was logical in view of the NEA's expanding role as formulator of national education policy. If the NEA was to become America's equivalent of a ministry of education, what better place to locate it than in the nation's capital? Besides, the NEA had gotten a new charter from Congress in 1906, signed by President Theodore Roosevelt.

The publication of the Cardinal Principles in 1918 by the U.S. Office of Education gave it the look of a government document, the aura of government approval and wide distribution throughout the nation. In a sense, the progressives had staged the most successful political coup in American history by capturing public education and using it to steer America in a socialist direction, and enlisting the help of the federal government to do it. There can be no doubt that the progressive educators set the stage for Roosevelt's New Deal in 1933 and the welfare state that came with it. The progressives were convinced that capitalism was dying anyway. Dewey had said, "The schools, like a nation, are in need of a central purpose which will create new enthusiasm and devotion, and which will unify and guide all intellectual plans."

For the godfathers pulling the strings, the NEA became an indispensable tool for controlling national policy. Tyack writes:

> Through building hidden hierarchies in such professional associations—in effect, powerful private governments—and in less evident ways in other groups such as the Cleveland Conference and their own placement networks, they gained an awesome power to define their own solutions to educational problems. Their solutions, accepted as standard by a growing number of educators, helped to create a potent professional consensus despite the formal decentralization of power in American public education.[1]

The formation of a "commission" became the accepted means of developing national education policy, and by putting the right people on the commission, the string pullers could get the results they wanted.

With America's entry into World War I in 1917, the NEA formed a Commission on the Emergency in Education with George D. Strayer of Teachers College at its head. The commission's progress report was read at the NEA convention in the summer of 1918 and NEA president, Mary Bradford, called it "a complete national plan for education." In 1920 the plan was fashioned into a bill and put before Congress. It proposed making the federal Office of Education into a Department of Education with cabinet status; appropriating money to reduce illiteracy; Americanize immigrants; and promote physical education and teacher training. It also advocated partial payment of teachers' salaries by the federal government.

The response of Congress fell dismally short of what the educators wanted. But it marked the beginning of the NEA's permanent role as an initiator of legislation in favor of "education." Throughout its history the NEA had made efforts to get favorable legislation passed on a variety of issues, but the efforts were haphazard. In 1920, the association formed a permanent Legislative Commission which, henceforth, would propose legislation and lobby Congress on a regular basis. It would take years for the NEA to perfect its lobbying skills. Also, the NEA began to build a little bureaucracy of its own. Membership had grown from 10,104 in 1918 to 52,850 in 1920. Business was booming.

In 1919 the NEA purchased the four-story Guggenheim mansion at 1201 Sixteenth Street, Northwest, for $98,000. Strayer of Teachers College was president of the NEA in that year of enormous growth, and the future indeed looked rosey for the progressives.

The year 1920 also saw a major change in the governance of the NEA. While teachers had always provided most of the NEA's revenues, the association was essentially run and controlled by an elite group of men. Pressure was mounting from the large membership of women classroom teachers to have greater say in the management of the association. Out of these internal conflicts came the idea of a Representative Assembly. The idea was finally adopted in 1920. The first meeting of the Representative Assembly was held in 1921 with 463 local associations and 44 state associations sending delegates.

The new set-up might have made it a bit more difficult for the string pullers to control the association, but it expanded their influence enormously among the teachers, especially through such publications as the NEA *Journal* which began publication in 1922 under the editorship of William C. Bagley of Teachers College. The NEA was becoming more of an association for classroom teachers than for college and university professors. Thus, while the philosophy of the association would still be shaped by the educational trust simply because it controlled teacher education in America, the NEA itself would reflect more and more the interests of the teachers. According to Tyack:

From time to time Judd and some of his peers in the educational trust had doubts about the utility of the politically volatile NEA, seeing it as "moribund" and "threatened with dissolution." He regarded the Department of Superintendence as "infinitely more influential as a gathering genuinely interested in educational reports and hitherto relatively free from 'the blighting influence of selfish politics." There the educational scientists could speak of their work to men who had the power to put the new designs into effect.[2]

It was inevitable that a clash of interests would develop between the lowly classroom teachers and the exalted professors of education within the NEA. This clash became particularly evident as the more radical teachers began to identify themselves more as workers involved in the class struggle than as professionals. As a result, the pressure to unionize teachers began to grow. Margaret Haley, a paid organizer for the Teachers' Federation in Chicago, told an NEA audience in 1904:

Two ideals are struggling for supremacy in American life today: one the industrial ideal, dominating thru the supremacy of commercialism, which subordinates the work to the product and the machine; the other, the ideal of democracy, the ideal of the educators, which places humanity above all machines, and demands that all activity shall be the expression of life.[3]

It all sounded very John Deweyan. Teachers had to join the workers in their "struggle to secure the rights of humanity thru a more just and equitable distribution of the products of their labor." Only then could teachers become free to "save the schools for democracy and to save democracy for the schools."[4] Dewey, it should be noted, was issued the American Federation of Teachers' first membership card.

It was the NEA's ambivalence about its role as a quasi-governmental body formulating national education policy and that of a mere labor union that made it possible for its rival, the American Federation of Teachers, to grow, particularly in the large cities. As a pure labor union, the AFT could concentrate on fighting for higher teacher salaries, tenure, and pensions, regardless of philosophies of education. But union organizers like Margaret Haley in Chicago and Kate Hogan in New York were also militant progressives who supported women's suffrage, child labor legislation and other measures on the progressive political agenda. Tyack describes what the new feminist militancy was doing to the NEA:

> As a member of the old guard, Nicholas Murray Butler bitterly resented Haley and her allies. Once the NEA had been a meeting ground of the educational aristocracy, he wrote in his autobiography, "not only men of great ability, but men of exceptional character and personality." In the twentieth century, however, it "fell into the hands of a very inferior class of teachers and school officials whose main object appeared to be personal . . . advancement." Haley saw the NEA governing clique as part of a "powerful, persistent, silent and largely successful conspiracy to make a despotism of our entire public school system," and she decided to try to oust the old guard by electing a sympathetic woman.[5]

Thus it was that in 1910 Ella Flagg Young, superintendent of schools in Chicago and a strong advocate of Dewey's philosophy, was elected the first woman president of the NEA. Young had been supervisor of instruction at Dewey's Laboratory School, and it was thought that her election would not only aid the cause of progressive education but also open the NEA to feminine leadership. The next three years, in which militant women teachers openly challenged the old guard, were the most discordant in NEA history. But ways were found to keep the elite's control in tact. Tyack writes:

> In the NEA the challenge of women was deflected as new governance arrangements secured continuing power for male administrators while it gave women certain symbolic concessions. And although women teachers continued to experience some freedom of action in the privacy of their classrooms, reforms largely proceeded from the top down and administration remained hierarchical as well as male dominated.[6]

What happened in the NEA is very similar to what happened in politics. After women got the vote in 1920 it was thought that large numbers of them would enter politics. But today the number of women in Congress is nowhere near their proportion in the population. Even after the NEA adopted the Representative Assembly form of governance, women did not make the kinds of gains that were expected. At the first convention under the new system in 1921, out of 553 delegates there were only 81 elementary teachers, compared with 297 administrators, mostly male. The women did gain a symbolic victory when it was agreed that a woman would be president of the NEA every other year. But continuity of control would remain in the hands of the executive secretary who has always been a male.

Meanwhile, in order to deal with such matters as teachers salaries, tenure, retirement benefits and conditions of employment, the NEA, in 1922, created a Research Division with a monthly *Research Bulletin*. The *Bulletin* provided statistics, guidelines, studies, and comparative data for local associations, superintendents, school boards, legislators, etc. While the NEA insisted that teachers were "professionals" it recognized that it had to supply such information to the many small school districts so that teachers, superintendents and school boards could negotiate suitable terms of employment. Thus, through its Research Division, the NEA could perform some of the functions of a labor organization while maintaining its public image as a professional association.

In 1935 Crabtree retired as executive secretary of the NEA. He went on to become secretary-general of the World Federation of Education Associations. Under Crabtree the NEA had expanded its membership to 190,944 in 1935.

Crabtree was succeeded by Willard E. Givens who had gotten his Master's degree at Columbia in 1915 and studied there until 1917. He was superintendent of public instruction in Hawaii (1923–25), Assistant Superintendent of Schools in Oakland, California (1925–27), Superintendent of Schools in San Diego (1927–28), and Superintendent of Schools once more in Oakland (1928–35). He had been president of the

California State Teachers Association (1932–35). He was the perfect organization man.

Like Dewey, he also believed in socialism. At the 1934 session of the NEA's Department of Superintendence, he told the conferees that "many drastic changes must be made. A dying 'laissez-faire' must be completely destroyed and all of us, including the 'owners,' must be subjected to a large degree of social control. A large section of our discussion group maintain that the credit agencies, the basic industries and utilities cannot be centrally planned and operated under private ownership." Givens then recommended "taking these over and operating them at full capacity as a unified national system in the interest of all the people."

Givens took power at a time when Marxist radicalism was at its height at Teachers College, his alma mater. George S. Counts, the leftist professor at Teachers College who had toured the Soviet Union several times and written glowing accounts of its social "experiments," published *Dare the School Build a New Social Order?* in 1932. He urged "that the teachers should deliberately reach for power and then make the most of their conquest."

Cremin writes in his history of Teachers College:

> Counts's position was that teachers should play a primary role in formulating desirable societal goals and then consciously seek to attain them. . . . The course for American teachers was clear: they would have to gain power and use it to help create a great new society.[7]

Meanwhile at Teachers College intense verbal warfare broke out between communists and socialists. The former preached revolution, the latter advocated gradual evolution. Dewey, who numbered himself among the latter, wanted a socialist society as much as any communist, but he differed on methods. He wrote in *Liberalism and Social Action* in 1935:

> The Communist Manifesto presented two alternatives: *either* the revolutionary change and transfer of power to the proletariat *or*

the common ruin of the contending parties. Today, the civil war that would be adequate to effect transfer of power and a reconstitution of society at large, as understood by official communists, would seem to present but one possible consequence: the ruin of all parties and the destruction of civilized life. This fact alone is enough to lead us to consider the potentialities of the method of intelligence.[8]

The "method of intelligence" pointed directly to the schools. To Dewey, the obstacles to socialism were the ingrained habits, the "institutional relationships fixed in pre-scientific age." These obstacles could be removed through education. To Dewey, science was "socially organized intelligence" and the function of liberalism was to facilitate social change in the socialist direction. He wrote:

> Organized social planning . . . is now the sole method of social action by which liberalism can realize its professed aims. . . .[9]
>
> When I say that the first object of a renascent liberalism is education, I mean that its task is to aid in producing the habits of mind and character, the intellectual and moral patterns, that are somewhere near even with the actual movement of events.[10]

It was under Givens that the movement within the NEA to unify the teaching profession began in earnest. In 1944, at the Pittsburgh convention, resolutions to increase dues and unify membership were adopted. The unification plan provided for the enrollment of members in the local, state and national associations in one transaction. Hitherto, a member of a local or state teachers association did not have to join the national association. Under the new scheme, unified membership would be compulsory in states that adopted it. The system would automatically increase NEA membership, revenues and power.

Oregon was the first state to adopt unification in 1944. The next year Hawaii and Montana followed suit, and by 1950 Arizona, Idaho and Nevada were also unified. After that, the process virtually stopped. From 1950 to 1960 only one state voted for unification, indicating that there was no great enthusiasm for the idea among teachers. Radicalism might have been popular among the professors at Teachers College, but it meant little to most of the teachers in the classroom. Nevertheless, by the time Givens ended his administration in 1952, NEA membership had grown to 490,968.

9. The Biggest Lobby in Washington

In 1952, William G. Carr succeeded Willard Givens as executive secretary of the NEA. Carr had gotten his B.A., M.A., and Ph.D. at Stanford University, the domain of godfather Cubberly. In 1924–25, at the age of 23, Carr taught at a junior high school which immediately qualified him to become a professor of education at Pacific University, Forest Grove, Oregon, in 1926–27. While working for his Ph.D he served as director of research for the California Teachers Association, and on receiving his Ph.D. in 1929 became assistant director of research at NEA headquarters in Washington. He then became director of research (1931–40), associate secretary (1940–52), and finally executive secretary.

Carr was also instrumental in creating UNESCO and the World Confederation of Organizations for the Teaching Profession (WCOTP), of which he served as secretary-general from 1946 to 1970. He was dedicated to the idea of world government.

Carr's tenure at NEA, which lasted until 1967, was a period of transition. He became executive secretary in the same year that Eisenhower became President and John Dewey died at age 92. The vast curriculum and philosophical changes advocated by the educational mafia were in place and most of the leading godfathers were either dead or in retirement. Their teachings were being carried forward by their disciples, some of whom took things to further extremes, particularly in the field of behavioral psychology.

In 1914 Thorndike had said, "the progressives in psychology think of a man's mind as the organized system of connections or bonds or associations whereby he responds or reacts by this or that thought or feeling or act to each of the millions of situations or circumstances or events that befall him. . . From this point of view educational achievement consists, no, in strengthening mystical general powers of the mind, but in establishing connections, binding appropriate responses to life's situations, 'training the pupil to behavior' ('behavior' being the name we use for 'every possible sort of reaction on the circumstances into which he may find himself brought'), building up a hierarchy of habits, strengthening and weakening bonds whereby one thing leads to another in a man's life."

Following Thorndike came John B. Watson, who is often referred to as the true father of behaviorism. Watson had gotten his Ph.D. at the University of Chicago in 1903 under James R. Angell and John Dewey. He decided to dispense with the human mind altogether. Watson wrote in 1924:

> Behaviorism . . . holds that the subject matter of human psychology is the behavior of the human being. Behaviorism claims that consciousness is neither a definite nor a usable concept. The behaviorist . . . holds, further, that belief in the existence of consciousness goes back to the ancient days of superstition and magic. . . . The great mass of people even today has not yet progressed very far away from savagery—it wants to believe in magic. . . . Almost every era has its new magic, black or white, and its new magician. Moses had his magic: he smote the rock and water gushed out. Christ had his magic: he turned water into wine and raised the dead to life. . . .
>
> The extent to which most of us are shot through with a savage background is almost unbelievable. . . . One example of such a religious concept is that every individual has a *soul* which is separate and distinct from the body. . . . No one has ever touched a soul, or seen one

in a test tube, or has in any way come into relationship with it as he has with the other objects of his daily experience. . . .[1]

The behaviorist asks: Why don't we make what we can *observe* the real field of psychology? Let us limit ourselves to things that can be observed, and formulate laws concerning only those things. Now what can we observe? We can observe *behavior—what the organism does or says.* And let us point out at once: that *saying* is doing—that is, *behaving.* . . .

The rule, or measuring rod, which the behaviorist puts in front of him always is: Can I describe this bit of behavior I see in terms of "stimulus and response"? By stimulus we mean any object in the general environment or any change in the tissues themselves due to the physiological condition of the animal, such as the change we get when we keep an animal from sex activity, when we keep it from feeding, when we keep it from building a nest. By response we mean anything the animal does—such as turning toward or away from a light, jumping at a sound, and more highly organized activities such as building a skyscraper, drawing plans, having babies, writing books, and the like. . . .[2]

The interest of the behaviorist in man's doings is more than the interest of the spectator—he wants to control man's reactions as physical scientists want to control and manipulate other natural phenomena. It is the business of behavioristic psychology to be able to predict and to control human activity. . . .[3]

Why do people behave as they do—how can I, as a behaviorist, working in the interests of science, get individuals to behave differently today from the way they acted yesterday? How far can we modify behavior by training (conditioning)? These are some of the major problems of behavioristic psychology.[4]

By 1952, behavioral psychology had not only become the "scientific" foundation of American pedagogy, but it had changed our textbooks, revised the classroom curriculum, and redesigned the American school building. If you detect something mindless about American education, it's because the mind has been taken out of it. Only visible behavior counts. The NEA not only accepted all of this but was one of the main instruments for diffusing this educational philosophy among teachers.

But the public was beginning to wake up. An article in the January 1955 issue of the *NEA Journal* by Teachers College historian Lawrence Cremin drew special attention to the problem. He wrote:

> For two years, beginning with Dean Harold Benjamin's "Report on the Enemy" to the NEA in 1950, the profession had been made increasingly aware of persistent and acrimonious attacks on the public schools. Communities from Englewood, New Jersey, to Pasadena, California, had become the scenes of sharp encounters over educational policy.

The "enemy" were a growing number of "new organized anti-public school groups suggesting insidious relationships between public education and communism, socialism, subversion, delinquency, atheism, and ignorance."

Apparently the public knew that something had gone wrong in public education but simply did not realize the extent of the problem they were dealing with. There were lots of complaints that children weren't learning to read. In fact, American children by the thousands were suddenly deemed to be afflicted with a newly discovered condition called "dyslexia." All of which prompted Rudolf Flesch to write a book called *Why Johnny Can't Read,* which told a startled public:

> The teaching of reading—all over the United States, in all the schools, in all the textbooks—is totally wrong and flies in the face of all logic and common sense.[5]

Flesch then went on to explain how beginning reading instruction in American schools had been radically changed by the professors of education from the traditional alphabetic-phonics method to a new whole-word, or hieroglyphic method. What astonished so many parents was how thoroughly the traditional method had been replaced by the new method. It indicated the power the progressives had to make such drastic fundamental changes in every classroom in the nation without public awareness that it was even happening. Flesch explained how it was done:

It's a foolproof system all right. Every grade-school teacher in the country has to go to a teacher's college or school of education; every teachers' college gives at least one course on how to teach reading; every course on how to teach reading is based on a textbook; every one of those textbooks is written by one of the high priests of the word method. In the old days it was impossible to keep a good teacher from following her own common sense and practical knowledge; today the phonetic system of teaching reading is kept out of our schools as effectively as if we had a dictatorship with an all-powerful Ministry of Education.[6]

In the September 1955 issue of the *NEA Journal,* Arthur I. Gates, Thorndike's disciple at Teachers College, blasted Flesch in an article with the headline, "Why Mr. Flesch Is Wrong." He wrote:

Close reading of Mr. Flesch's book, in fact, makes it apparent that his aim is to discredit American education in general. And no attack has yet appeared which is more flagrant in its misrepresentation of the facts.

Gates had another reason for wanting to discredit Flesch. Aside from inheriting Thorndike's prestigious post at Columbia, he was the editor of one of the most widely used basal reading programs in the country published by Macmillan. A lot of money was at stake for both editor and publisher. Another article blasting Flesch appeared two months later in the *NEA Journal,* plus a defense of progressive education by Hollis L. Caswell, president of Teachers College, who, in the previous year, had awarded executive secretary Carr an honorary doctor's degree.

The mid-fifties also saw the construction of a new multimillion dollar NEA building on the site of the Guggenheim mansion to house a growing bureaucracy. Membership in 1956 stood at 627,000. There were 65 state and 5,815 local affiliated associations, plus a Representative Assembly of 5,000 delegates, 30 departments, 13 headquarters divisions, 24 commissions and committees, 51 directors, 5 trustees, 11 members of the executive committee, and a staff of 560 employees in 39 units, 25 of whom reported directly to the executive secretary. Out of all of this flowed 20 monthly magazines, 181 bulletins, 36 yearbooks and over a thousand miscellaneous publications.

The United States didn't need a Department of Education. It already had one, and it had become the largest single lobby in Washington. Each year the NEA's Legislative Commission drew up its legislative shopping list for Congress. In 1955 that list included proposals for:

General federal aid to education
School-building construction
Federal aid for disaster areas
Aid to federally affected areas
Public school assistance for federally affected areas
Aid for teachers salaries
Revenues from federally controlled natural resources
Teacher retirement and social security
Separation of church and state
Tax exemption for retirement incomes
Legislative investigations
National Board of Education
U. S. Office of Education
Aid for vocational education
Civil defense
International relations
Teacher and student exchange
Narcotics
The right to vote at age 18
Child labor
Educational use of the mails
Rural library service
Equal-status amendment (ERA)

Although the NEA found many friends in Congress willing to do its bidding, there was strong opposition to federal aid to education from a variety of sources: those who argued that federal support would mean federal control of local schools; those in the parochial schools who would be ineligible for federal aid; and liberal Congressmen who insisted on withholding federal funds from racially segregated school districts.

Nevertheless, the NEA persisted, each year missing passage of their bills by smaller margins. Yet, in 1956, Congress appropriated over $500 million for a variety of educational programs. But what finally opened the federal spigot wide was the alarm set off by the Soviet launching of Sputnik, the first man-made satellite, in 1957. The following year Congress passed the National Defense Education Act, the first major act of general federal support of public education to the tune of $1 billion. This may not seem like much today, but in 1958, the entire federal budget was a mere $73.9 billion.

The election of liberal Democrat John F. Kennedy to the presidency in 1960 brightened NEA hopes that its legislative agenda would find easier sailing in Congress than under the Republicans. But Kennedy had won by a very small margin, and Congress was still the stumbling block. Executive Secretary Carr told NEA members in January 1960:

> Now is the time for American citizens to tell members of Congress that federal support for education is essential. . . .
> Public schools today cost the nation over $15 billion a year. . . . Clearly the federal government must join in the partnership (with state and local governments).
> I call upon every member of NEA to help the American people express their views to Congress.

At that time, the idea of NEA members becoming a militant political force was still just an idea. The classroom teachers who made up the bulk of NEA membership were not interested in politics. They had a paid staff in Washington which lobbied Congress on a full-time basis, and if the NEA's legislative proposals were not being made into law, perhaps the American people didn't want them.

But Carr was convinced that the public wanted large-scale federal support of education, and that Congress did not really reflect the views of the public as expressed in opinion polls. Nevertheless, Carr realized that the teachers of America needed the support and trust of the public and he did not want the NEA to engage in activities that might alienate that trust and support.

Yet, calls for educators to become politically active were being voiced with increasing frequency. At the NEA convention in 1955, Dr. Earl James McGrath, president of the University of Kansas City and former U.S. Commissioner of Education, urged educators to organize for political action. In 1956 the executive secretary of NEA's Legislative Commission, James L. McCaskill, urged NEA members to "check for yourself the voting record of your Congressman." Teachers were urged to register to vote, to write their Congressmen, visit their offices. An article in the January 1957 *NEA Journal* went further:

> Your help is needed in translating into action NEA policy which supports or opposes a particular piece of legislation. You can help set up a committee on federal legislation in your local association to study the pending legislation and to develop a program of local support or opposition, whichever seems called for. Then enlist the help of organizations and individuals outside the profession.

In 1958, the NEA Representative Assembly approved a new statement of principles calling for "informed participation by teachers in the consideration of all legislation that would affect the quantity and quality of education either directly or indirectly."

In 1961, when the 87th Congress failed to pass a bill in support of federal aid to education, the NEA concluded that "not enough pressure from supporters of public education" was responsible for the defeat. The only solution was for teachers to get involved in party politics.

In January 1962, President Kennedy presented a budget calling for the largest expenditure for education in U.S. history: $2.5 billion, or 2.6 percent of the total budget. But the Congress rejected it. The NEA concluded that "the forces favoring federal support of education are not in control of Congress."

In 1963, Congress voted $3 billion for education by passing the Higher Educational Facilities Act, the Vocational Education Act, an "impacted areas" aid program, and extending the National Defense Education Act. But elementary and secondary educaton—which NEA considered the most important area of all—was still left out in the cold. Nevertheless, after John F. Kennedy's assassination, President Johnson called that session "the education Congress."

The 1964 presidential campaign between Barry Goldwater and Lyndon Johnson presented the issues to the NEA in very clear terms. The *NEA Journal* printed statements from both candidates. Johnson told NEA members that "new and imaginative methods of financial aid must be explored," while Goldwater told them, "I have consistently opposed federal aid to elementary and secondary schools as unnecessary and unwise." It was the policy of the NEA not to endorse any presidential candidate, but the statements by the candidates made it quite clear which one NEA members would vote for.

The October 1964 *NEA Journal* published an article on "The Teacher's Role in Politics," and in the following month appeared an article entitled "Education Is a Political Enterprise." Both articles were clarion calls to political action.

Lyndon Johnson's sweeping victory over Goldwater in November 1964 set the stage for what was to be the NEA's biggest legislative victory. In January 1965 the NEA's Legislative Committee submitted its proposal for a $1.5 billion federal aid program for elementary and secondary education. On March 1, 1965 President Johnson met with 220 NEA members and leaders in the East Room of the White House summoned from all over the country by the NEA's Legislative Commission. Allan West, an NEA executive, describes the occasion:

> Attendance at the conference was one of my most memorable Washington experiences. I had attended conferences in which educators had expressed such faith in education. But I had never heard such unrestrained commitments from a President of the United States.[7]

In Johnson the NEA had always had a powerful friend, for LBJ himself had graduated from a teachers college and had actually taught school. He addressed the group as "fellow educators." The result was the passage of the Elementary and Secondary Education Act of 1965, the single largest federal aid to education program ever enacted by Congress. It opened the floodgates of federal money, and public education has never been the same since.

The role the NEA played in helping Johnson get the law passed was crucial. According to Allan West:

> During the entire period that [the bill] was before Congress, the NEA shuttled hundreds of state and local leaders in and out of Washington to work with their congressmen to furnish information, write speeches, and produce other materials as needed.

NEA consultants were actually used by Congressional committeemen to help write the final version of the bill. For all practical purposes, it was everything the NEA wanted. According to Robert E. McKay, chairman of the NEA's Legislative Commission:

> There was written into the act specific prohibitions against the allocation of any funds by the states . . . for direct support of private or parochial schools and the use of any of the money from the act to finance or enchance or to promote in any way religious instruction.[8]

When the bill was about to be passed, LBJ told the jubilant educators: "We are going to get it started, but we are never going to get her stopped." The September 1965 *NEA Journal* spread the news to its members all across the country: "We've got it started. The Elementary and Secondary Education act of 1965 is only the beginning. . . . NEA hopes that President Johnson was correct in his estimation that, once started, federal aid to education will never be stopped."

PART THREE

The War Against the Independent Mind

10. The Road to Academic Disaster

The passage of the Elementary and Secondary Education Act (ESEA) of 1965 marked the beginning of a new era for both the educators and taxpayers of America. For the educators it meant hitting the federal jackpot with untold prosperity for themselves and their suppliers. For the taxpayers it meant a new, never-ending, ever-increasing tax burden with little or no academic improvement to show for it. In fact 1965 marks the year when the SAT scores began their toboggan slide downward.

The ESEA and its numerous Titles had something for everyone. Title One provided initially $1 billion for compensatory education for economically and culturally deprived youngsters. By 1984 the accumulated appropriations for Title One would reach over $42 billion, 70 percent of which would be designated for reading programs. In its first year, Title II provided $100 million to school libraries and media centers for books, audio-visual equipment, etc. Title III provided $100 million for supplementary educational centers and services, such as educational television, language labs, and other aids to "intellectual development." Title IV provided enough millions for educational "research" to make it a booming industry for years to come. Title V provided $25 million in grants to state departments of education ostensibly to "strengthen" them—whatever that meant.

And, of course, new Titles were added every year or so. In 1966 Title VI was added to help the education of the handicapped, and in 1968 Title VII was added to finance bilingual education. Title VIII, the Indian Education Act, came aboard in 1972 as well as Title IX, the Ethnic Heritage Program.

Meanwhile other "Acts" came fast and furious. In 1970 Congress passed the Environmental Education Act, to fund curricula, research, and demonstration projects concerning the environment, and the Drug Abuse Education Act to pay for grants, training programs, workshops, institutes and a never-ending parade of conferences and seminars. In 1972 the big spenders passed the Emergency School Aid Act to facilitate the school desegregation process with a billion dollars worth of remedial services, teachers aides, guidance counselors, curricula development and other assorted goodies.

And we haven't even mentioned the School Lunch Program which started in 1946, or the Headstart Program started in 1964 and followed up in 1967 by Follow Through. In short, by the middle of the 1970s the public educators of America were literally swimming in money. Never in the history of the world had a nation poured so much of its treasure into its education system with such dismal results. But as much as it was, it would never be enough, and the NEA would keep asking for more and more and more.

(In 1984, the so-called austerity budget of President Reagan, who had been accused by the NEA of starving education to death, provided $15.4 billion in federal funds to education, and the proposed 1985 budget provided $15.5 billion.)

For years the NEA had argued and pleaded that federal money was needed to improve public education in quantity and quality. Well now that they had the money, what were the results? Was the taxpayer's federal investment a good one? We can get an idea by looking at the scores of the Student Aptitute Tests (SATs) which are taken each year by millions of high school students seeking college entrance. From 1952 to 1963 the SAT verbal mean score rose a modest two points, from 476 to 478. But three years later, in 1966, it was down a full eleven points to 467. In 1970 it was down another 7 points to 460, and in 1977 it had plummeted to 429, a staggering decline of 48 points from 1963.

The *Boston Globe* of August 29, 1976 described it as:

> . . . a prolonged and broad-scale decline unequalled in U.S. history. The downward spiral, which affects many other subject areas as well, began abruptly in the mid-1960s and shows no signs of bottoming out. . . .
>
> Only recently have facts become available that reveal the magnitude and disturbing nature of the achievement decline, its pervasiveness and consistency across all academic areas and all segments of American education.

What was the reaction of the educators to this unprecedented decline in academic achievement? The article went on:

> For the most part, educators and those connected with schools and colleges have tried to ignore or discount the significance of the achievement decline. At a national conference of school administrators earlier this year, for example, it was alluded to as the "big lie" being perpetrated against education.

But who was doing the lying? The fact is that the educators themselves had been doing all in their power to hide the decline that was taking place from parents and the public at large. The article states:

> At the same time as declining achievement engulfs the nation's schools and colleges, American education is beset with another problem: wholesale grade inflation. From high school through college, "A" and "B" grades have become the common currency for work which probably would have earned a "C" grade 10 years ago. "C" grades are

now relatively few, and "D" and "F" grades are all but nonexistent. . . .
Grade inflation at least partially blinded many to the reality of the
achievement decline.

Anyone who knew anything about education knew, of
course, that the reading problem was at the heart of the
general academic decline, for if you couldn't read well, you
could hardly be expected to do well in all the other subjects
which required reading. The seriousness of the situation was
graphically described by Karl Shapiro, the eminent poet-
professor who had taught creative writing for more than twenty years at the University of California (Davis). He told the
California Library Association in 1970:

> What is really distressing is that this generation cannot and does not
> read. I am speaking of university students in what are supposed to be
> our best universities. Their illiteracy is staggering. . . . We are
> experiencing a literacy breakdown which is unlike anything I know of
> in the history of letters.

Rudolf Flesch had warned the public in 1955, but the warning had been wasted on the educators. There was no doubt,
however, that if blame for the decline of literacy was to be
placed anywhere, it had to fall on the heads of the progressive
educators who got rid of traditional phonics instruction and
replaced it with their whole-word, look-say methods and textbooks. The nation was now reaping a bitter harvest of growing
illiteracy while paying through the nose for universal compulsory education.

The cost to the taxpayer in remediation expenditures could
be calculated in billions of dollars. But the emotional cost to
the students, intellectually crippled by this widespread educational malpractice, can never be calculated. Some parents
have tried to sue school systems for graduating students who
can't read well enough to get a decent job. But the courts have
dismissed such suits. The state and its educators have refused
to accept responsibility for the damage they have caused and
continue to cause.

Strangely enough the origin of this educational malpractice can be traced back to the earliest days of the public school movement in this country. In fact, it had a rather benign beginning. The whole-word method was invented in the 1830s by Thomas H. Gallaudet, the founder of the Hartford Asylum for the Deaf and Dumb, as a method of teaching the deaf to read.

Since deaf-mutes have no conception of spoken language, they could not, in Gallaudet's time, learn a sound-symbol system of reading. Instead, they were taught to read by way of a purely sight method consisting of pictures and whole words. Thus, as far as the deaf pupil was concerned, the written language was a series of strange little images, like Chinese ideographs, each of which consisted of an arbitrary number of "letters" arranged in an arbitrary sequence. Thus, to the deaf pupil, printed word images were hieroglyphics or word pictures representing objects, feelings, actions, and ideas and had nothing to do with sounds made by the tongue and vocal chords. Gallaudet thought that this method of beginning reading instruction would work even better with normal children, and he wrote a primer based on that method. It was called the *Mother's Primer,* the first look-say primer ever to appear, and it was published in 1835.

In 1836 the Boston Primary School Committee decided to try Gallaudet's primer on an experimental basis. Horace Mann, who became secretary of the Massachusetts Board of Education in June 1837, was very critical of the traditional alphabetic teaching method, and he heartily endorsed the new method as a means of liberating children from Calvinist academic tyranny. In November, the Primary School Committee reported favorably on the Gallaudet primer, and it was officially adopted for use in the Boston primary schools. The teachers had indeed observed that most children could learn to read some whole words before learning their letters. What they couldn't have known was that the reading problems associated with look-say would not become apparent until the pupil was in the second and third grades and required to read books with larger and more difficult vocabularies.

All of this took place in the context of a great movement for universal public education, which was expected to eradicate the ills of mankind by applying science and rationality to education. In 1839 Mann and his fellow reformers established the first state-owned and operated school for teacher training—the Normal School at Lexington, Massachusetts. In the very first year of the very first state teachers college in America, the whole-word method of teaching reading was taught to its students as the preferred and superior method of instruction. Also, the world's first course in educational psychology was given. It was called Phrenology. Thus, educational quackery not only got a great running start with government-controlled teacher training but became a permanent part of it.

During the next five years, Mann's *Common School Journal* became the propaganda medium not only of the public school movement and the state normal schools but of its quackery—particularly the whole-word method. But finally, in 1844, common sense made a comeback. A group of Boston schoolmasters, who had had enough of the nonsense, published a blistering attack on Mann and his reforms. Included in the attack was a thorough, incisive critique of the whole-word method, the first of its kind ever written.

The attack ignited a bitter dispute between Mann and the schoolmasters which lasted more than a year but resulted in a return to traditional primary reading instruction. The state normal schools, fledgling institutions at best, were simply not powerful enough to exert a decisive influence in the local classroom. Professors of education were still a long way off in the future. So the alphabetic method was restored to its proper place in primary instruction. But the whole-word method was kept alive in the normal schools as a legitimate alternative until it could be refurbished by a new generation of reformers in the new progressive age.

The man who did more than anyone else to keep look-say

alive during the period when McGuffey's Readers and other phonics primers dominated the scene was Col. Francis W. Parker, whom John Dewey called the father of progressive education. Parker, born in New Hampshire in 1837, decided to make teaching his career at the age of 16. He read the works of contemporary educational theorists and, after the Civil War, spent two and a half years in Europe soaking up more advanced pedagogical theory. When he returned to the U.S. he was determined to make changes in American education.

In 1873 Parker became superintendent of schools in Quincy, Massachusetts. There he made progressive reforms which brought him attention and fame. From Quincy he went to Chicago to become principal of the Cook County Normal School in 1883. From 1899 to 1901 he was principal at the University of Chicago's School of Education. When John Dewey came to the University of Chicago in 1894, Parker was his neighbor and he got to know him well. Dewey used many of Parker's ideas in creating the Laboratory School where reading was taught via the sight, or look-say, method. It was Dewey's book about the Laboratory School experiment, *School and Society,* published in 1899, that catapulted him to leadership in the progressive movement. With this book Dewey had provided the movement with a blueprint for restructuring American education, and when Parker died in 1902 Dewey became the undisputed philosophical leader of the movement.

Dewey's aim was to create among the students a spirit of social cooperation, and he believed that an emphasis on the mastery of the symbols of learning turned children inward and made them competitive and independent of their peers. Socialism demanded a strong sense of interdependence and, in Dewey's school, cooperative activities in the classroom were the means to develop it. The ABC method of teaching reading provided no social motive. It was selfish and private. Dewey criticized the prevalent mode of education as:

... dominated almost entirely by the medieval conception of learning. It is something which appeals for the most part simply to the intellectual aspect of our natures, our desire to learn, to accumulate information, and to get control of the symbols of learning; not to our impulses and tendencies to make, to do, to create, to produce, whether in the form of utility or of art.[1]

Of course Dewey was wrong. Nowhere in the world were men doing more, creating more, and producing more than in the United States where the rewards of free enterprise provided strong incentives to do, create, and produce. Under socialism, however, a sense of brotherly spirit was supposed to provide the incentive. But as history has shown, socialist societies, because of oppressive economic controls, become stagnant and dull. The contrast between West Berlin and East Berlin, Hong Kong and Peking, South Korea and North Korea demonstrate the productivity and vitality of free enterprise as opposed to drab, depressing, regimented socialism. But in 1894 socialism was still only a dream. Dewey would live long enough to see the horror of its fulfillment in the Soviet dictatorship, but he never gave up hope that a democratic socialism was possible.

It was James McKeen Cattell who got Dewey to come to Columbia in 1904. Cattell had known Dewey since their days at Johns Hopkins in the early 1880s when G. Stanley Hall was their teacher. And it was Cattell who conducted the reaction-time experiments in Wundt's Leipzig laboratory that would later be used to provide a "scientific" basis for look-say. Cattell had observed that adults could read whole words just about as fast as they could read individual letters. From that he assumed that a child could be taught to read simply by showing him whole words and telling him what they said—look-say.

But Cattell knew that look-say needed an authoritative textbook, with the seal of approval of the New Psychology, if it was to be adopted by teachers. Apparently Cattell was not much of a writer. So he got one of G. Stanley Hall's students, Edmund Burke Huey, to write a book arguing in favor of the look-say method as opposed to the traditional alphabetic method. In 1908 the book was published with the authoritative title, *The Psychology and Pedagogy of Reading*. That book, which was neither inspired nor written by anyone who had ever taught a child to read, instantly became the bible of progressive educators on the matter of reading instruction. The book achieved the status of authority so quickly, that when Paul Monroe, a Teachers College professor, compiled his *Cyclopedia of Education* in 1911, Huey's book was used as the *sole* authority for its article on reading.

What is even more shocking is that by 1908 Cattell and his colleagues were already aware that the look-say method was producing inaccurate readers, which was one of the reasons why it had been discarded in Boston back in the 1840s. So Huey turned a negative into a positive and defended inaccuracy as a virtue! He wrote:

> Even if the child substitutes words of his own for some that are on the page, provided that those express the meaning, it is an encouraging sign that the reading has been real, and recognition of details will come as it is needed. The shock that such a statement will give to many a practical teacher of reading is but an accurate measure of the hold that a false ideal has taken of us, viz., that to read is to say just what is upon the page, instead of to *think,* each in his own way, the meaning that the page suggests.

In other words, what an author has to say is less important than what the reader *thinks* he has to say. And each reader is free to interpret "each in his own way" the message of a written page. Therefore precision of thought and language belongs to a "false ideal" from which teachers have got to shake themselves loose. Dr. Huey continues:

> Inner saying there will doubtless always be, of some sort; but not a saying that is, especially in the early reading, exactly parallel to the forms upon the page. It may even be *necessary,* if the reader is to really tell what the page suggests, to tell it in words that are some-

what variant; for reading is always of the nature of translation and, to be truthful, must be free.

Of course, every adult reader is free to interpret or paraphrase whatever he reads provided he can at least read accurately what the writer has written. But to encourage children to misread the written word in early stages of learning to read can create disastrous reading habits in later life. Anyone who has tried to remediate a "reading disabled" child will know what I am talking about. However, Dr. Huey has more to say:

> Both the inner utterance and reading aloud are natural in the early years and are to be encouraged, but only when left thus free, to be dominated only by the purpose of getting and expressing meanings; and until the insidious thought of reading as word-pronouncing is well worked out of our heads, it is well to place the emphasis strongly where it really belongs, on reading as *thought-getting,* independently of expression.

So, according to Dr. Huey, we have to get it out of our heads that accuracy in reading the written word is important. In fact, it's downright insidious. But if accuracy in reading is unimportant, then what about accuracy in writing? Why should authors take pains to choose the right words, fashion the right sentences if the reader is going to substitute words of his own?

It is hard not to believe that intelligent men like Dewey, Thorndike, Cattell and Huey had an ulterior motive in promoting poor reading habits. The socialists have told us over and over again that the schools must be used as the means to change human nature so that a socialist society can be brought about. Was planned illiteracy part of their scheme? If it was, then we can say that they have been incredibly successful, for never has functional illiteracy and reading disability been more widespread in America, despite the highest expenditures for education in the history of mankind. What is the money being spent for? Not to produce literacy, but to produce socialism.

11. The Conspiracy Against Literacy

Nothing has mystified Americans more than the massive decline of literacy in the United States. Children spend more time in school and the government spends more money on education than ever before. Yet, reading ability keeps declining. What has gone wrong?

The Department of Education estimates that there are 24 million functional illiterates in the United States, *virtually all of whom have had from eight to twelve years of compulsory public schooling*. Contrast this with the figures for illiteracy in 1910 issued by the U.S. Bureau of Education and quoted in the January 30, 1915 issue of James McKeen Cattell's own weekly publication, *School and Society:*

> Statistics compiled by the Bureau of Education for use at the Panana-Pacific Exposition, show that of children from 10 to 14 years of age there were in 1910 only 22 out of every 1,000 who could neither read nor write. In 1900 there were of the same class 42 per 1,000. . . . The following states report only 1 child in 1,000 between the ages of 10 and 14 as illiterate: Connecticut, District of Columbia, Massachusetts, Minnesota, Montana, New Hampshire, North Dakota, Oregon, Utah, and Washington. . . .
>
> It is evident that the public schools will in a short time practically eliminate illiteracy.[1]

So apparently they knew how to teach children to read in 1910. Also, there was no such thing as "functional illiteracy," that is, a kind of low, inadequate reading ability which is the product of faulty teaching methods in our schools. The illiteracy of 1910 was the result of some children having no schooling. Functional illiteracy is the result of the way we actually teach children to read in our schools, for our teachers today, whether they know it or not, have been deliberately trained to produce functional illiteracy.

To believe that such massive functional illiteracy is an unplanned phenomenon beyond the control of anyone is to believe that our educators with all of their doctoral degrees literally don't know what they are doing. After all, teaching children to read is no big mystery. Teachers have been doing it for the last 3,000 years, and as the U.S. Government's own statistics show they were doing it well in 1910 and up to about the 1930s when the big switch took place in teaching methods.

It is always possible for educators to make mistakes. But what is an equally strange phenomenon is the intense resistance the educators have put up to any suggestion of reform of reading instruction methods in our schools. For example, the Reading Reform Foundation was founded in 1963 to attempt to restore phonics to its proper place in reading instruction in American schools. Since its inception, the Foundation has met nothing but hostility and resistance from the educational establishment. Many individual teachers have responded to the Foundation's message, but the establishment as a whole has simply ignored, discounted, or resisted it.

This writer was taught to read in the public schools of New York City back in the early 1930s. In those days they still used phonics—that is, they taught the alphabet and the sounds the letters stand for, and before you knew it, you could read. In those days dyslexia was unknown and there were no functional illiterates or "reading disabled" children. Organically caused dyslexia did indeed exist, but it was so rare that most people had never even heard of it. Everyone in school, including the not so bright and the culturally disadvantaged minorities, learned to read. Today, even the very bright have a terrible time learning to read. Why?

It was John Dewey who first formulated the notion that high literacy is an obstacle to socialism. The authors of *The Dewey School,* in recounting the history of the Laboratory School, wrote in 1936:

> Too much emphasis cannot be laid upon the fact that undue premium is put upon the ability to learn to read at a certain chronological age.... The entertainment plus information motive for reading conduces much to the habit of solitary self-entertainment which ends too often in day-dreaming instead of guided creative activities, controlled by objective success or failure.[2]

All of this echoed what Dewey had written in 1896, after the Laboratory School had been in operation for nine months:

> It is one of the great mistakes of education to make reading and writing constitute the bulk of the school work the first two years. The true way is to teach them incidentally as the outgrowth of the social activities at this time. Thus language is not primarily the expression of thought, but the means of social communication.... If language is abstracted from social activity, and made an end in itself, it will not give its whole value as a means of development.... It is not claimed that by the method suggested, the child will learn to read as much, nor perhaps as readily in a given period as by the usual method. That he will make more rapid progress later when the true language interest develops ... can be claimed with confidence.[3]

Thus, Dewey knew then that the new teaching methods would not produce better readers. He assumed that their reading would improve "later." Incredible as it may seem, for Dewey the social goals justified the use of these new reading instruction methods. But why, you might ask, did Dewey consider high literacy to be incompatible with his social goals? He provides the answer.

To Dewey, the greatest enemy of socialism was the private

consciousness that seeks knowledge in order to exercise its own individual judgment and authority. High literacy gave the individual the means to seek knowledge independently. To Dewey it created and sustained the individual system which was detrimental to the social spirit needed to build a socialist society. In *Democracy and Education,* published in 1916, Dewey devoted a good deal of the book to show how individualism had to adapt itself to the needs of collectivism. He wrote:

> [W]hen knowledge is regarded as originating and developing within an individual, the ties which bind the mental life of one to that of his fellows are ignored and denied.
>
> When the social quality of individualized mental operations is denied, it becomes a problem to find connections which will unite an individual with his fellows. Moral individualism is set up by the conscious separation of different centers of life. It has its roots in the notion that the consciousness of each person is wholly private, a self-inclosed continent, intrinsically independent of the ideas, wishes, purposes of everybody else.[4]

What better way to undermine this independent individualism than by denying it the necessary tool for its development: high literacy. Dewey wrote in *School and Society* in 1899:

> [T]he tragic weakness of the present school is that it endeavors to prepare future members of the social order in a medium in which the conditions of the social spirit are eminently wanting. . . .
>
> The mere absorbing of facts and truths is so exclusively individual an affair that it tends very naturally to pass into selfishness. There is no obvious social motive for the acquirement of mere learning, there is no clear social gain in success thereat.

Some pages later, Dewey wrote:

> The introduction of active occupations, of nature-study, of elementary science, of art, of history; the relegation of the merely symbolic and formal to a secondary position; the change in the moral school atmosphere . . . are not mere accidents, they are necessities of the larger social evolution. It remains but to organize all these fac-

tors, to appreciate them in their fulness of meaning, and to put the ideas and ideals involved into complete, uncompromising possession of our school system.[5]

Note how emphatically Dewey put it: "the relegation of the merely symbolic and formal to a secondary position," as well as the other curriculum changes, *"are not mere accidents"* but a necessity "of the larger social evolution."

Dewey based all of his new reforms on the new psychology developed at Leipzig and brought to this country by Hall, Cattell, Judd and others. He wrote in the same book:

> Earlier psychology regarded mind as a purely individual affair in direct and naked contact with an external world. . . . At present the tendency is to conceive individual mind as a function of social life—as not capable of operating or developing by itself, but as requiring continual stimulus from social agencies, and finding its nutrition in social supplies. The idea of heredity have made familiar the notion that the equipment of the individual, mental as well as physical, is an inheritance from the race: a capital inherited by the individual from the past and held in trust by him for the future. The idea of evolution has made familiar the notion that mind cannot be regarded as an individual, monopolistic possession, but represents the outworkings of the endeavor and thought of humanity.[6]

Dewey never explained how someone with low literacy skills would be able to enjoy the intellectual inheritance of the race if he couldn't read! Although Dewey never minced any words, the American public has never really been fully aware of Dewey's intense hostility to individualism and what he did in his attempt to destroy it. Max Eastman once wrote that "Dewey concealed the dynamite of his educational theories in a pile of dry hay." How true! Perhaps Dewey's view is best summed up in a line he wrote in 1935 in *Liberalism and Social Action:*

> The last stand of oligarchical and anti-social seclusion is perpetuation of this purely individualistic notion of intelligence.[7]

Thus, the goal was to produce inferior readers with inferior intelligence dependent on a socialist educational elite for guidance, wisdom and control. Dewey knew it, Cattell knew it, and Huey knew it. After the publication of Huey's book in 1908, G. Stanley Hall, Huey's mentor, went so far as to extol the virtues of illiteracy. He wrote:

> Very many men have lived and died and been great, even leaders of their age, without any acquaintance with letters. The knowledge which illiterates acquire is probably on the whole more personal, direct, environmental and probably a much larger proportion of it practical. Moreover, they escape much eyestrain and mental excitement, and, other things being equal, are probably more active and less sedentary. It is possible, despite the stigma our bepedagogued age puts upon this disability, for those who are under it not only to lead a useful, happy, virtuous life, but to be really well educated in many other ways. Illiterates escape certain temptations, such as vacuous and vicious reading. Perhaps we are prone to put too high a value both upon the ability required to attain this art and the discipline involved in doing so, as well as the culture value that comes to the citizen with his average of only six grades of schooling by the acquisition of this art.[8]

Commenting on Huey's book, Hall wrote:

> The best pedagogues are now drifting surely, if slowly, toward the conclusion that instead of taking half the time of the first year or two of school to teach reading, *little attention should be paid to it before the beginning of the third year,* that nature study, language work, and other things should take the great time and energy now given to this subject. Huey collected nearly one hundred primers, and classifies reading methods as alphabetic, phonic, phonetic, word, sentence, and combination methods. . . . Primary reading should no longer be made a fetich. This should always be secondary and should have a purpose—that is, there should be no reading for the sake of reading, for this is never an end, but should always be a means of gratifying an interest.[9]

When the educational leaders of America, the teachers of our teachers, keep drumming into the heads of their Ph.D. students that the development of literacy in school children is not only not important but socially undersirable, you get a school system geared to turning out illiterates.

It took some years before the views advocated by Dewey, Cattell, Hall, Huey, Thorndike, Judd and others were translated into practice in every classroom of America. Textbooks had to be written. Teachers had to be trained. The new methods had to be slipped into the schools without undue public notice. After all, parents don't send their children to school to become functional illiterates.

The simple truth is that the NEA played a key and significant role in advancing this conspiracy against literacy. It was a conspiracy because the American people were never informed of what was taking place nor given a choice. They were never asked if they wanted their children to be taught in a manner that would turn them into functional illiterates. They were never asked if they wanted their children's education to be tailored for socialist ends. The children were never given a choice between individualistic intelligence and socialist adaptation. All of this was imposed from above by educators, psychologists and philsophers imbued with a messianic mission to transform America into a socialist society. It would have been hard to impress the parents of America with the virtues of illiteracy. You had to have a Ph.D. to be impressed with that kind of lunacy.

In 1922 the NEA launched a monthly magazine for its members, the *Journal* of the National Education Association. For all practical purposes it became the house organ of the progressive movement. Cattell, who had been publishing his own weekly magazine, *School and Society,* since 1915 was especially active in planning the editorial content with the *Journal's* first editor, William C. Bagley of Teachers College, Columbia. Cattell had been expelled from Columbia in 1917 by Nicholas Murray Butler because of his pro-Socialist, anti-conscription radicalism. But he continued to be active and highly influential among educators and psychologists until his death in 1944.

In 1923 Cattell organized The Psychological Corporation, a private company to do psychological consulting and research for education, industry and government. The stock of the corporation had been sold exclusively to Wundtian and behavioral psychologists. The roster of stockholders was listed in the NEA *Journal* of June 1923. It included the foremost psychologists of the time. These were the men who were transforming every aspect of American education to conform with the theory of evolution and materialism. They included Edward L. Thorndike; G. Stanley Hall (President of Clark); Charles H. Judd (University of Chicago); John B. Watson, father of behaviorism; James R. Angell (President of Yale); William McDougall (Harvard); C. E. Seashore (University of Iowa); Robert M. Yerkes, who built Yale's first primate laboratory; Lewis M. Terman (Stanford), inventor of the I.Q.; and others.

In describing the purpose of the corporation, Cattell wrote:

> If everybody were trained and selected for work there might result a revolution in industry as great as that brought about through the introduction of machinery. . . . The scientific control of conduct may become of greater economic importance than the uses of electricity or of steel. . . . It is not unreasonable to assume that the production of national wealth would be doubled if everyone, from the feeble-minded child to the President of the Nation, were allowed to do the work he can do best and were trained to do it in the best way.

Implicit in the "scientific control of conduct" was a coercive society in which psychologists decided who would be trained for what. It is the system they now use in Communist China. As of now, they have not found a better way to produce wealth than the capitalist system which has made Hong Kong and Taiwan far more productive and wealthy than the People's Republic.

Meanwhile, the look-say method had begun to find its way into the schools of America. At first it was adopted by the small, private progressive schools, many of which later dropped it when its negative results became apparent. But its adoption by the public schools on a large scale would have to wait until the 1930s.

However, its first use on a large scale in public schools took place in Iowa. It wasn't long before the schools there were plagued by "reading problems." Indeed, the problems were so serious that they came to the attention of Dr. Samuel T. Orton, a professor of psychiatry at Iowa State University. Orton, a neuropathologist who specialized in speech disorders, was so alarmed by what he saw that he wrote an article entitled "The 'Sight Reading' Method of Teaching Reading as a Source of Reading Disability" which was published in the February 1929 issue of the *Journal of Educational Psychology*. Orton was almost apologetic in the way he approached the subject, for Harold Rugg, an associate of Dewey and Thorndike, edited the journal, and Arthur Gates, Thorndike's protégé, was on its editorial board. Perhaps they published it because it confirmed their theory that the new teaching method would destroy the high literacy they wanted to get rid of. Orton wrote:

> I feel some trepidation in offering criticism in a field somewhat outside of that of my own endeavor but a very considerable part of my attention for the past four years has been given to the study of reading disability from the standpoint of cerebral physiology. This work has now extended over a comparatively large series of cases from many different schools and both the theory which has directed this work and the observations garnered therefrom seem to bear with sufficient directness on certain teaching methods in reading to warrant critical suggestions which otherwise might be considered overbold.
>
> I wish to emphasize at the beginning that the strictures which I have to offer here do not apply to the use of the sight method of teaching reading as a whole but only to its effects on a restricted group of children for whom, as I think we can show, this technique is not only not adapted but often proves an actual obstacle to reading progress, and moreover I believe that this group is one of considerable size and because here faulty teaching methods may not only prevent the acquisition of academic education by children of average capacity but may also give rise to far reaching damage to their emotional life.

This was the first article in which a trained neuropathologist stated in no uncertain terms that "the sight method of teaching reading" could cause reading disability and be "an actual obstacle to reading progress" rather than a help. He also made it clear that these "faulty teaching methods may not only prevent the acquisition of academic education by children of average capacity but may also give rise to far reaching damage to their emotional life."

The case against look-say could not have been spelled out more clearly and in more alarming terms. But the NEA *Journal* said nothing. In fact it devoted its December 1929 issue to a celebration of John Dewey's 70th birthday, awarding America's premier socialist philosopher-educator with a Life Membership in the NEA. The magazine was filled with tributes from countless university presidents and other notables. It left the reader with no doubt as to who stood beside Horace Mann on the pedestal of public education. It also indicated to what extent the progressives now had complete control of American public education. It was hardly to be expected that one article in a professional journal owned and operated by the progressives would deter them in their plans to socialize America.

12. The NEA Helps Promote Functional Illiteracy

By 1930, the progressives were ready to launch their drive to get look-say textbooks into every primary classroom in the nation. The two leaders in the drive were William Scott Gray, Dean of the University of Chicago's School of Education, and Arthur I. Gates, Thorndike's protégé at Teachers College. Gray had gotten his M.A. at Teachers College in 1914 and his Ph.D. in 1916 at the University of Chicago under godfather Charles H. Judd. The latter had gotten his own Ph.D. in 1896 in Leipzig under Wundt. In 1907 Judd became director of the Psychology Lab at Yale, and in 1909 went to the University of Chicago where be became head of the School of Education. He translated Wundt's *Outlines of Psychology* into English in 1907 and wrote *Reading, Its Nature and Development* in 1918. He also became president of the American Psychological Association in 1909.

All during his career Judd was a dominant force within the NEA. He was a stockholder, along with Thorndike, in Cattell's Psychological Corporation. In the NEA he was particularly active and influential in its Department of Superintendence. His ability to get good jobs for his graduate students, particularly during the Depression, was a key to his influence. He too was anxious to implement the Dewey educational revolution.

In December 1930, the NEA *Journal* began publishing a series of articles on reading instruction by Gray whom it described as "the most eminent authority in the field of reading." The final article appeared in June 1931. No other educator had ever been given so much space in the NEA *Journal*. For Gray and his publishers it was free advertising, for in 1930 Scott Foresman had just published the first edition of Gray's "Dick and Jane" primers. In a few short years they would become the dominant reading textbooks in America's primary schools. Both publisher and author would make millions of dollars while at the same time causing a national epidemic of reading disability.

It is interesting that in his May 1931 article in the NEA *Journal* entitled "Remedial Reading Cases in Class," Gray wrote:

> The types of poor readers may be classified roughly into several groups, namely: non-readers, including those who encounter unusual difficulty in learning to read; those who can read to some extent but who are notably deficient in all phases of reading; those who encounter difficulty primarily in recognition, in comprehension, in rate of reading, or in oral interpretation; and those who are not interested in reading or who have narrow rather than diverse reading interests or who exhibit undesirable tastes in reading.

Nowhere in the article did Gray use the term dyslexia, or any other exotic medical term to describe the cause of poor reading.

Yet in April 1935, only five years after "Dick and Jane" had gotten into the schools, Gray, in an article in the *Elementary English Review* described a whole new syndrome of problems that were causing reading disability: mental deficiency or retardation, defective vision, auditory deficiencies, congenital word blindness, developmental alexia, congenital aphasia, dyslexia, congenital alexia, strephosymbolia, cerebral dominance, handedness, eyedness, ambidexterity, emotional instability, etc. Dr. Orton had been right. The sight method would indeed cause reading disabilities on a massive scale.

It was also in 1930 that Macmillan published Arthur I. Gates's primers. Both "Dick and Jane" and the Gates *Program of Reading* primers were based on the teaching methods developed by Thorndike: the use of a small number of sight words serving as stimuli and repetition of the same words as the conditioning response. The social content of the books followed John Dewey's prescription in *School and Society*. Dewey opposed using myths and fairy tales in primers. They stimulated private imagination rather than the social spirit. He wrote:

> Some writers appear to have the impression that the child's imagination has outlet only in myth and fairy tale. . . . The John and Jane that most of us know let their imaginations play about the current and familiar contacts and events of life—about father and mother and friend, about steamboats and locomotives, and sheep and cows.

Thus, the focus in the new look-say primers was on home relationships in which the child's social development was stressed. Dewey wrote:

> Little children have their observations and thoughts mainly directed toward people: what they do, how they behave, what they are occupied with, and what comes of it. . . . Its intellectual counterpart in the story-form . . . the holding together of a variety of persons, things, and incidents through a common idea that enlists feeling. . . . Their minds seek wholes, varied through episodes, enlivened with action and defined in salient features—there must be go, movement, the sense of use and operation.[1]

The result was such literary gems composed by Dr. Gray as:

Dick
Look, Jane.
Look, look.

See Dick.
See, see.
Oh, see.
See Dick.
Oh, see Dick.
Oh, oh, oh.
Funny, funny Dick.

Also, the books had lots of pictures, for Dewey had said in *My Pedagogic Creed:* "I believe that the image is the great instrument of instruction."

Of course, that contradicted all of human history in which it had been proven since the beginning of time that language, not image, is the chief instrument of both learning and instruction. Only the deaf rely on image more than language, and even they must master language to achieve any high degree of learning.

Both "Dick and Jane" and Gates's primers—which later became the "Nick and Dick" books—appeared during the Depression when the schools were strapped for money. But Gates tried to persuade schools that buying new books was, in fact, a way of economizing. In an article entitled "Printed Material: Economy or Extravagance?" in the April 1933 NEA *Journal,* Gates wrote:

> Under the present conditions, when the need for reduction of expenditures is insistent, a marked extension in the use of books and printed learning materials, instead of being an extravagance, is the most obvious and certain means of economizing without impoverishing education.

Actually, the Depression probably saved millions of children from becoming functional illiterates, for many schools were unable to afford the new look-say textbooks and thus continued to use the old phonics books until they wore out. However, when it came time to buy new books, they bought look-say. Indeed, they had no choice. Phonics books were no longer being published, and unless you had an old teacher who could teach phonics from her own experience or parents who could teach you to read at home, you now stood a good chance of becoming reading disabled.

Another strange phenomenon took place in the early 1930s that smells of conspiracy. The old primers began disappearing from the libraries of America at a time when book theft was unheard of. Charles F. Heartman in the 1934 edition of his *Bibliographical Check-list of The New England Primer,* writes:

> The most curious fact is the impossibility of locating some New England Primers sold during the last thirty years. They seem to have vanished for all efforts to locate some of them have proven futile. A number of copies located in the first and second edition of this book cannot be found now. Some have disappeared even from the libraries, probably due to the crime wave which spread, a few years ago, over all the libraries in the country.

Was it a mere coincidence that while the progressives were in the process of changing reading instruction in America, all of the old primers that were used in the past to achieve high literacy vanished into thin air? Was this done to make sure that future teachers could not go back to the old methods, or to prevent some enterprising publisher from reprinting them?

In October 1934, a Macmillan ad in the NEA *Journal* for the Gates *Program of Reading* boasted: "It has achieved tremendous success in all sections of the country, actually revolutionizing the teaching of reading in modern times and is acknowledged generally as the leading method today."

But it didn't take long before the negative effects of the method became obvious. The October 1936 NEA *Journal* began publishing a series of articles on reading problems by Arthur I. Gates and Guy L. Bond, in which it was pointed out "that there are probably nearly a half million children in the first four grades of American schools whose educational career is blocked by serious disabilities in reading." Surely Gates must have known that it was Thorndike's conditioning method that was causing the blockage. But this was only a preview of things to come. The articles were entitled "Failure in Reading and Social Maladjustment" (October 1936), "Reading Disabilities" (November 1936), "Prevention of Disabilities in Reading" (December 1936 and January 1937).

What was diagnosed as causing all the trouble? According to Gates the new look-say primers introduced too many sight words too soon and repeated them too few times. Gates wrote in the December article:

> The typical reader introduces a new word in about every 15 running words. Experiments have shown that this vocabulary burden is very heavy for even the brightest pupils and that it is overwhelmingly difficult for the slow learners.

What was his solution to the problem? Fewer words and more repetitions. Gates explained:

> All these experiences have indicated, indeed, that it would be desirable for each first-grade child to have 200 or 300, or even more, running words of reading matter for each and every new word introduced, instead of from 15 to 40 which represents the typical range.

In other words, you won't have any reading problems if you teach the children fewer words and have them repeat them interminably. And so the look-say primers were revised accordingly. In *The New Illiterates,* published in 1973, I compared the earlier and later editions of Dr. Gray's pre-primer. The revisions made in 1951 were a virtual admission of look-say's utter and dismal failure as a reading instruction method:

> In 1930 the Dick and Jane pre-primer taught 68 sight words in 39 pages of story text, with an illustration per page, a total of 565 words and a *Teacher's Guidebook* of 87 pages. In 1951 that same pre-primer had been expanded to 172 pages, divided into three separate pre-primers, with 184 illustrations, a total of 2,613 words, and a *Guidebook* of 182 pages to teach a sight vocabulary of only 58 words! . . .
>
> In 1930 the word *look* was repeated eight times in the pre-primer. In 1951 it is repeated 110 times. In 1930 the word *oh* was

repeated twelve times, in 1951, 138 times. In 1930 the word *see* was repeated 27 times, in 1951, 176 times![2]

Did the revisions do any good? Apparently not, for the problems of reading disability continued to grow in scope and complexity. But what was especially significant was Gates's acknowledgment that slow learners in particular found look-say "overwhelmingly difficult." That would explain why, before look-say was adopted, slow learners learned to read without great difficulty via the alphabetic phonics method. That fact was recently confirmed in the updated edition of Dr. Jeanne Chall's book, *Learning to Read: The Great Debate.* She wrote:

> Enfield's (1976) study was concerned with a group below average in reading readiness tests, scoring below the 25th percentile. In her pilot study, she compared 15 children receiving an experimenter-designed synthetic phonics program with a matched sample receiving an analytic phonics program [look-say] in a popular basal-reading series. In all comparisons—reading comprehension, word recognition, and spelling—the direct-synthetic group was significantly ahead. She extended this study with 192 first graders, comparing their progress with similar children the year before. The results also favored the direct-synthetic on all three measures.[3]

You may be confused by the technical language, but "analytic phonics" is the kind of incidental phonics taught in look-say reading programs as phonetic clues. Synthetic phonics refers to the alphabetic phonic method, sometimes known as "phonics first." Despite this recent research evidence overwhelmingly in favor of phonics, *most of the schools in America still teach look-say in one version or another,* to the particular detriment of slow learners who unquestionably *need* intensive phonics in order to succeed.

In the late thirties, Gray and Gates and other look-say authors revised their reading programs to accomodate the problems they were causing. However, the situation only got worse. By the 1940s the term "dyslexia" had become a household word. In April 1944 *Life* magazine ran a major article on the subject, reporting:

Millions of children in the U.S. suffer from dyslexia which is the medical term for reading difficulties. It is responsible for about 70% of the school failures in 6- to 12-year-age group, and handicaps about 15% of all grade-school children. Dyslexia may stem from a variety of physical ailments or combination of them—glandular imbalance, heart disease, eye or ear trouble—or from a deep-seated psychological disturbance that "blocks" a child's ability to learn. It has little or nothing to do with intelligence and is usually curable.

The article went on to describe the case of a little girl with an I.Q. of 118 who was being examined at the Dyslexia Institute of Northwestern University. After her tests, the doctors concluded that the little girl needed "thyroid treatments, removal of tonsils and adenoids, exercises to strengthen her eye muscles." The article concluded:

Other patients may need dental work, nose, throat or ear treatment, or a thorough airing out of troublesome home situations that throw a sensitive child off the track of normality. In the experience of the institute these range from alcoholic fathers to ambitious mothers who try to force their children too fast in school.

Gray, Gates, Thorndike, Cattell and Judd must have had a good laugh over that one! The method was working beyond their wildest dreams. What is particularly significant is that Dr. Orton, Dr. Gates himself, and *Life* magazine all described the problem as a "blockage" to learning. Men as skilled in psychology as Gates and Thorndike knew exactly what was causing the blockage, yet Gates denounced criticism of look-say to the very end.

Meanwhile, *Collier's* magazine of November 30, 1946 published an article entitled "Why Can't They Read?" After stating that "A third of all school children are illiterate," the magazine went on:

It's nothing new, it's been going on for years. It is common knowledge among educators that at least one third of our school children lag behind their age and grade in reading, all the way through school. Thousands emerge from high school totally unable to read and comprehend so much as the daily paper. As for reading for pleasure—only a lucky minority ever learn to do that.

Now that the Deweyites had confirmation that they could induce massive illiteracy in the classroom by using their methods, there was nothing to stop them from eradicating that hated independent intelligence that stood in the way of socialism. They would fight tooth and nail any attempts to go back to the old methods of teaching reading. And that's exactly what they did when *Why Johnny Can't Read* was published in 1955. The book was important because it identified the cause of the reading problem: the look-say method. Other writings in popular and education magazines had told about the reading problem, but none of them had identified and pin-pointed its cause. Rudolf Flesch had done it in no uncertain terms, and he named the professors by name.

And that's why their reaction to Flesch was so vehement. He made them appear stupid, as if they really didn't know what they were doing. Flesch presented eleven research studies that proved phonics to be superior to look-say as a method of teaching reading. He seemed to say: "Look, you silly fools, phonics works better than look-say." What Flesch didn't know is that the professors already knew that. They knew it when they devised the look-say method. Dewey had in fact admitted that children taught by look-say would not read as well as those taught by phonics. Huey happily admitted that children taught by look-say would misread all over the lot, Hall had shamelessly extolled the virtues of illiteracy, and Gates had acknowledged that slow learners found look-say "overwhelmingly difficult."

It is obvious that Gray and Gates knew exactly what their mentors' aims were since they were the very disciples chosen and groomed to carry them out. It is naive to assume that the disciples were not as devoted to these aims as were their masters, for the key to their advancement within the hierarchy was the degree of devotion they brought to their mentors' cause.

The dangers posed by Flesch and other critics of look-say prompted Gray to create an organization that could exert much stronger control over the teachers of reading in America, one that would create a united front against growing parental dissatisfaction. The spread of reading disability had created a need for remedial teaching, and two organizations had been formed for professional purposes: the National Association of Remedial Teaching (1946) and the International Council for the Improvement of Reading Instruction (1948). In 1956 Gray and his colleagues decided to merge these two groups into one major professional organization, the International Reading Association (IRA). It would, in a few short years, become the impregnable citadel of the look-say method. Gray, as expected, was elected its first president, and most of the presidents who followed have been look-say textbook authors.

In 1956 the IRA had a mere 7,000 members; in 1983 it had 65,000. It now publishes four journals and holds an annual convention that attracts as many as 13,000 registrants. In addition, many of its regional and state organizations hold annual local conventions of their own. Also, it collaborates closely with the NEA. So if you are one of the many Americans who wondered why nothing improved after Flesch's book came out, there's the answer.

Meanwhile the NEA did its job in discrediting Flesch and keeping the teachers in line. In the September 1955 NEA *Journal* Gates blasted Flesch, accusing him of trying to "discredit American education." In the October 1955 issue, an article by one of Gates's graduate students, Nila Banton Smith, then professor of education at New York University, reminded teachers of the important social purposes behind reading. Professor Smith wrote:

> We are on the brink of a new epoch in reading instruction. . . . In the future, reading instruction must concern itself with much more than pedagogy. It must mesh more directly with the gears of vital social problems and needs.

The November 1955 NEA *Journal* published another blast at Flesch entitled "Why Can't Rudy Read." The authors wrote:

> Most of the book is simply opinion (unsupported by any objective evidence), quotations out of context, accounts of Flesch's limited personal observations, and some amusing (tho occasionally vicious) rhetoric.
>
> . . . Either Flesch is deliberately attempting to mislead and deceive the American people, or Flesch can't read.

At no time did the NEA *Journal* offer Flesch the opportunity to reply to his critics, nor did it ever suggest that the dispute over phonics and look-say could be resolved by independent research. For an organization known for its propensity to form commissions, it's surprising that the NEA has never sponsored a commission to investigate the cause of the reading problem.

But then, in 1967, a book was published which indeed caused the look-say establishment a bit of embarrassment. The book, *Learning to Read: The Great Debate,* was written by Dr. Jeanne Chall, a respected member of the International Reading Association and a professor at the Harvard Graduate School of Education. After several years of intensive research into a mountain of studies done on beginning reading instruction, Chall came to the conclusion that the phonics, or code approach, produced better readers than the look-say method. In short, it was a clear vindication of what Rudolf Flesch had asserted 12 years earlier.

Since the book had been written for the educational rather than the popular market, it did not make the kind of waves in the general press that Flesch's book did. Still, Chall had given ammunition to the progressives' worst enemies, and the profession dealt with her in its own way. The reviewer in the IRA's *Journal of Reading* (January 1969) wrote:

> What prevents Chall's study from achieving respectability is that many of her conclusions are derived from a consideration of studies that were ill-conceived, incomplete and lacking in the essen-

tials of suitable methodological criteria. In her eagerness to clarify these studies she allowed her personal bias toward a code emphasis to color her interpretations of the data. . . .

It seems rather odd that a researcher intent upon dispelling confusion should have allowed herself to be moored on a reef of inconclusiveness and insubstantiality.

Other reviewers in the *Reading Teacher, Elementary English,* and *Grade Teacher* were equally critical of Chall, seriously reducing the impact of her findings. However, in deference to her position as a member in good standing of the educational establishment, the NEA permitted Dr. Chall to air her views in the February 1969 NEA *Journal.* In an article entitled "Beginning Reading: Where Do We Go From Here?" Dr. Chall voiced cautious optimism that reading instruction would improve, with more phonics being taught earlier. However, the *Journal* of April 1969 ran an article by Lyman C. Hunt, director of the Reading Center at the University of Vermont, which was quite critical of Chall's views. The NEA would not permit Chall to have the last word. Nevertheless, in response to the Hunt article, Donna Connell, a teacher from California, wrote (September 1969):

> The research is overwhelmingly in favor of a decoding emphasis in *beginning* reading. . . . Without decoding skills, early sight readers are completely dependent upon the teacher. . . .
>
> Auditory discrimination is at its peak in early childhood, when children all over the world effortlessly learn their native language. Postponing decoding, the bridge between sound and sight, until this peak of neurological readiness has passed (about age five and a half) is imposing an unnecessary handicap.
>
> All my kindergarten children, regardless of IQ or economic background, read, some up to middle second grade level on the Stanford Achievement Test. Decoding may be dull and difficult for older children, but it is a fascinating experience for the younger ones.

If some teachers had switched from look-say to phonics, it was because phonics had begun to make something of a comeback in 1963 when several publishing houses came out with new phonics-oriented reading programs, the first since the 1930s. But the major look-say publishers still retained at least 85 percent of the market. After all, the graduate students of Gray, Gates and other look-say professors were in key positions throughout the educational establishment. Their criticisms of Chall's book created almost as much controversy and confusion over her findings as they did over Flesch's. Also their influence on textbook selection committees guaranteed the continuation of look-say in the schools despite frantic pleas from parents for phonics. Twenty-two states have statewide textbook adoption procedures. In 1980, for example, Texas chose *only* look-say primers for its primary schools, and in 1982 California did virtually the same, thus guaranteeing the perpetuation of the reading problem in two of our largest states well into the 21st century.[4]

Despite Chall's influence, reading scores continued to decline. In New York City, for example, the 1972 reading scores were the worst ever recorded. Only 32 percent of the pupils were reading at or above grade level. In 1973 the Board of Education in New York became jubilant because that figure had risen to 33.8 percent, a 1.8 percent improvement over the previous year. And in 1974 New York was satisfied because the scores held steady at 33.8 percent. At the same time it was revealed that there had been widespread cheating on the tests, so the real scores were probably a lot lower than the recorded ones.

This is what look-say had done to the nation's largest public school system which, prior to the introduction of the whole-word method, had taught hundreds of thousands of children from immigrant families to read fluently and competently.

Meanwhile, the progressives found other ways to counter their critics. They changed the vocabulary of the debate. The whole-word method was no longer referred to as look-say. It became known as "psycholinguistics." The educator who brought that word into usage was Dr. Kenneth S. Goodman, a look-say author and one of Gray's most promising disciples.

Goodman obtained notoriety when he told a *New York Times* reporter (July 9, 1975) that it was perfectly all right if a youngster read "pony" for "horse," because it meant that the youngster had gotten the meaning. Somehow it didn't matter to Dr. Goodman if the youngster didn't know the difference between a pony and a horse—or a car and a truck, or an ape and a man.

After William S. Gray's death in 1960—he accidentally fell off a horse, not a pony, although he might have thought he was on a pony—Goodman became look-say's new leader. He was particularly adept at defending whole-word textbooks against the new phonics competition. He wrote in the May 1967 *Journal of the Reading Specialist:*

> The teacher's manual of the Lippincott *Basic Reading* incorporates a letter by letter varians in the justification of its reading approach: "In short, following this program the child learns from the beginning to see words as the most skillful readers see them . . . as whole images of complete words with all their letters."
>
> In place of this misconception, I offer this: "Reading is a selective process. It involves partial use of available language cues selected from perceptual input on the basis of the reader's expectation. As this partial information is processed, tentative decisions are made to be confirmed, rejected or refined as reading progresses."
>
> More simply stated, reading is a psycholinguistic guessing game.

We must be grateful to Dr. Goodman for being so honest in proclaiming what he believes reading is: a guessing game, albeit a "psycholinguistic" one. Ancient hieroglyphics required a lot of guessing, and so do modern Chinese ideographs. And that's why the alphabet was invented, to eliminate the guessing and to make reading an exact skill. Once you are trained in translating written sound symbols into the exact spoken words they represent, precision in reading becomes automatic. Perhaps, Dr. Goodman doesn't consider precision in reading important, except when negotiating contracts with his publisher, or defining the benefits in his retirement plan, or knowing the schedule of his appointments. We live in a highly technological civilization that demands precision in virtually every working aspect of life. But Dr. Goodman and his colleagues are preparing American children for a world of guessing and imprecision more attuned to the stone age than the age of the computer.

The year 1981 was an important one. It was the year in which Rudolf Flesch came out with *Why Johnny Still Can't Read* and Kenneth Goodman became president of the International Reading Association. Flesch wrote: "Twenty-five years ago I studied American methods of teaching reading and warned against educational catastrophe. Now it has happened."

What was NEA's reaction? Their contempt for both Drs. Flesch and Chall was best expressed by their declaration in the 1983–84 Annual Edition of *Today's Education* that "the overemphasis on phonics with beginners" is now "ready for the scrap heap." In their lists of books recommended for "Must Reading," they neither listed Flesch's new book nor Dr. Chall's updated edition of *The Great Debate*. They listed *Language and Literacy: the Selected Writings of Kenneth S. Goodman*. Need more be said?

13. The Soviet Connection

The success of the conspiracy against literacy in the United States can be measured by comparing two simple statistics: the first from Cattell's *School and Society* of January 30, 1915 in which the U.S. Bureau of Education reported that in 1910 only 1 out of 1,000 children between ages 10 and 14 in Massachusetts were illiterate; the second from an editorial in the *Boston Globe* of March 11, 1984 stating that "about 40 percent of the city's adult population is believed to be functionally illiterate." What a staggering difference—and at a time when "science" is supposed to have taught us more about education than our highly literate ancestors ever knew!

Never have we had more reading experts, remedial specialists, and doctors of education devoted to reading. Never has more money been poured into reading "research," and never have we had more illiteracy affecting every level of society. Several years ago, Prof. Steven Marcus of Columbia University wrote:

> What we are confronted with in higher education in America is a situation of mass functional illiteracy. The situation itself is not entirely new, but the scale is unprecedented. . . . Hence, one of the

127

historic functions of the first two years of higher education in America has been, and remains, reparative.[1]

This is the depth to which American literacy has fallen, thanks to the NEA and its friends.

What is even more shocking is that reading disability has now been classified as a handicap like deafness and blindness under a previously unheard of category called "learning disabled." In 1982–83 the federal government funded special education for 31,096 blind students and over 1.7 million "learning disabled" students. The cruel tragedy is that most of the learning disabled acquired their handicap in the classroom through widespread educational malpractice—at the taxpayer's expense.

According to *Education Week* of April 24, 1984:

> Since the enactment in 1975 of the federal law guaranteeing handicapped children the right to an education, the number of learning-disabled students receiving special services in the nation's schools has risen by 948,658 children to 1.7 million, a 119-percent increase over a seven-year period. During that same time, overall enrollment in public schools dropped by about 11.5 percent, according to federal statistics.
>
> Learning-disabled students represented 40 percent of the more than 4 million students served in special-education programs throughout the country during the 1982–83 school year, according to data collected by the U.S. Education Department.

Most of the increase in learning disability is taking place in states with large urban minority populations. For example, in New York, the number of learning-disabled students increased 68 percent in *one* school year—between 1981–82 and 1982–83. In Philadelphia the number of learning-disabled students enrolled in full-time classes has increased 496 percent since 1977–78—from 1,113 students to 6,640. And that doesn't include another 5,402 enrolled in part-time programs. It costs Philadelphia about $5,092 a year to educate each full-time special education student, more than twice the

$2,300 needed to educate a regular student. In all, American schools spent more than $10 billion in added costs for special education services during the 1980–81 school year.

For the NEA, the "special education" bonanza has meant a new lucrative source of employment for its members at a time of declining school enrollment. In 1981–82, there were 235,386 special-education teachers in the schools. In 1984–85 that number is expected to increase to 280,000.

For the NEA and the educational establishment massive functional illiteracy has proven to be the greatest financial boon in the history of public education. It has provided such multimillion and billion dollar programs as Title One, the National Right to Read Effort, the Office of Basic Skills, Head Start, Follow Through, Special Education, and an unending flow of federal grants into "research" on reading—as if the teaching of reading were a mysterious, unknown process recently discovered by professors of education. When will it all end? If the NEA gets its way—never!

Which brings us to an even more sinister aspect of this conspiracy. It is known that in 1934, when the negative effects of look-say were already becoming known to the professors who were promoting the method, a group of about 200 Americans spent the summer in the Soviet Union attending the Anglo-American Institute of Moscow University. They were offered a variety of courses in education, psychology, economics, sociology, etc., all taught by Soviet professors in English. We do not know if there were any teachers of reading among them, but the *New York Times* of July 23, 1934 reported that politically and socially the students were "of many types, ranging from members of students' radical organizations to Groton graduates planning to enter Harvard or Yale next Fall."

According to researcher K. M. Heaton, one of the courses taken by Americans was something called "Psychopolitics," that is, the application of psychology and the principles of mental health to the conquest of the United States by the communists.[2] It is well known that Soviet psychologists had experimented with methods of artificially inducing behavioral disorganization in human beings. In fact, the major experimental work in that field was conducted by Soviet psychologist Aleksandr R. Luria, whose book, *The Nature of Human Conflicts,* was translated into English and published in the United States in 1932. The translator was Dr. W. Horsley Gantt of Johns Hopkins University who himself had spent the years 1922 to 1929 in the Soviet Union, working for five of those years in the laboratories of Prof. Pavlov on the physiology of the brain. In 1930 Gantt established the Pavlovian Laboratory at the Phipps Psychiatric Clinic at Johns Hopkins University. He also founded the Pavlovian Society for Research and was editor-in-chief of the *Pavlovian Journal of Biological Psychiatry.* Thus, by the 1930s, a very cordial and intimate relationship existed among Soviet and American psychologists and psychiatrists.

In the preface to his book, Dr. Luria wrote:

> The researches described here are the results of the experimental psychological investigations carried on at the State Institute of Experimental Psychology, Moscow, during the period of 1923–1930. The chief problems of the author were an objective and materialistic description of the mechanisms lying at the basis of the disorganization of human behavior and an experimental approach to the laws of its regulation. . . . To accomplish this it was necessary to create artificially affects and models of experimental neuroses which made possible an analysis of the laws lying at the basis of the disintegration of behavior.

In Chapter One, Luria writes:

> Pavlov obtained very definite affective "breaks," an acute disorganization of behavior, each time that the conditioned reflexes collided, when the animal was unable to react to two mutually exclusive tendencies, or was incapable of adequately responding to any imperative problem.

It is known that by imposing look-say teaching techniques on an alphabetic writing system, one can artificially induce dyslexia, thereby creating a learning block or reading neurosis. Reading disability is a form of behavior disorganization induced by the look-say method, because look-say sets up two mutually exclusive tendencies: the tendency to look at written English as an ideographic system, like Chinese, and the tendency to look at written English as a phonetic system because it is alphabetic.

The alphabetic system is in harmony with the spoken language because it is based on it. But the ideographic look-say system is in opposition to the spoken language because it is an entirely separate system of graphic symbols with no direct relation to any specific spoken language. Arabic numbers are a perfect example of such a system, because they can be read in any language. But numbers, when spelled out alphabetically in a particular language, can only be read in that language. In look-say, the written word is treated as a picture that can be interpreted by the reader in any way he or she wishes. As Prof. Goodman has said, it doesn't matter if the child reads the written word "horse" as "pony"—or, for that matter, "hundred" as "thousand"—for he's getting the meaning!

It is obvious that American psychologists know as much about all of this as the Russians. In fact, the article on reading in the 1911 edition of the *Cyclopedia of Education,* written by Henry Suzzallo of Teachers College, explained all of this quite clearly. And Luria's experiments indicate that psychologists know how to artificially induce dyslexic behavior. True dyslexia is so rare a condition, that it was virtually unheard of before 1930. But artificially induced dyslexia is today the most common learning disability in the United States. And that is why in the Soviet Union, *look-say is not taught.* Soviet children are taught to read by intensive phonics, the very method advocated by Rudolf Flesch and opposed by Gates, Gray and the look-say establishment. The behaviorist educators have always known that artificially induced dyslexia could be eliminated overnight by switching the primary schools back to intensive phonics. But the conspiracy against literacy is now so powerful that even the state of Texas cannot prevail against it. For this reason, if literacy is ever to gain ascendancy in the United States, it will have to be done outside the public education system which is totally controlled by the behaviorists.

Does a conspiracy of such magnitude and diabolical evil really exist to destroy American literacy? Perhaps the most convincing evidence is to be found in the *Journal of Reading* of December 1981, a special issue devoted to education and literacy in Communist Cuba. In an article entitled "Teaching reading in the Cuban primary schools," we are told that in the 1970s, Cuban "teams of curriculum experts" were given the job of "developing a unified methodology" for Cuban schools. "After reviewing the relevant research, these curriculum specialists chose the Phonic/Analytic/Synthetic method of teaching reading which was originally developed and researched in the Soviet Union and is still in use there. This method and the curriculum materials which evolved from it now constitute the official approach to the teaching of reading in the Cuban primary schools, and are used throughout the public education system."[3]

The article then goes on to tell us that the "psychological roots" of the Soviet method "can be traced to the work of Lev Vygotsky, Alexander Luria (one of Vygotsky's students), and their associates." Since American psychologists are familiar with Luria's work on the disorganization of behavior, it is hard to believe that they are not familiar with what he wrote about teaching reading. The article tells us:

> Following Vygotsky, Luria characterizes reading and writing as an integrated process developmentally progressing through various stages. He recognizes that the reading process differs with different languages. For example, largely nonphonetic writing systems like Chinese are not dependent on auditory decoding as are phonetic codes. The conventional symbols of Chinese do not record the phonetic

composition of words, but rather ideas and concepts. In such a writing system, the visual modality is primary and, therefore, most developed. But, for languages which have alphabet writing systems based on phonics (such as Spanish or English), Luria believes that reading should be approached primarily through the auditory channel.

. . . Consequently, methodologies for teaching reading should be based on the principle that comprehension of written, as well as oral, language is fundamentally related to the sound structure of the word and this is so whether the written word is perceived as a whole, in syllables, or as separate letters. . . .

While many children learn to read by the "sight" approach, they usually do not develop the "phonematic hearing" which results from the auditory analysis and synthesis of word sounds. Thus, they are hampered in their development of the other language skills of spelling, writing, and speech articulation. To bypass such auditory training is to deprive the child of an important key to language. From this perspective, the methodology used in the teaching of reading assumes unexpected importance.

Are there any reading instruction programs in the United States based on the same principles as the Soviet teaching methods? The article informs us:

In the United States, the approach closest to the Phonic/Analytic/Synthetic Method was developed in the late 1930s by Anna Gillingham, an educator, in collaboration with Samuel Orton, a neurologist interested in dyslexia. Orton decried the use of the "sight" method in the schools and emphasized the importance of the auditory blending process.

A number of methods adapted to classroom use qualify to be termed as "Orton" approach, such as those of Spalding and Spalding (1957), Traub (1977), Slingerland (1967) and Pollack (1979). What is characteristic of all of them is . . . they are intensive phonic approaches moving from sound/symbol relationships to words, phrases, sentences and then on to extended connected discourse.

The Orton approach is known to be particularly effective in teaching dyslexic students because of their great difficulty with the sequence of sounds in words.

Orton, as we pointed out in an earlier chapter, was the neuropathologist who first sounded the alarm, pointing out the negative learning and emotional effects of look-say back in 1929. The teaching methods he helped develop were used mainly to retrain the thousands of children who had become reading disabled in the classrooms of America. Yet, Orton's warnings were disregarded by Gray, Gates, Thorndike, Judd and others who knew what psychologists like Pavlov and Luria were doing in their Soviet laboratories. As trained psychologists they were smart enough to know that look-say would cause behavioral disorganization on a massive scale. The fact that they actually increased the dosage of look-say poison when it became known that look-say was producing reading failure is perhaps the most incriminating evidence of all. They resisted all pressures to return to intensive phonics.

If they didn't know what they were doing, then one would have to conclude that they were not only inferior to their Russian counterparts but also grossly incompetent. The fact that the Russians were well acquainted with the work of their American counterparts and learned much from them indicates that the Americans knew what they were doing. Pavlov, like his American colleagues, had been trained at Leipzig. The experimental work being done in the Russian laboratories was based on the methodology developed at Leipzig. Also, Thorndike's work on animal intelligence was first published in 1899. Pavlov's book on conditioned reflexes wasn't published until 1927. Indeed, Gantt, the American psychologist, worked with Pavlov in his laboratory for five years and then translated Luria's work into English. The only reason why work similar to Pavlov's and Luria's could not be conducted in American laboratories is because the law may have precluded the use of animals and human beings in such cruel experiments. But the American psychologist-educators decided to do the Russians one better. They decided to convert the entire American public school system into one gigantic behavioral laboratory using American children as their subjects. There is no conspiracy in history to compare with this one, and our schools are still very much in its grip thanks to the NEA and the International Reading Association.

Thus, the Soviet-American connection among psychologists can be traced as far back as 1924 when Gantt started working in Pavlov's laboratory. In 1925 the Soviet government established a Bureau of Cultural Relations Between U.S.S.R and Foreign Countries (VOKS) which in 1927 set up a subsidiary in the United States, the American Society for Cultural Relations with Russia (ASCRR). William Allan Neilson of Smith College was president, and John Dewey and Stephen P. Duggan were among the vice presidents. The main work of the ASCRR was to facilitate the exchange of students, professors and scientists between the two countries.

For us to believe that Gates, Gray, Thorndike, Judd and Dewey didn't know or had no interest in how the Russians were teaching their children to read when the radical change of reading instruction in America was a major part of the entire progressive education program, is to stretch credulity to the breaking point. Dewey had visited Soviet schools in 1928, and Prof. Counts of Teachers College had toured the Soviet Union in 1927 and 1929. During his visits, Counts conferred with virtually all of the people in charge of Soviet education, including Lenin's widow, N. K. Krupskaya, who wrote in her *Reminiscences of Lenin* how phonics was used to teach illiterate Red Army soldiers to read during the civil war in 1919. She writes:

> At the Extra-School Education Congress which Ilyich (Lenin) addressed a resolution was passed calling on the delegates to go out to the front. Many of them went. Among them was Elkina, an experienced school-teacher. She went to the Southern Front. The Red Army men asked to be taught to read and write. Elkina started giving them lessons based on the analytic-synthetic method of the textbooks then in use: "Masha ate *kasha* (porridge)." "Masha made butter," etc. "What are you teaching us!" the Red Army men started protesting. "Who the dickens is Masha? We don't want to read that stuff!" And

Elkina constructed her ABC lessons on different lines: "We are not
slaves, no slaves are we."

It was a success. The Red Army men quickly learned to read and
write. This was the very method of combining instruction with real
life that Ilyich had been urging all the time. There was no paper to
print new textbooks on. Elkina's textbook was printed on yellow
wrapping paper. . . . The Red Army men quickly learned to read and
write by Elkina's ABC book.[4]

All of which proves how simple and inexpensive it is to
teach reading if the proper methods are used. Today, American schools use the most expensive, lavish primers in history,
but they aren't worth the paper they're printed on. In any case,
back in 1927 George Counts had much freer access to the
Soviet educational hierarchy than Americans have today, and
it is certain that his colleagues at Teachers College were
aware of his findings.

Thus, by the time the Moscow summer school got underway
in 1934, the groundwork had been thoroughly done. Stephen
P. Duggan, director of the Institute of International Education, which sponsored the Moscow summer schools, explained
how the arrangements were made in a letter to the *New York
Times* published May 4, 1935:

In the Fall of 1933 I was invited by the Soviet Government to go
to Moscow to advise with it as to the best methods to develop cultural
relations between the United States and the Soviet Union. . . . Before
leaving for Russia I invited a number of distinguished educators to
form an advisory council. Every one invited accepted the invitation,
and during the following years two meetings of the advisory council
were held.

In order to discover from those who attended the Moscow Summer session the relative success of the enterprise, I requested a
confidential report from each student at the close of the session. These
reports were very illuminating. One criticism upon which there was
almost unanimous agreement was that each professor who conducted
a course thought it necessary to give the background of the Soviet
philosophy of political and social organization to show how his particular course fitted into it. As there were thirteen courses, the stu-

dents naturally grew tired of the repetition. Hence this Fall a subcommittee of the advisory committee conferred with the representatives of the Soviet educational authorities as to ways in which the Summer School might be improved. I suggested that one fundamental course in the principles of the collective society should be given which would be a prerequisite for all students who did not give evidence of a previous familiarity with that system.

Recently the statement appeared in the *New York American* that the particular course just mentioned was organized by the Soviet Government. This letter is to correct that statement. If any blame is attached to the action it does not belong to the Soviet Government. It is mine.

Obviously, Prof. Duggan was sympathetic to the Soviet Union, and his sympathy must have rubbed off on his son Laurence, who succeeded him as director of the Institute of International Education. On December 20, 1948, Laurence Duggan, at the age of 43, fell, jumped, or was pushed to his death from the window of his sixteenth floor office in New York after having been implicated by Whittaker Chambers as belonging to a communist spy ring. He had already been interviewed by the FBI and was scheduled to testify the next day before a Congressional committee investigating the infiltration of the U.S. government by communist agents. It is not known what he would have said, but it is believed that he was ready to name names.

It would be interesting to read the reports of those students who attended the Moscow summer school in 1934 and to see where their careers led them. The summer school of 1935, which was promoted by a full page ad in the NEA *Journal,* was abruptly cancelled after about 200 Americans had arrived in Moscow. Apparently some of the Soviet professors had fallen victim to Stalin's massive purge of the communist party. It was probably also feared that some of the Americans might be Trotskyite agents. In any case, the purge of the Trotskyites hardly seemed to put a dent in the ongoing infiltration of American institutions by Stalinists. Nor did the purges deter American progressives from pursuing their socialist goals.

Meanwhile the NEA has established cordial relations with Soviet and Nicaraguan teachers who use intensive phonics to teach their children to read. Yet, the NEA keeps pushing look-say, the thalidomide of primary education, on American children. The crucial question is: do they know any better, or are they just dumb?

PART FOUR

Teachers Become a
Political Force

14. The NEA Becomes a Labor Union

The NEA is probably the most intellectually dishonest organization in America. It is part union, part professional organization, and part political party. Its object is to control the Congress, the fifty state legislatures, the Democratic Party, the curriculum in all the schools, public and private, and the entire teaching profession. Its interest in academics is subordinate to its radical political and social ends.

Although the NEA pays much lip service to the idea of quality education, it has since 1918 promoted only the progressive variety and, for the last sixty years, has played a key role in the conspiracy against literacy. Although the public schools are supposed to be for all children and all parents, the NEA has waged warfare against conservatives for as long as it has known that there were Americans who opposed their radicalism. Today that warfare has reached a hysterical state.

From 1857 to about 1900 the NEA was little more than a discussion club for superintendents, state education officers, and college presidents. Its conventions were commercially self-serving, philosophically stimulating, but politically inconsequential. The new evolution-based psychology revolutionized education at the turn of the century, and the NEA became its organized voice. In 1893 and again in 1918 the NEA assumed the role of "Ministry of Education," setting down educational policy for the nation's public schools.

Its move to Washington in 1918 made the NEA into an educational lobby under full control of the progressive mafia. Even though its new charter of 1920 created the Representative Assembly whereby the member teachers could express their views and vote on resolutions, the NEA was still a professional organization, run by an entrenched secretariat, promoting legislation and national education policies through its various appointed commissions. The control of the organization by a small inner group is well-illustrated by the fact that one man, Joy Elmer Morgan, was editor of the NEA *Journal* for 34 years, from 1921 to 1954, in which time the progressive philosophy was promoted ad nauseam in issue after issue. From 1918 to 1967 only three men served as executive secretaries. Few national associations have been so tightly run by a small inner circle.

As for teachers' working conditions, these were left up to the local associations which dealt directly with school boards and superintendents. The NEA's Research Division supplied the local affiliates with guidelines and statistics on salaries, tenure, class size, pensions, retirement benefits, etc., which were helpful to the school boards. The NEA shunned the idea that it was a union.

Actually, the unionization of teachers had begun in 1899 when the National Teachers Federation was created in Los Angeles and reorganized in 1901 with membership limited to classroom teachers only. To these teachers, the NEA reflected the interests of the staid eastern university people like Charles Eliot and Nicholas Murray Butler. It hardly represented the teachers at all. The attempts of the teachers to gain power within the NEA culminated in the election of Ella Flagg Young to the NEA's presidency in 1910. But since the real power lay with the board of directors and executive secretary, the teachers' victory meant very little.

In New York City, the United Federation of Teachers (UFT) was founded in 1916 and its first membership card was issued to John Dewey. In those early days of the socialist movement, when the schools were still conservative institutions, many teachers identified themselves with the workers in the class struggle against capitalism. In 1935, the UFT was taken over by a communist faction. Its leadership withdrew to form a new organization, the Teachers Guild.

Thus, the creation of teachers unions actually preceded the NEA's move to Washington and the setting up of its own bureaucracy. The NEA argued that it could do more for teachers by getting Congress to vote for federal aid to education than by union activities. Besides, state affiliates were active in getting state legislatures to enact laws favorable to teachers. In fact, more teachers belonged to the state affiliates than to the national organization. For example, in 1945, 733,409 teachers belonged to the state affiliates, while less than half of them, only 331,605, belonged to the national organization, which is one of the reasons why the unification drive was started at about that time.

There was also a basic disagreement in philosophy between the NEA and the unions. The NEA saw the public schools as serving the state with teachers acting as loyal agents of the state, while the union regarded teachers as "workers" in constant conflict with management. The two philosophies were basically incompatible, involving the rivalry of two power gangs: the progressive mafia and the labor bosses.

The NEA and the progressive mafia were concerned with formulating national education policy and controlling all of America's public schools. No labor union could assume such an expansive function for itself. The NEA was involved in the deep social and philosophical problems of America. Unions were only interested in employee benefits. For example,

Thomas H. Briggs of Teachers College, chairman of the NEA's Committee on the Orientation of Secondary Education, set forth its program in the March 1937 NEA *Journal*. It offered such sweeping views as the following:

> The transition of society from the philosophy of individualism to the new emphasis on group goals and cooperative action produces vexing problems in secondary education. . . .
>
> A characteristic product of the era of individualism was the report on the "Cardinal Principles of Secondary Education." . . . However, these principles no longer furnish a philosophy adequate to guide education thru the social and economic transformation of the century. . . .
>
> Another basic principle must be found and accepted. This we have enunciated in the following: "The state maintains free public education to perpetuate itself and to promote its own interests. Free public education is a long-term investment that the state may be a better place in which to live and in which to make a living."
>
> This implies that education of the future will be concerned with the welfare and progress of the individual only as the welfare and progress of the individual contributes to the welfare and progress of society. . . .
>
> Only education which seeks the reconstruction of society is consistent with and capable of realizing and perpetuating the fundamental principles of democracy. . . .
>
> Teachers should play an active part in securing acceptance by their communities of new social ideas and ideals by their communities. . . . Ideals accepted by teachers and pupils after critical examination should not be suppressed even though such ideals are at variance with those of the local community.

And so, in the NEA's view, the purpose of the public schools was to guide American education through the social and economic transformations of the century, to help America make the transition from an individualistic society to a collectivist one. Not only did an NEA commission develop this policy, but it was making sure that the teachers of America knew about it, for the teachers would have to play the major role in implementing it. And to be effective, the teachers had to have the trust and confidence of the public. Union activities would only undermine that confidence.

Thus, in April 1947, an NEA *Journal* editorial, entitled "A Declaration of Professional Independence," boldly stated its policy on unionization:

> Shall teachers form unions and affiliate with labor organizations? The answer is emphatically NO—if teachers value the future of their profession and country. . . .
>
> . . . Are not teachers in our free public schools employed by all the people, paid by all the people, to teach the children of all the people, to foster the search for truth and good living without bias to class or creed or party? . . .
>
> Teachers unions are born of desperation and thrive on catastrophe.

This view was quite compatible with the progressive position that the public schools served the state which maintained them, and that therefore teachers represented the state. Teachers could no more strike against the state than could the army.

But leaders in organized labor had other ideas. As union membership began to decline in the 1950s among blue-collar workers, union organizers began to eye the large white-collar work force and the public employee as a vast untapped source of new membership. Although white-collar workers in 1962 made up 43 percent of the labor force only 3.2 percent of them were union members.

It was Walter Reuther of the AFL-CIO who decided that teachers were potentially the best group of public, white-collar, quasi-professional employees to organize. If he could organize them, then other white-collar workers and public employees would be less resistant to the idea. After all, if a union was good enough for teachers, it would be good enough for them too.

Reuther chose New York City in which to launch a drive for exclusive representation of teachers in collective bargaining.

It was a good choice. New York was a strong union town with a pro-labor mayor, and the NEA was virtually non-existent there.

Although teachers and other public employees had never had the right to strike, there were occasional illegal strikes which made headlines. The most famous, of course, was the Boston policemen's strike of 1919, of which Calvin Coolidge, then Governor of Massachusetts, said, "There is no right to strike against the public safety by anybody anywhere at any time."

In 1959, however, the state of Wisconsin passed a law permitting public employees to organize and bargain collectively. It was probably one of the worst mistakes ever made by a body of lawmakers in American history.

In 1960, Reuther's organizers formed the United Federation of Teachers (UFT) by merging the New York Teachers Guild, an affiliate of the American Federation of Teachers, and the High School Teachers Association. The UFT inherited the Guild's AFT charter. The UFT then asked New York's Board of Education for approval to hold a referendum to determine whether or not the teachers wanted collective bargaining. When the Board failed to respond affirmatively, the UFT called an illegal one-day strike. The Board caved in, agreeing to let Mayor Wagner appoint a fact-finding panel to study the matter. The panel, made up of three well-known labor leaders, naturally recommended collective bargaining for teachers. However, the Board decided to get a second opinion from a commisson headed by a professor of industrial relations. The commission recommended a referendum for the teachers.

The issue at stake was whether or not public employees should have the right to unionize, bargain collectively, and even strike. It was an issue the public should have had a part in deciding, but never did. Public officials simply found it more in their interest to please the unions than the taxpayers.

It was at this point that a group of New York teachers who

did not like the idea of being lumped in with organized labor, approached the NEA for help. They knew that after the teachers voted in favor of collective bargaining, another election would be held to determine which union would have the exclusive right to represent them: the UFT or some other organization. The dissenting teachers wanted the NEA to organize a local affiliate and take part in the election.

The time had come for the NEA to make a choice. But it really had no choice. While it clung to the idea that teachers were "professionals,'" it had to face the reality of labor's drive to organize public employees with little resistance from liberal public officials. The NEA's executive committee in Washington authorized sending a team to New York to form a local affiliate and take part in the election.

In 1961 the UFT finally got approval from New York's Board of Education to hold a referendum among teachers in June. As expected, a majority voted in favor of collective bargaining. An election to determine which union would be the teachers' exclusive bargaining agent was to be held in December 1961.

In New York the NEA team formed a coalition of nineteen local organizations to compete with the UFT in the election. When the ballots were counted on December 15, 1961, the UFT had won with 20,000 votes, the NEA coalition receiving 10,000 votes. About 10,000 to 13,000 teachers hadn't voted. It looked like the public officials of New York had simply handed over the teachers to organized labor.

Concerning the election, Carr wrote in January 1962: "The NEA will continue to promote the principle that the unique responsibilities of the profession require it to avoid becoming a subordinate part of any other single segment of American society." For Carr, joining the AFT meant surrendering independence of action.

Meanwhile, the defeat was a blow to the NEA's prestige even though the UFT had spent much more money on the election than the NEA. Above all, it meant that the NEA would have to become a union if it was not to lose its urban members to the AFT. For organized labor, the New York victory opened a whole new world of potential union membership among public employees.

Labor's cause was then given a tremendous boost when on January 19, 1962—only a month after Reuther's victory in New York—President John F. Kennedy signed Executive Order 10988 recognizing the right of certain federal employees to collective bargaining. It was a serious defeat for the taxpayer. Although the Order prohibited strikes and stipulated that all collective bargaining agreements had to meet civil service regulations, it triggered a whole series of new bargaining laws for public employees in strong union states like New York, Michigan, Pennsylvania and Washington. One even heard talk of eventually unionizing the armed services! By 1980, 31 states had passed laws permitting public employees to unionize.

It is obvious that Democratic politicians were paying their debts to labor by voting for the unionization of public employees, much to the detriment of the taxpayer and general public. The public employee unions adopted the principles of majority rule, exclusive representation and collective bargaining. They also wanted the right to strike, but even the politicians couldn't grant them that and still face. the taxpayers on election day. So there were lots of illegal strikes which began to wake up the public. It was one thing to strike General Motors, it was another to strike the subways of New York and leave the public stranded. But as usual, Democratic politicians were reluctant to restrain labor, so the public suffered and the courts issued injunctions. However, it was President Reagan's strong stand against the air controllers' strike in 1981 that served notice to public-employee unions that there was a limit beyond which they could not go.

In 1962, the NEA decided to lose no time in becoming a full-fledged union. The rule of exclusive representation left them no choice. The Representative Assembly could have voted somewhere along the line to make the NEA an affiliate of the AFL-CIO, but this would have meant submerging the teachers within the labor movement and the complete loss of independence.

Executive Secretary William G. Carr told NEA convention delegates in 1962 that "the difference between an independent professional organization and a branch of organized labor is not superficial. . . . The public school serves all the children of all the people. Its personnel should not be affiliated with any one segment of the population."

What Carr meant was that the power and prestige of the teachers of America would be seriously jeopardized if they lost the confidence of the public. Once that confidence was lost, it would be difficult for the NEA to impose its national education policy on the public schools.

To meet the AFT challenge, the NEA hired some expensive legal talent to develop procedures to use in collective bargaining, which they later preferred to call "professional negotiation." The relationship of teachers to school boards was a complex one fraught with problems. The NEA also set up an Urban Project to work on the problems of organizing the teachers in large cities where the AFT was most active and to develop legislation for the states outlining negotiation procedures. As for NEA's policy on strikes, Secretary Carr made his stand known at the Denver convention in 1962:

> The members of the National Education Association, whatever others may do, . . . will never walk out on the students in their charge.

But not all NEA members agreed with Carr. Some wanted the right to strike. Between 1941 and 1961 there had been over 100 teacher strikes, and to those who favored strikes, a union without the power to strike lacked its most potent weapon.

To answer such arguments, Dr. Arthur Corey, executive

secretary of the California Teachers Association, addressed the delegates. He told them: "The strike, as a weapon for attaining economic and professional ends by teachers, is first, inappropriate; second, unprofessional; third, illegal; fourth, outmoded; and fifth, ineffective."

In its place he recommended that "a system of professional sanctions be instituted by which the collective influence, not of just a local group but of the whole profession—state-wide and nation-wide—be brought to bear upon a school district which refuses to correct unsatisfactory conditions in its schools."

Corey's arguments persuaded enough delegates so that the Assembly passed a resolution favoring the use of professional sanctions to "provide for appropriate disciplinary action by the organized profession."

For all practical purposes the 1962 convention put the stamp of approval on the NEA's transformation from a professional organization into a union. Of course, the NEA would go on maintaining the myth that it was still a professional organization with all of the rights and powers of a professional organization, but its future behavior would clearly demonstrate that the NEA's interest was more in political power than in professionalism.

After the convention "local affilitates were urged to return home and, together with their school boards, formalize those negotiation procedures already in use by preparing written documents recognizing the right of teachers to negotiate with their employers and outlining the procedures by which the negotiation should take place. Further, local affiliates were requested to file copies of the signed agreements with the NEA."[1]

As a result of the 1962 convention, the NEA drafted model collective bargaining statutes covering teachers which by 1980 were enacted into law by 31 states. Unionization also gave much impetus to the unification movement. By 1976, all of the states had unified membership—meaning that a member of a local affiliate was forced to join the national organization and pay its dues. Unionization also meant that a number of affiliated organizations had to sever their formal connections with NEA and go out on their own. These included the American Association of School Administrators, the Association of Elementary School Principals, the National School Public Relations Association, and the National Association of Education Secretaries.

Meanwhile, forced membership through unification increased the number of NEA members from 713,994 in 1959–60 to 1,700,000 in 1983. It also expanded the NEA's budget from $5 million in 1957 to $67 million in 1979–80. A new constitution adopted in 1972 mandated unified membership and restructured the NEA to fit its new role as a labor union. Also the IRS reclassified the NEA as a Labor Organization under Section 501(C)(5). However, in order to continue receiving tax-deductible grants, the NEA, in 1969, established the National Foundation for the Improvement of Education. Despite all of this the NEA still maintains that it is a professional organization and wants control of the profession, including teacher certification and who may or may not teach.

Unionization has also created an ongoing rivalry between the American Federation of Teachers (AFT) and the NEA. In reality they are like two gangs fighting over the same turf. Organized labor is using the teachers to help spread unionism throughout the white collar and public sectors. Charles Cogen, UFT president, wrote in the January 15, 1964 issue of *The United Teacher:* "The United Federation of Teachers has become a symbol of what can be accomplished in the white collar area." And Nicholas Zonorich, an executive in Walter Reuther's Industrial Union Department, put labor's strategy in these terms: "How long will a file clerk go on thinking a union is below her dignity, when the teacher next door belongs?"[2]

Also, the UFT's constitution states that UFT's first objective is "to cooperate to the fullest extent with the labor movement and to work for a progressive labor philosophy; to awaken in all teachers a labor consciousness and a sense of solidarity with labor." Union teachers were expected to preach the gospel of unionism among their high school students.

Between 1963 and 1965 union elections were held in 36 school systems involving 51,000 teachers who voted. NEA affiliates won 23 and AFT won 13. But the number of votes gotten by each organization was just about even—22,500 for NEA affiliates and 21,600 for AFT affiliates. In 1965–66 the NEA won 176 elections out of a total of 206. Of the AFT's 29 victories, 18 of them were in Michigan.

Although there have been periodic talks about merging the NEA and AFT, both organizations have decidedly different goals. For the AFT, the unionization of teachers has been a means of bolstering the labor movement. For the NEA, becoming a union was a means of keeping its control over the teaching profession as well as maintaining its control over the social content of public education. Neither the AFT nor the NEA has the interests of the public, the parents, or the children as central to their activities. Their chief interest is power.

In 1973 the NEA joined with other public employee unions to form the Coalition of American Public Employees (CAPE). The coalition had been formed so that public employees could exert stronger pressure on legislators who were reluctant to raise taxes. President John Ryor of the NEA said: "We must acknowledge our common destiny with other public employees and work cooperatively to ensure that we are no longer treated as second-class citizens."

There was a time when public employees considered themselves fortunate because they had the security of a government job with excellent benefits, vacations, pensions and pleasant working conditions. Yet, according to the NEA, they really felt like second-class citizens!

By 1981 the teachers had lost that precious independence that William Carr considered too important to give up. The teachers were now organized public employees lumped in with the rest of them. Not only were they now part and parcel of the labor movement, but they had become the *leaders* of the labor movement because of the enormous power and connections of the Association.

15. The Drive For Power

It was the progressives who first advanced the idea that teachers should seek power in order to transform America into a socialist society. Professor George S. Counts of Teachers College put it quite bluntly in his 1932 book, *Dare the School Build A New Social Order?* He wrote:

> That the teachers should deliberately reach for power and then make the most of their conquest is my firm conviction.

Counts had been to Russia and seen communism in action. He was thrilled by what he had seen. But he saw no possibility of a Russian-style revolution in the United States. The process would be evolutionary, with the schools playing the major role. Lawrence Cremin, in his history of Teachers College, writes:

> Counts's position was that teachers should play a primary role in formulating desirable societal goals and then consciously seek to attain them. . . . The course for American teachers was clear: they would have to gain power and use it to help create a great new society.[1]

The only problem was that, apart from the radical teachers in big cities like New York, most American teachers had little interest in politics. They were more concerned with doing their jobs in the classroom than joining a political party.

It became the primary role of the NEA to indoctrinate the teachers in progressive political and social ideas and then activate them politically. The process was a slow one, but in time the goal would be reached.

Actually, the NEA began getting into politics at its very first founding meeting in which it called for the creation of a Department of Education with cabinet status. That called for lobbying Congress. In 1867 Congress created a Department of Education, but without cabinet status. In 1869 the "department" became a bureau within the Department of Interior with a commissioner. In 1889 a committee of the NEA urged that "the Bureau of Education should be restored to its original position as an independent department." But the bureau became the U.S. Office of Education and remained that way until 1979 when President Carter paid his debt to the NEA by getting Congress to create a Department of Education with cabinet status. The NEA waited 122 years to get what it wanted. It has a great deal of patience and staying power. It also wants socialism, and it expects to get it.

The NEA started lobbying for federal aid to education long before it set up its headquarters in Washington and created its Legislative Commission in 1918. The NEA developed and drafted legislation which it began submitting to Congress in 1918. It urged NEA members to write their Congressmen and organize local support to get these bills passed. Although they had to wait until 1965 for the big breakthrough in federal aid, they succeeded in getting such legislation passed as the Smith-Lever Act for Agriculture and Home Economics Education (1914), the Smith-Hughes Act for Vocational Education (1917), Child Labor Laws (1900–1924), the abolition of loyalty oaths for teachers in the District of Columbia (1937), exclusion of teachers from the Hatch Act (1938–1942), and they helped defeat a tax-limitation amendment that would have limited federal income taxes in peacetime to 25 percent.

When they achieved victory in 1965 with the passage of the Elementary and Secondary Education Act, they hailed it not as the culmination of their efforts, but as the beginning of a new era of open ended federal aid to education. As President Johnson told the NEA: "We'll get it started. But we'll never get it stopped."

All of this lobbying for legislation required a great deal of political activity. State NEA affiliates have always been particularly active in getting their state legislatures to enact laws favorable to public education. For example, according to *The Wall Street Journal* of October 10, 1983, some 450 bills were introduced in the Illinois legislature in 1983 directly or indirectly related to public education, and 165 of them ultimately passed. The article comments: "The unions' unbridled success in milking the legislature for costly special-interest legislation is especially remarkable in view of the fact teachers comprise less than 1% of the population in Illinois."

Many state teachers associations maintain their headquarters in the state capital and are considered the single most powerful interest group in their states. When one considers that 50 percent or more of an average state's budget is devoted to public education, it is easy to see why NEA state affiliates are so powerful. The NEA has used state laws to weave a web of legal and bureaucratic control that have benefited the education establishment but stifled education. The state associations have been particularly powerful in deciding governorships, legislator and school board elections, taxation policies, school bond referenda, etc. These affilates are well skilled at lobbying and local politicking.

But getting the average teacher to become politically active is another story. The prodding would have to come from the leaders. From its very first issue in 1921, the NEA *Journal* made sure that its readers knew about the Association's intense lobbying efforts in Washington. Every issue of the *Jour-*

nal had a report on the status of the NEA legislation being pushed in Congress. And, of course, each yearly convention included a detailed report by the chairman of the NEA's Legislative Commission. Although for the first twenty years there wasn't much success to report, the NEA was learning through direct experience with Congress what it would take to achieve success: more Congressmen and a President who believed what they believed.

In 1926, when the NEA's New Education Bill was being lobbied in Congress, the *Journal* urged teachers to write their Congressmen, circulate petitions and discuss the bill in faculty meetings. "Every teacher has a stake in the New Education Bill," they were told. But the bill never got out of committee. The fear of federal control of education was its greatest handicap.

In November 1934, John K. Norton of Teachers College wrote an article for the *Journal*, "Shall We Enter Politics?" While he thought it unwise for teachers to enter partisan politics, he predicted that in the future teachers would play "a more dynamic role in the political arena." In October 1936, the NEA *Journal* demonstrated its political impartiality in the upcoming Presidential election by giving both candidates, Gov. Alf Landon of Kansas and President Roosevelt, equal space in which to present their views on education. Meanwhile, various NEA initiatives in Congress for federal aid to education met with defeat.

In May 1942, the NEA proposed still another bill for federal aid to education. "Every member of the NEA can do something to make this bill a law," wrote H. M. Ivy, chairman of the NEA's Legislative Commission. In subsequent months NEA members were urged to contact their Congressmen and given helpful hints on how to write effective letters. But in September 1943, Exec. Secretary Givens was forced to admit that, "The Association's chief weakness is in the field of teacher welfare and in mustering legislative pressure where rapid and integrated action is demanded." Regardless of their leaders, most American teachers were simply not interested in forcing their fellow citizens to accept laws and taxes they didn't want.

In December 1943, Secretary Givens was still fighting for federal aid to education. "We will take this fight to the people in the 1944 elections if necessary," he warned. In January 1944 the NEA enlarged its lobbying staff and also conducted a poll to prove that "the people favor federal aid."

In December 1944, the NEA alerted its members to a new menace to public education, a proposed constitutional amendment, which would limit federal taxation in peacetime. The *Journal* wrote:

> The NEA opposes any amendment to the United States Constitution which provides for a limitation on federal income, inheritance, and gift taxes, and recommends to state education associations their vigorous opposition to such amendment.

In 1946 the NEA launched another legislative campaign in Congress by creating a Bipartisan House Committee for the Support of Federal Aid for Public Schools. But the opposition was still too strong. The September 1946 *Journal* identified the sources of opposition as, "(1) the economy-at-any-price advocates who place dollars above children; (2) the fear, actual or assumed, of federal control; (3) and the private-and-sectarian school bloc which opposes federal aid to public schools unless the federal government also assumes responsibility for assisting in financing private and sectarian education."

In February 1948 Secretary Givens was still telling NEA members, "Federal aid can be achieved in the present Congress if sufficient support is mobilized." One year later NEA members were urged to "work for it now with all your strength and resources." And in May 1949 NEA members were asked, "Have you written your Congressman?" Month after month teachers were urged, persuaded, admonished and cajoled into working for federal aid to education. But there was always just enough opposition in Congress to frustrate the NEA.

In 1952 William G. Carr succeeded Willard Givens as Executive Secretary of the NEA. Like his predecessor, Carr was a strong believer in federal aid to education and under his administration the NEA intensified its lobbying efforts. That was not difficult to do, for by 1956 the NEA had grown into a considerable empire, with over 600,000 members and 1,085,000 affiliated members. In addition, in 1954 construction began on a new $3-million NEA Center in Washington.

In 1956 another program for federal legislation was launched. NEA members were told: "The success of this program will depend not so much on direction from NEA's Washington headquarters as upon the initiative and leadership of NEA members throughout the country."[2]

When a school-construction aid bill was defeated, NEA members were told to "check for yourself the voting record of your Congressman." The NEA *Journal* of September 1946 published the pictures of 16 Congressmen who strongly supported the bill.

Nevertheless, the Second Session of the 84th Congress (1956) appropriated over a half-billion dollars for a variety of educational programs. But the NEA still hadn't gotten what it wanted, general federal aid to public education.

In January 1957 members were told by their new president:

> Your help is needed in translating into action NEA policy which supports or opposes a particular piece of legislation. You can help set up a committee on federal legislation in your local association to study the pending legislation and to develop a program of local support or opposition, whichever seems called for. Then enlist the help of organizations and individuals outside the profession. . . .
>
> I firmly believe the success of our federal legislative program lies in the direction of getting more of the rank and file involved in promoting sound federal educational legislation and a sound federal policy in the field of education.

In 1958 the NEA's Representative Assembly inched its members closer to political activism by revising its statement of principles and calling for "informed participation by teachers in the consideration of all legislation that would effect the quality or quantity of education either directly or indirectly." NEA leaders were particularly jubilant that year by the passage of the National Defense Education Act of 1958. However, Sputnik had more to do with getting that bill passed than the NEA.

In March 1959 the *Journal* published an article by Congressman Lee Metcalf of Montana entitled "Congressmen Want Your Letters." Metcalf had coauthored the Murray-Metcalf Bill for federal support of education. In support of the bill, Secretary Carr told NEA members in January 1960: "Now is the time for American citizens to tell members of Congress that federal support for education is essential. . . . I call upon every member of NEA to help the American people express their views to Congress."

The February 1960 *Journal* instructed NEA members in "How to Campaign Effectively for School Bonds and Taxes" and "How to Answer Certain Questions on Federal Support for Public Schools." In October 1960 the *Journal* published side-by-side statements of the two presidential candidates, John F. Kennedy and Richard M. Nixon. The NEA's policy was still not to endorse any particular candidate.

During his administration President Kennedy backed the NEA's proposed bill for federal aid to education, but he was unable to get it through Congress. In 1963, however, Congress enacted into law more than $3-billion in aid to education, including a $1.5 billion omnibus measure boosting federal assistance to vocational schools, expanding and extending the National Defense Education Act, and a $1.2 billion college classroom construction program. But the NEA was not satisfied yet. It wanted general acceptance of the idea that the federal government was an equal partner in public education, and should fund its share—one third.

The October 1964 *Journal* continued to urge teachers to get interested in politics: "Political decisions not only affect the amount of financial support for the schools but also determine such crucial issues as school districting, integration, and teacher welfare," the article said.

But the boldest statement was made by Stephen K. Bailey, dean of the graduate school of citizenship and public affairs at Syracuse University in the November 1964 *Journal*. In an article entitled "Education Is A Political Enterprise," he wrote:

> If Education is to receive the moral and financial support of citizens, political forces must be mobilized in its behalf. . . .
>
> Education is one of the most thoroughly political enterprises in American life. More public money is spent for education than for any other single function of state and local government. . . .
>
> It seems to me . . . that we . . . should face squarely the politics of mobilizing support for public education and that we should understand how the process works. . . . In every case where a major breakthrough in increasing state aid to education, the state teachers associations . . . have either been at the forefront or in the middle of the political campaign for increasing such state aid. . . . It is evident that effective political leadership is the keystone to the arch of educational finance.

We must be grateful to Dean Bailey for telling it like it is. Public education is indeed one of the most thoroughly political enterprises in American life, and that is probably the main reason why it does such a poor job of educating. Education should no more be a political enterprise than religion. A separation of school and state would be as beneficial as our separation of church and state. But as long as Americans insist on maintaining a politicized public education system, they will never be free of the insoluble financial, social and academic problems that come with it.

President Johnson's sweeping reelection in November 1964 brought into power one of the most liberal Congresses in American history. In 1965 it finally gave the NEA what it wanted, the Elementary and Secondary Education Act of

1965, a virtual key to the federal treasury. But for the NEA this was only the beginning. The May 1965 *Journal* gave an account of how the bill was concocted, lobbied and passed.

By November 1965 the NEA was ready to cross the political Rubicon. An article in the *Journal* entitled "Teachers—A Political Force" said: "Many teachers are tipping their toes in the political pond and others have decided to jump right in." The new activism, spurred by unionization, was also creating political fever. The NEA's victories over the AFT began to give NEA leaders a sense of unlimited potential power. Finally the moment came for the NEA to announce that it intended to use the incredible power it had quietly accumulated since 1918. In July 1967 Secretary Carr retired and Sam M. Lambert, the NEA's Research Division director, was chosen to succeed him. Like his predecessors, Lambert had worked his way up through the ranks. Starting out as a teacher of mathematics in West Virginia, he became a staff member of the West Virginia state school agency and then a director of research for the West Virginia Education Association. In 1950 he joined the staff of the NEA Research Division and in 1956 became its director. Lambert was very much an Association man and the Association had grown fat and powerful. It had beaten its rival union, it had hit the federal jackpot in Congress, and through mandated unification it now had over one million members. In addition, in 1966 the NEA had formally merged with the American Teachers Association, the national black teachers organization. Also, a whole new generation of young militant teachers had invaded the profession and were ready to use the classroom to carry forth the revolution toward socialism. What Sam Lambert had to say in his inaugural speech no doubt made them feel that the millennium had arrived. The message was clear:

> NEA last year had 1,030,000 members; and by the end of this year we will have at least 1,100,000. . . . We are already four times as large as any other professional organization in this country. Within a few years we will be six or seven times as large. And, beginning now

we are going to put our power and influence to work for the things that are most important:

NEA will become a stronger and more influential advocate of social changes long overdue. . . .

NEA will become a political power second to no other special interest group. . . .

NEA will have more and more to say about how a teacher is educated, whether he should be admitted to the profession, and depending on his behavior and ability whether he should stay in the profession. . . .

And, finally, NEA will organize this profession from top to bottom into logical operating units that can move easily and effectively and with power unmatched by any other organized group.[3]

These were pretty militant words coming from a supposedly benign group of public servants. But what Lambert was telling America is what Dean Bailey had told it three years earlier, that public education is a political enterprise and had to be considered as such. It might take a while for Americans to get used to the idea, and there was a good chance they never would. But only time would tell. However, as of 1967, the NEA was not particularly concerned with public opinion, probably because the teachers had gotten a lot of encouragement from liberal politicians who wanted the NEA to become more political. Politicized teachers would help liberals get elected and stay elected, and that's all that mattered in Washington and fifty state capitals.

But before political action could take place there had to be political training. What better place to start than at the local level? Beginning in 1964 the NEA had sponsored Teacher-in-Politics weekend training workshops all across the country. The purpose of these "political clinics" was to teach teachers how to win school-bond elections in their local communities, elect pro-NEA candidates to school boards and local office, and mobilize local groups to support NEA objectives. As long as local school boards were in the hands of those friendly to the NEA, the teachers would get their way.

The voters, however, were a little harder to control. In 1972, for example, voters defeated 53 percent of the bond-issue elections, an approval rating of 47 percent, down from 69 percent in 1967 and 62 percent in 1968.[4] But the voters probably would have defeated more of them had it not been for NEA activists. Clearly, the public at the local level was growing increasingly dissatisfied with public education and its miserable academic record. Now, more than ever, NEA activism was needed at every level, but particularly the federal, for that's where the megabucks are.

16. NEA-PAC: Political Octopus in the Making

No sooner did Sam Lambert proclaim the NEA's new political manifesto than the board of directors began planning the creation of a national political action committee—an NEA-PAC that would be unlike any other PAC in the nation, one that would enable teachers to participate legally in political action and openly support candidates.

The biggest problem was finding suitable ways to fund the PAC and coordinating the national PAC with the state affiliate PACs. In November 1969 the NEA decided to publicly voice opposition to President Nixon's nomination of Judge Clement Haynsworth to the U.S. Supreme Court because of the judge's civil rights record. All members of the Senate were notified of the NEA's disapproval of Haynsworth and also of Judge G. Harrold Carswell, another Nixon nominee.

That was the NEA's first open involvement in political action. To what extent it influenced the Senators is difficult to determine. But we do know that the nominations were withdrawn, which means that the NEA achieved victory its first time at political bat. It must have given the board of directors a very good feeling.

In April 1970, NEA president George Fischer interviewed both Rogers Morton, Chairman of the Republican National Committee, and Fred Harris, Chairman of the Democratic National Committee. Since the NEA was already in the process of creating a PAC, it wanted to find out what the politicians thought about teachers getting into politics. As expected, both politicians were all for it. Morton said, "Get in there and fight, but make sure you're right." Harris said, "I want to see more politically active teachers and I think most politicians would be very interested in any help from people in the education field." Morton had voiced a little caution; Harris none.

Going to the politicians for advice on political action was like going to an alcoholic for advice on drinking. But the interviews indicated that the NEA's leadership wanted reassurance from others that what they were doing was right. Unfortunately, they got that reassurance from the wrong people.

But it really didn't matter. The NEA had committed itself to political action, and there was no going back. Fischer expressed it well when he said: " Whether we like it or not we're getting into a lobby-mad, power-mad world. We are realistic enough to know that the great lobbies have power, and that if we're going to get a share of the pie, we'd better move in alongside of them." One had hoped for nobler sentiments from our "educators."

In September 1970, the NEA's new president, Helen Bain, told *Journal* readers: "Whether we like it or not, education is in the political arena. . . . The recent stab in the back of education by the dagger of a Presidential veto is a measure of the cutting edge of political considerations." Nixon's crime was his reluctance to pump another $7 billion into the educational pipeline while the educators could barely digest the billions already in it. National expenditures for public elementary and secondary schools had risen from $26.2 billion in 1966 to $40.6 billion in 1970, an increase of about 65 percent in 4 years!

With more money came more teacher dissatisfaction and militancy. In 1969–70 there were 180 teacher strikes in 26 states and the District of Columbia. Michigan had the greatest number, 43, and Los Angeles, the longest, lasting 23 days.

Meanwhile, the plans to develop NEA-PAC were going full speed ahead. All that was needed was the setting up of the machinery to comply with the Federal Corrupt Practices Act and the Internal Revenue Code. The Association was concerned with protecting its tax status as a nonprofit organization. How it had been able to keep its tax-exempt status as an active legislative lobby all these years has never been explained.

Also, it was necessary to develop procedures with state PACs concerning the endorsement of candidates. The national PAC and the state PACs had to coordinate their choices of candidates to support. Another problem was how to collect contributions from NEA members for the PACs and how to distribute the money.

By February 1972 all of the presidents, executive secretaries and chairmen of state PACs had met and reached agreement on the purpose of NEA-PAC and funding procedures. In June the launching of NEA-PAC was officially announced at a fund-raising reception in Washington. After that, events moved swiftly. According to Allan West:

> By September, NEA-PAC had adopted a strategy for the 1972 national election which was outlined in a Telex statement to the state affiliates. The statement said the NEA would elect candidates for national offices who would support education; urge members to elect Senate and House candidates who were strong supporters of education; and step up its campaign activities, including financial and other assistance, in an intensive grass-roots effort to achieve this goal.[1]

The NEA did not support a candidate in the Nixon-McGovern presidential race, but the NEA's executive committee issued a statement charging the Nixon administration with "callous disregard for education." Apparently, the educators, still gorging themselves on the billions provided by the ongoing entitlements of the Elementary and Secondary Education Act of 1965, were not satisfied. Having grown fat, they wanted to become obese. So in 1968 the NEA's Legislative Commission proposed a new $6 billion federal-aid-to-education program. No one charged the NEA with a "callous disregard for the taxpayer." That disregard was built into the psyche of the NEA, whose greed was only matched by its ingratitude. If anyone had a "callous disregard for education" it was the NEA which might have stopped a moment in its march toward political power to find out why the SAT scores had plummeted to their lowest levels in U.S. history.

At the 1973 convention, NEA President Catherine Barrett, told the Representative Assembly: "In 1972, teacher political activity reached its highest level . . . teachers played an active role in electing 30 percent of the House of Representatives, and 40 percent of the 33 candidates elected in the Senate. NEA-PAC became a reality last September. It supported 32 candidates. Twenty-six of them won." She also told them that 44 states already had functioning PACs.

One wonders if there was a correlation between SAT scores reaching their lowest levels and teacher political activities reaching their highest level. But don't expect educational researchers to bother investigating that interesting phenomenon.

It was in 1973 that the NEA also chose a new executive secretary, Terry Herndon, and adopted a new constitution tailored to its new role as a national labor-political organization with unified compulsory membership of every state and local affiliate. The incoming president, Helen Wise, outlined the NEA's new political agenda:

> Our first major objective, politically and legislatively, will be to reverse the national leadership in Washington and put a friend of education in the White House and more friends of education in Congress.
>
> We will initiate a grass roots campaign that will bring about the

victories that we must have in 1976, and if that means building a war chest to get friends of education elected—then we need to keep the old lid open and continue to plunk in the money.

One thing is certain—the NEA will never again sit out a national election.

In fact, we will build NEA's political force over the next two years to the point where the Presidential candidates will seek NEA endorsement.[2]

The teachers had finally fashioned an organization that would have gladdened the hearts of Prof. Counts and John Dewey. The educators were on the march to political power, which the progressives had always considered to be a necessary step on the road to socialism.

Was socialism the NEA's purpose? The September 1969 *Today's Education*—the *Journal* had adopted a new name—characterized NEA members as "agents of constructive change." To change what into what? "The NEA is not content to wait for something to happen," the article continued, "it is making things happen. . . . The profession now has massive resources at its command. The job ahead is one of mobilizing and directing these resources with precision and purpose. The reorganization of NEA's vital internal machinery will be a long step in that direction."

For an organization that talked so much about direction, precision, and purpose, they seemed awfully vague about what that purpose was aside from extorting more money from the taxpayer. The September 1970 *Today's Education* was a little more explicit about the activities of the "change agent":

The change-agent teacher does more than dream, however; he builds, too. He is part of an association of colleagues in his local school system, in his state, and across the country that makes up an interlocking system of change-agent organizations. This kind of system is necessary because changing our society through the evolutionary educational processes requires simultaneous action on three power levels.

Apparently there must be a master plan somewhere so that this "interlocking system of change-agent organizations" can be directed with precision and purpose. Will the NEA please tell us what the plan is and who the people are directing it?

In 1974 the NEA developed its procedures for endorsing presidential candidates by way of a 58 percent majority vote of the Representative Assembly at the annual convention or by mail. The endorsement of primary election candidates was to be made by a 58 percent majority vote of the 123-member Board of Directors.

In 1973, *Today's Education* became a bimonthly magazine. In the September-October issue, NEA President Helen D. Wise told the readers:

> The professional classroom teacher is no longer the quiescent, compliant teacher of 30 or even 20 years ago. . . .
>
> But reaching this stage has required militancy, for it has meant forcing two dramatic changes—moving people from a plane of apathy to a stage of activism and upsetting the power structure which has thwarted the teacher movement. . . .
>
> Now, the muscle of teacher organizations must be used to become politically effective in every election throughout the country.

The teachers were beginning to sound more like left-wing agitators than simply civic-minded participants in the democratic process. In the November-December issue, Terry Herndon, wrote:

> We are highly organized, and our organization pervades every state and nearly every local community. . . . The complete unification of membership among NEA, state affiliates, and local affiliates has been mandated. . . . This concept of inseparable mutuality is essential to the fulfillment of our purpose.

The NEA's "purpose" seemed to be to create a professional dictatorship with the help of federal funding. In the January-February 1974 *Today's Education*, NEA president Wise again stressed the importance of politics:

History tells us that virtually every educational decision is a *political* decision. . . .

Teachers are 2 million strong, and any politician who can count knows how much power an active, determined group of that size can generate. . . . But I believe that our efforts in the political arena must move swiftly to a new dimension: *activity by each and every one of us within the party system* to help assure that education is a top priority in party platforms and that pro-education candidates are nominated.

Activity within the party system meant, among other things, becoming a delegate to the party's national convention. And wouldn't you know that by 1980 the NEA would have 302 delegates and 162 alternates at the Democratic National Convention?

Meanwhile, in that same issue of *Today's Education,* two liberal politicians lauded the NEA for its invaluable help. Senator Claiborne Pell of Rhode Island described how the Rhode Island Education Association got him elected, and H. John Heinz III of Pennsylvania told of how 1,500 teacher volunteers from the Pennsylvania State Education Association labored for his election. These were two Congressmen who owed their political survival to NEA. Whom would they represent? NEA or the people in their states? After the election Pell had said: "My election is a victory for teacher power. Before the teachers began to help me I was a two-to-one underdog. Now, thanks to an army of teachers who knocked on thousands of doors and made thousands of phone calls, I have won by more than 33,000 votes."

In 1973, the NEA also decided to join with other public employee unions—namely the American Federation of State, County and Municipal Employees (AFSCME), the American Federation of Teachers (AFT), and the International Association of Fire Fighters (IAFF)—to form CAPE, the Coalition of American Public Employees. The obvious purpose of the coalition was to give public employees and liberal politicians a permanent stranglehold on the taxpayer. The public servants had decided to become the public's masters.

The NEA was also an important factor in winning the Presidency for Jimmy Carter over incumbent Gerald Ford in 1976. It was the first time in its 119-year history that the NEA had endorsed a presidential candidate. The endorsement made the crucial difference in such states as Pennsylvania, Ohio and Florida where teachers were particularly active, for President Ford lost by a relatively small margin against a virtually unknown newcomer to national politics.

Carter's victory was celebrated by the NEA as proof of teacher political power coming of age. Hamilton Jordan, Carter's campaign manager, said after the victory: "The massive support of teachers was critical to our winning this election. All over the nation, we turned to the NEA for assistance . . . and they delivered."[3] And Carter delivered, too, in 1979, by giving the NEA its Department of Education with cabinet status which it had been seeking since 1857.

In that 1976 election NEA-PAC scored an 83 percent win record in Congress. Of the 323 House candidates it endorsed, 272 won; and of the 26 Senate candidates it endorsed, 19 won.

This impressive record of victories was being closely examined by the politicians. Allan West writes:

> One of the gratifying developments of the more aggressive political action policy, according to NEA leaders, is that more and more candidates are consulting with them prior to the election on the Association's legislative goals and priorities.[4]

In other words, if an aspiring politician wanted NEA backing, all he had to do was find out what the teachers wanted and promise to give it to them. After all, a job in Congress or a state legislature was worth it. You got power, prestige, privilege, excellent pay and other benefits. And all you had to do is vote the way the NEA told you to vote.

Meanwhile, everything was working according to plan. NEA president John Ryor had said in 1975, "We must become the foremost political power in the nation." The NEA was well on its way to becoming just that.

The NEA's Legislative agenda for 1977-78 included a Federal Collective Bargaining law, lots more federal funding of public education, National Health Insurance and other social benefits. They succeeded in getting some more funding of already existing federal programs and something entirely new, a Teacher Center Bill which appropriated $75 million annually to establish teacher centers all around the country. The NEA had proposed the centers as a place where teachers could go for help in curriculum development. But we suspect that these centers were wanted as places for training teachers to become effective change agents away from the scrutiny of parents and school boards.

In the 1978 elections, NEA-PAC spent $335,347 helping its candidates and achieved a 77 percent win record, with 197 House candidates winning out of 247 endorsed by NEA, and 13 Senate candidates winning out of 24 endorsed by NEA.

But 1980 was considered to be the big year for NEA political action. The February-March 1980 issue of *Today's Education* carried an 18-page special feature entitled "Politics 1980." The message was clear:

> This 1980 political year presents a special challenge for teachers because adversaries of public education are out in full force. The National Right to Work Committee, for example, is a member of the leadership workshop of the New Right which helped defeat several friends of education in the 1978 Congressional elections. And a substantial number of pro-education incumbents in Congress have been targeted to be replaced by New Right candidates in the November elections.

> Active in raising political money, the New Right is committed to electing extremist candidates, Republicans and Democrats alike, who vote against education issues when they come up in Congress.

> This extremist coalition works vigorously to defeat much of the legislation that teachers support. . . .

It was easy to scare teachers by labeling conservatives as "New Right extremists." Members of the NEA were urged to increase their support of NEA-PAC and their local affiliate PACs. Members were also urged to become active in their parties so as to become delegates to the state and national political conventions. According to the magazine, "NEA's teacher members were the largest single delegation at both major political party national nominating conventions in 1976."

The cover of the November-December 1980 *Today's Education* pictured President Carter and Vice President Mondale, both of whom the NEA had endorsed for reelection. Willard McGuire, NEA's President, wrote:

> This year's presidential election will have a tremendous impact on our country throughout the rest of this century. Whoever is elected will have enormous impact on all facets of American life—including our education system.

The NEA's Board of Directors had voted 118 to 4 to endorse the Carter-Mondale ticket. Carter had spoken at the NEA convention in Los Angeles in July reviewing what his administration had done for the NEA. He stressed the mutual goals that he and NEA were working for including ratification of the Equal Rights Amendment. The 7,500 delegates to the Representative Assembly then voted 3 to 1 to endorse President Carter for reelection.

The defeat of Carter and the victory of Ronald Reagan confirmed the NEA's worst fears of a rising reaction against liberalism in America. Mary Futrell, NEA secretary-treasurer, put it this way: "We realize that Congress has changed. We lost men and women whose leadership was important to the continuation of the fight for civil-rights and human-rights issues. But we have not lost the heart of our commitment. We have a rebuilding job to do."

Surprisingly, a good many teachers voted for Reagan, suggesting not only that NEA's leadership was and is far to the left of NEA's rank and file membership, but that its propaganda is unable to control what teachers do in the voting booths. Curiously enough, a survey in the May 1972 *Today's Education* had indicated that 43 percent of teachers were Democrats, 34 percent were Republicans, and 22 percent were non-affiliated.

The February-March 1981 *Today's Education* published several letters from teachers who disagreed with NEA policy. Two teachers from California wrote:

> We're extremely annoyed about the cover and the editorial "Carter-Mondale—A Clear-Cut Choice" (November-December). For many of us, the Carter-Mondale ticket was not a clear-cut choice. No intelligent voter votes for a President on his education record alone.

A teacher from Massachusetts wrote:

> Your November-December cover is highly offensive to many of my colleagues and me. I did not support the reelection of Carter-Mondale and would not have been persuaded to support them simply because Carter created the Department of Education.
>
> I regard the Department of Education as simply another example of the way the federal bureaucracy wastes my taxes. The NEA, like the federal government, has become a self-serving monopoly that is out of touch with local associations.

A Michigan teacher wrote: "By endorsing any candidate—instead of providing an educational forum for all candidates—you have done a disservice to the Association and the profession as well."

In 1981, organized labor decided to celebrate its 100th anniversary with a huge Solidarity Day march on Washington. The NEA leadership decided to use the occasion to raise the labor consciousness of its members and bring them into the mainstream of the labor movement. An editorial by NEA president Willard McGuire in the November-December 1981 *Today's Education* virtually sealed the NEA's transformation into a labor organization. McGuire wrote:

> In the spirit of solidarity NEA salutes a century of accomplishment. . . .

NEA is proud to be a professional organization. We are also proud to be part of the labor movement and are proud to have joined together with the AFL-CIO, the NAACP, and other national and regional organizations—on September 19, *Solidarity Day*—in protest against the Reagan Administration's economic policies.

Today, NEA is a leader in the American labor movement. . . . while we are no better than any other labor group, we are different, and we see our organization, clearly, as having the strength, expertise, and clout to get important jobs done. . . .

We call on everyone within the labor movement to join us in a rededication to quality education. We in turn pledge to continue our efforts to ensure dignity and justice and equity for all workers, in all endeavors, throughout the workplace of our nation—and of the world.

All of this was music to the ears of not only organized labor but to American communists who saw this movement of the NEA into the ranks of labor as a sign that teachers were joining the class struggle. Robert Moir, a reporter from the *Daily World,* official newspaper of the Communist Party, USA, attended the NEA's Minneapolis convention in 1981 and wrote this in the July 25, 1981 edition under the heading "NEA: Moving toward labor unity":

The attacks of the Reagan Administration on education and educational employees was keenly felt, and there was much more of an inclination to fight back. Delegate after delegate referred to the NEA as "our union," or referred to other union members as "our union brothers and sisters." This was a remarkable development for an organization that once officially deplored strikes.

The convention's enthusiastic vote in favor of a motion by the New Jersey delegation to support the September 19 Solidarity Day March in Washington, called by the AFL-CIO, represented a high point in labor consiousness. . . .

If the NEA is moving toward the mainstream of organized labor, it is also taking the lead on a number of issues, particularly in the area of foreign policy.

By condemning the Salvadoran government and demanding an end to U.S. military support, the 1981 convention showed not only a strong democratic feeling, but also an enlightened self-interest.

Education suffers when the military budget is increased, and the NEA has historically been opposed to increases in the military budget. The government of Guatemala was also condemned for repression by the Organization, and support for world peace and multilateral disarmament was reaffirmed.

The NEA has no ties with the infamous AIFLD (American Institute for Free Labor Development), a red-baiting, scabbing outfit supported by the AFL-CIO and run by the CIA. NEA's international affiliate is the World Confederation of Organizations of the Teaching Profession, which takes strong stands against repressive military regimes and in support of the right of teachers to organize and strike everywhere.

If, as according to the reporter, the AIFLD is controlled by the CIA, is it not possible that the WCOTP is controlled by the KGB? The reporter then made a very astute observation:

> Nowhere in the basic documents of NEA, in their resolutions or new business items, are there any anti-Soviet or anti-socialist positions. . . .
>
> . . . It seems unlikely that the path NEA is now taking will be reversed. It has chosen a position in opposition to transnational corporations, to racism, to the Pentagon, and to the Reagan Administration. In doing so, it will increasingly be fighting shoulder-to-shoulder with fellow trade unionists as the class struggle intensifies.

The Solidarity Day march in Washington brought a half-million unionists, including members of the NEA, to protest the Reagan Administration. A strong anti-Reagan labor coalition had emerged as the political strategy of the radical left. George Meyers, chairman of the Labor and Farm Department of the Communist Party, explained the goal of the strategy in the *Daily World* of November 25, 1981:

> The key to the 1982 elections is the day-to-day involvement of the Solidarity Day coalition in grassroots struggle against the impact of Reagan's budget cuts. . . .
>
> Solidarity Day . . . has placed organized labor in the leadership of the economic and democratic struggles of the people. It dare not falter

or retreat. September 19th has created conditions for labor-led struggles that will guarantee a crushing defeat for the Reagan Administration and its politics of poverty on election day, Nov. 2, 1982.

Willard McGuire, NEA president, echoed these views in his editorial in the April-May 1982 *Today's Education,* in which he characterized the Reagan budget cuts as "callous, reckless, and potentially crippling." He then said:

> We joined thousands of citizens in the Solidarity Day protest against the Reagan Administration's economic policies. We devoted time and money to help defeat—by a 9 to 1 margin—Washington, DC's tuition-tax-credit proposal. With our National Day of Conscience for Public Education, January 17, we alerted the nation to the threat to its children posed by the continuing assault on public education. When the President unveiled, on January 17, his plan to dismantle the Department of Education, we mobilized forces against this blueprint for disaster. . . .
>
> After the long year, we know who the friends of public education in government are. We know also those who are not our friends. Both are voting today on issues that affect us. When, next November, we enter the voting booth, we will remember how they acted.

These were words to send fear down the spines of many politicians. The NEA had evolved into a formidable political machine. From 1972 to early 1982 NEA-PAC had supported 1,413 candidates for federal office and achieved a 78 percent win record. The 1982 elections would be another important test.

At the 1982 NEA convention in Los Angeles, Willard McGuire told the delegates:

> There can be no educational excellence without political power in our country today. Let us declare an all-out effort to elect a pro-education Congress and a pro-education Administration by November 1984. . . .
>
> I submit that we are in a war today. It is not a war on foreign soil, but a war that is taking place in every schoolroom and in every state capital and in every congressional district. It is a war for the survival of public education.

Jane Fonda, who had given our enemies in North Vietnam the encouragement to continue killing American soldiers who were trying to defend the freedom of South Vietnam, also addressed the NEA convention. She told the delegates: "I thank you for teaching our children that we are all equal. You teach that you can't kill an idea."

The Representative Assembly voted to promote a massive petition drive against President Reagan's tuition tax credit plan and to initiate court challenges in any state that provided tuition tax credits.They also approved of a new NEA legislative proposal—the American Defense Education Act—which would funnel some $10 billion in federal funds to the public schools, increasing the Department of Education's budget by about 66 percent.

In October 1982, the NEA began publication of *NEA Today,* a monthly tabloid newspaper. The magazine, *Today's Education,* was turned into an annual. In November 1982 McGuire told NEA members:

> Get out and vote on November 2. More and more often critical elections are being decided by margins of only one or two votes per precinct. With 4,000 to 6,000 NEA members in each of the nation's 435 congressional districts, together we can make the difference in many vital races on Election Day.

The NEA's efforts paid off. NEA-PAC had endorsed 302 House candidates of which 224 won, and it had endorsed 32 Senate candidates of which 20 won, thus achieving a 73 percent win average. Not bad for an organization that was shouting hysterically that public education was on the verge of destruction.

It was Senator Gary Hart who introduced the NEA's American Defense Education Act in the new Senate, but as of May 1984 it had not gotten out of committee.

The 1983 NEA convention in Philadelphia in July was another full-blown exercise in national politics. The 7,200 delegates elected Mary Hatwood Futrell as their new president. Futrell, an ERA activist, was a former business education teacher from Alexandria, Virginia, who had served as secretary-treasurer and a member of the executive committee of the NEA for several years. For all practical purposes, it was now the nine-member executive committee that ran the NEA.

The convention was also attended by five Democratic presidential candidates seeking their party's nomination. Former Vice President Walter Mondale, and Senators Gary Hart of Colorado, Alan Cranston of California, John Glenn of Ohio, and Ernest Hollings of South Carolina greeted delegates at candidate-hosted receptions. Each promised to spend lots more money on public education. Also, ten-minute videotapes of all the candidates' views on education were shown to the delegates. President Reagan was sent an NEA questionnaire on educational issues—the prerequisite for NEA endorsement consideration—but he declined to respond. He must have felt, somehow, that the deck was stacked against him.

On August 27, 1983, at least 1,000 NEA members took part in the demonstration in Washington organized by the left to celebrate the 20th anniversary of Martin Luther King Jr.'s famous March on Washington. Mary Futrell was one of the speakers who resoundingly denounced the Reagan Administration. The Communist *Daily World* had written on July 7, 1983:

> The newly-elected NEA President, Mary Futrell, an Afro-American woman, is one of the national conveners of the Jobs, Peace and Freedom demonstration.
>
> The teachers' union has contributed significantly to the August 27 effort by donating office space in Washington to the national organizing committee, the New Coalition of Conscience.
>
> NEA is calling on all teachers from around the country to march behind a united teachers contingent.

As a convener of the march, Futrell shared top billing with such well-known personalities of the left as former Congresswoman Bella Abzug, Representative John Conyers of Michigan, Jesse Jackson, and William Winpisinger, president of the

International Association of Machinists and Aerospace Workers. Mr. Winpisinger managed to make a trip to Moscow before the demonstration. The *Daily World* of August 25, 1983 reported the trip thus:

> William Winpisinger . . . met with Yuri Andropov, general secretary of the Communist Party of the Soviet Union, in Moscow earlier this month. . . . Winpisinger headed a trade union delegation which is travelling in the Soviet Union at the invitation of the All-Union Central Council of Trade Unions and the Central Committee of the Heavy Engineering Industry Workers' Union of the USSR.
>
> Andropov stressed that the Soviet Union is in favor of union-to-union contacts, on the basis of equality and mutual respect, without any discrimination. . . .
>
> The maintenance of peace was a major subject of discussion. Winpisinger stressed the powerful desire and demands of U.S. working people for peace, and for peaceful relations. Andropov pointed out that, despite differences of view on some matters, there are many interests which concern both Soviet and U.S. workers, peace being one of them.
>
> Andropov presented Winpisinger with a plaque showing two joined hands and the inscription: "In the spirit of friendship and striving for lasting peace for all people of Earth."

It should be noted that this trip was made while the communist government of Poland, under threat from Andropov, was in the process of suppressing the Solidarity movement for an independent union.

Winpisinger was not the only one who had made a trip to the Soviet Union. In 1971 Donald Morrison, NEA president, and Sam Lambert, executive secretary, had spent two weeks touring the USSR at the invitation of the Education and Scientific Workers Union of the Soviet Union. On his return, Lambert said: "I was impressed with the fact that their system of distributing goods and services seems to be working, and that the Soviets do seem to have eliminated extreme poverty." Of course the tour did not include any stops at slave-labor gulags. Morrison was impressed with the fact that the Russians had eliminated illiteracy. He didn't bother to ask them what teaching method they used. Had he asked, they would have told him: "Intensive phonics."

An earlier trip to the Soviet Union was made by NEA officials in November 1970. Among the visitors were Helen Bain, NEA president, and George Fischer, past president. The invitation came from the same Soviet Educational and Scientific Workers Union. At the end of the trip a joint statement was issued by the two groups, pledging cooperation and all-around good feelings for quality education.

17. Radicalism and the NEA

There is a myth believed by many observers of American education that the NEA was, until recently, somewhat of a conservative organization and that its present radical positions on social, economic and foreign policy issues are a late development. Nothing could be farther from the truth. The NEA became a radical organization when it was taken over by the progressives early in the century.

From the December 1923 issue of the NEA *Journal,* which published an article by socialist John Dewey, to the September-October 1981 issue of *Today's Education,* which featured an article by socialist Michael Harrington ridiculing George Gilder's brilliant defense of capitalism, the NEA has subjected its members to an unrelenting hatred of capitalism and an unceasing, uncritical benevolence toward socialism. The NEA became mildly anti-communist after World War II when many progressives and liberals were repelled by the excesses of Stalinism. But nowhere in any NEA publication will the reader find a kind word for the economic system that has made America the richest and most powerful nation in history.

From 1857 to the present, the NEA has worshipped two gods: Horace Mann, a statist, and John Dewey, a socialist.

The NEA *Journal* published Dewey's "My Pedagogic Creed" in May 1927, a sympathetic article on "The New Education in New Russia" in January 1928, an attack on American corporations by Dewey in February 1928, a favorable article on Communist youth in Russia in November 1928. The *Journal* devoted its December 1929 issue to a celebration of John Dewey's 70th birthday, at which time Dewey was awarded a Life Membership in the NEA. Tributes to Dewey from university presidents and foreign dignitaries filled the pages of the magazine. No other educator in American history has received the kind of adulation that was heaped on Dewey. Yet Dewey labored all of his professional life to turn America into a socialist society. In 1949, at the age of 90, Dewey was made honorary president of the NEA.

How ironic that the most celebrated educator in the greatest capitalist society that has ever existed should be a socialist! The NEA did its share to create that uncritical reverence for Dewey which bordered on deification and which is still a powerful influence today. One of the ways this was done was by making the word "democracy" synonymous with socialism. Dewey and the progressives used the two words interchangeably, creating a good deal of confusion in the minds of many intelligent people who favored democracy but opposed socialism and read little of what Dewey actually wrote. You had to have an intimate knowledge of the man's writings to be convinced of the full extent of his commitment to collectivism and the educational means he devised to bring it about.

The most frequent writer on economics in the NEA *Journal* during the 1930s and '40s was Stuart Chase, a popularizer of socialist ideas. Chase, who coined the slogan "New Deal," was a frequent speaker at NEA conventions and was particularly popular among superintendents. In May 1934 he wrote: "If it requires at least a decade to modify the psychology of stolid Russian peasants, it may require twice as long to modify the psychology of Wall Street."

In an article entitled "Government in Business" in the March 1936 *Journal,* Chase advocated a "minimum program" of economic and social planning for the United States which would include "the nationalization of banking and credit; the use of the income tax to redistribute income and purchasing power, so that savings will be spent; the use of government credit to create vast new industries in the sector of public works and services; the progressive control by government of natural monopolies; the collective control of agriculture; wage and hour controls; consumer protection; and the extension of social security."

He topped it all off by saying, "It is no longer a question of collectivism versus individualism, but of what kind of collectivism." However, after World War II, when the failures and brutalities of Russian communism became apparent to anyone who could read a newspaper, Chase decided to settle for a "mixed economy" in the Swedish mode.

Another frequent attacker of capitalism in the NEA *Journal* was the editor himself, Joy Elmer Morgan, whose monthly editorials were often a barrage aimed at corporations. In February 1934 he wrote: "The super-corporations threaten democracy in the United States. . . . So long as the school is free, so long as it is the House of the People where the entire community can gather in an effort to solve its own problems, democracy is safe." In December 1934, Morgan advocated government control of all corporations, which he called "America's economic oligarchy," "so that they serve the people." As editor, Morgan controlled everything that went into the *Journal* for 34 years, from 1921 to 1955. He had joined the NEA staff in 1920 and set up its division of publications of which he was director until his retirement. During that period, the progressive mafia maintained a firm grip on the NEA.

During the 1930s, the progressives were so sympathetic toward communist Russia that they began sponsoring summer schools for American teachers in the Soviet Union through the Institute of International Education. The courses were conducted at Moscow University in English by Soviet professors in such subjects as education, economics, psychology, philosophy, and socialized medicine. A course in Soviet experimental psychology and psychological research was offered to advanced students of psychology.

In the 1934 session, a staff of 22 Soviet professors instructed 212 American students. In 1935, two professors from Teachers College, Columbia University—George S. Counts and Heber Harper—acted as official advisors to the students. A full-page ad for the Moscow summer school with a picture of Lenin's tomb appeared in the March 1935 NEA *Journal*. We know virtually nothing about the teachers who attended these summer schools, what they were taught, and how they applied these teachings in American schools. We do know that among the advisory council of the Institute of International Education, were John Dewey; George S. Counts; Harry Woodburn Chase, chancellor of New York University; Frank P. Graham, president of the University of North Carolina; Robert M. Hutchins, president of the University of Chicago; Charles H. Judd, dean, School of Education, University of Chicago; William F. Russell, dean, Teachers College, Columbia; William Allan Neilson, president of Smith College; and others.

The brochure describing the summer school stated:

> The tremendous progress of the Soviet Union in the cultural field creates for Americans an unequalled observation ground for education, psychology, and the social sciences. The Soviet Union presents a unique opportunity for study of the processes of cultural change. The first and second Five Year Plans, by creating the foundations of a planned national economy, have brought about a complete reconstruction in the social attitudes and behavior of the Russian people.

The forerunner to the Moscow summer school was the American Society for Cultural Relations with Russia, a communist subsidiary founded in 1927. Its president was William Allan Neilson, president of Smith College, and its vice presidents included John Dewey and Stephen Duggan who later became director of the Institute for International Education. It had a large advisory council, including author Stuart Chase and Prof. Susan Kingsbury of Bryn Mawr, who also served on the National Advisory Council of the Moscow summer school.

Even before the United States established diplomatic relations with the Soviet Union, many Americans visited Russia, including John Dewey, who toured Soviet schools in 1928 and wrote a book about it, and George Counts, who also wrote a book about his 1930 tour. Counts had gotten his Ph.D. at the University of Chicago in 1916 under Judd and was a professor at Teachers College from 1927 to 1956. In 1934, Counts and his progressive colleagues launched a publication called *The Social Frontier*. In the prospectus he wrote:

> *The Social Frontier* assumes that the age of individualism in economy is closing and that an age marked by close integration of social life and by collective planning and control is opening. For weal or woe it accepts as irrevocable this deliverance of the historical process.

The idea that socialism was historically inevitable absolved Counts and many of his colleagues of having to make a moral choice. Their argument, basically, was that since socialism is inevitable, we might as well prepare young Americans for it as effectively as possible.

Obviously, the Moscow summer schools would help American teachers lead their students toward a new collectivist society, and they would try to shape the purpose of American education according to the Soviet model. In his 1931 book, *The Soviet Challenge to America*, Counts wrote:

> The general purpose of education in Soviet Russia has remained unchanged since the Bolsheviki seized power in 1917. ... Throughout the entire range of education institutions a systematic effort is made to change the very character of the people inhabiting the Union: to rear a generation steeped in the abstruse doctrines of dialectical materialism, imbued with the ideas of collectivism, internationalism,

and equality between the sexes, and thoroughly committed to the application of science to the problems of social life and particularly to the organization and development of the public economy. . . .[1]

The ideal of promoting individual success, which is so characteristic of education in the United States, is almost entirely absent in the schools of the Soviet Union. . . . In Russia, emphasis is always placed on service to the group, while in America the driving motive of education seems to be personal advancement. . . .[2]

The foreign student who visits the Soviet schools is impressed from the first with the activity of the children. . . . The initial conclusion usually drawn is that the Soviet schools are patterned after the progressive schools of Europe and America. As a matter of fact, nothing could be farther from the truth. In both instances there is great emphasis on activity, but in the schools in Russia it is activity with a purpose; it is activity with a strongly collectivistic bias; it is activity devoted to the promotion of the welfare of the surrounding community; it is, in a word, to a very large degree, *socially useful labor*. . . .[3]

In Soviet Russia the union of social planning with a collective economy is apparently making possible a far more intimate and natural relationship between education and society than exists under private capitalism. . . .[4]

No man of sensitive mind can remain long in the [Soviet] Union without feeling himself in a veritable furnace of the world where the elements composing human society are in a state of fusion and new principles of right and wrong are being forged. Under such conditions the commonplaces of American education sound like faint voices from a distant and mythical land. . . .[5]

Whatever may be said on the other side concerning the regimentation of opinion and the restriction of individual freedom, there exists in Soviet Russia today an idealism and a driving passion for human betterment which contrast strangely with the widespread cynicism of the United States.[6]

Unless industrial capitalism can go beyond the production of material things and meet the spiritual needs of men, it cannot and should not endure.[7]

Thus, according to Counts, American industrial society was spiritually bankrupt, and the products of its technology were being put to trivial use. In contrast, the Soviet Union had embarked on a historic revolutionary mission to create not only a new society but a "New Man." It was this idealism, energizing these vast cultural changes, that intoxicated men like Counts. He wrote:

> This cultural revolution possesses a single mighty integrating principle—the building of a new society in which there will be neither rich nor poor, in which the mainspring of all industry will be social need rather than private profit, in which no man will be permitted to exploit another by reason of wealth or social position, in which the curse of Eden will be lifted forever from the soul of woman, in which a condition of essential equality will unite all races and nations into one brotherhood.[8]

Admiration for the Soviet Union was always accompanied by harsh criticism of American society. But disillusionment with the great Soviet experiment began to set in around 1936 when Soviet dictator Stalin began to purge the communist party of Trotskyite elements. After Lenin's death in 1924, a mere seven years after the communist takeover of Russia, an intense power struggle took place between Leon Trotsky and Josef Stalin for control of the communist party. Stalin won and, in 1929, Trotsky was sent into foreign exile. The world communist movement split into two groups: Trotskyites and Stalinists. From 1936 through 1938 Stalin put on trial in Moscow many top communists whom he accused of being counter-revolutionaries. They were all found guilty and executed. Trotsky himself was tried in absentia, found guilty, and sentenced to death.

The Moscow trials had a tremendous impact on progressives in Europe and America. Trotsky had settled in Mexico in 1936. In 1937, John Dewey, at the age of 78, headed a commission of inquiry that went to Mexico to hear Leon Trotsky's rebuttal to Stalin's charges. The Dewey commission found the charges to be a complete fabrication. Trotsky's death sentence, however, was carried out in 1940 when a Soviet agent bludgeoned Trotsky to death with a pickaxe. Years later, when the killer was released from his Mexican prison, he returned to Russia and was awarded a medal for his work.

The Moscow trials, the Hitler-Stalin pact, the murder of Trotsky disillusioned many progressives. But many others remained loyal to Stalin. In fact, it was during the 1930s that communist agents made their most successful infiltration of the United States government, some of them reaching high policy-making positions. It was not until the 1950s that Americans became aware of the extent of the infiltration. By then many progressives and liberals had become anti-communist, and many communists had left the party.

In 1949 George Counts wrote a strongly anti-communist book warning his fellow liberals that they had better understand communist strategy for world conquest if they were to avoid the fate of those countries that had fallen behind the Iron Curtain. He was particularly disturbed by the cynical amorality of communist strategy. He quoted Lenin who, in 1920, encouraged communists to join non-communist labor unions in order to manipulate and control the working class. Lenin said:

> One must be prepared to make all kinds of sacrifices and overcome the greatest obstacles, in order to propagandize and agitate systematically, stubbornly, persistently, and patiently, precisely in those institutions, associations, and unions, even the most reactionary, where there is a proletarian or semi-proletarian mass. . . . One must be prepared . . . in case of necessity, even to resort to all kinds of tricks and ruses, to employ illegal measures, secretiveness, and concealment of truth in order to penetrate into trade unions, to remain in them, and to conduct Communist work in them at any cost.[9]

One wonders if the shift of the NEA from an organization for professionals to a highly politicized labor union with a strong working-class consciousness, was not the work of communists operating within the NEA. The interesting fact is that in the 1950s communists were banned from membership in the NEA. But that ban was lifted in the 1970s. Thus members of the communist party have been free to join the NEA and work within it since that time.

Most people do not understand how the American communist party, with only 10,000 members, can exert so much influence in large noncommunist organizations. As Lenin pointed out, they do it by infiltration and concealment. Communists have always been active in the labor movement because the central doctrine of communism is the class struggle between the workers, or proletariat, and the capitalists, or the bourgeoisie. The communists consider themselves to be the leaders of the working class whose dictatorship they aim to establish.

Thus, communists will try to gain control or influence large organizations in order to lead them toward their ultimate goal: a proletarian dictatorship under one leader. Concerning dictatorship Lenin wrote:

> There is absolutely no contradiction in principle between Soviet (that is, socialist) democracy and the assumption of dictatorial powers by particular individuals. . . . Absolute submission to a single will, for the purpose of achieving success in work, organized on the pattern of large machine industry, is unquestionably necessary.[10]

Lenin defined dictatorship as "unlimited power resting on force not law." His disdain for the democratic process was eloquently summarized in these words:

> Only scoundrels and half-wits can think that the proletariat must first win a majority of votes in elections conducted under bourgeois oppression, under the oppression of hired slavery, and only then seek to win power. This is the height of stupidity and hypocrisy.[11]

What will the communists do to the capitalist class once their dictatorship is established? Counts quoted a member of the Cheka, the Soviet secret police, which was set up after the communists took power in Russia:

> "We are not waging war against particular individuals," he said. "We are exterminating the bourgeoisie as a class. Don't look for evidence to prove that the accused acted by deed or word against the Soviet power. The first question you should ask him is: To what class

he belongs, what is his origin, his education, his training, and his profession? This should determine the fate of the accused. Herein lies the meaning and the 'essence of the Red Terror.' "[12]

Gus Hall, head of the Communist Party USA, outlined Communist strategy in the *Daily World* of June 25, 1981. That strategy consisted mainly of intensifying the class struggle and forming mass coalitions to defeat Reaganism. He said:

> There are no solutions along the line of class collaborations. For workers it leads only to a dead end. The only viable solutions are solutions along the path of militant class struggle. . . .
>
> More than any period since the 1930s, the most active and effective force has been and is the working class. This is adding a new dimension as well as a quality to the mass upsurge.
>
> The rank and file pressures have pushed the trade union movement into initiating and participating in most of the mass actions. In fact, many of the demonstrations were initiated, sponsored, endorsed and led by the trade union movement. A large section of trade union leadership is active in the surge. . . .
>
> The mushrooming coalitions and alliances are the main form of the mass upsurge. Some are still of the one-shot, ad hoc type. But increasingly they are coming together for long-range goals and longer periods. Some are still single-issue oriented. But increasingly they are dealing with multiple and related issues. . . .
>
> It is important to recognize and to understand the full significance of the coalitions and alliances and their growing interrelationships. This adds not only a new quantity, but a new qualitative dimension to the developing mass upsurge. . . .
>
> We should have the outlook of helping to build a huge network of thousands of grass roots formations, affiliated and connected to hundreds of coalitions—in every neighborhood, every community, every town, city and state.

The NEA, with its local affiliates in every school district of every town and city of America, is obviously an organization the communists would love to control or at least influence. And perhaps the communists already control it, for their reporter, Robert Moir, pointed out in July 25, 1981 that "Nowhere in the basic documents of NEA, in their resolutions or new business items, are there any anti-Soviet or anti-socialist positions. . . . It seems unlikely that the path NEA is now taking will be reversed."

Even the American Federation of Teachers, the NEA's arch rival, has strongly criticized the NEA for its reciprocal relations with the Soviet teachers union. In its brochure, *The AFT vs. the NEA,* the AFT states:

> The Communist governments consider it a great propaganda coup to have their phony "unions" accepted around the world as "true representatives of the workers." When the NEA establishes ties with these groups and agrees to have official exchanges with them, it plays right into the propaganda maneuvers of these totalitarian governments. . . .
>
> The NEA's cooperative activities with these so-called "unionists" from Communist countries have a very negative impact on the cause of freedom and the effort to build truly free and democratic unions. As Vladimir Borisov, a Soviet dissident who was exiled from that country in June of 1980 after a series of arrests and jailings by the KGB, explained in an impassioned statement following his release: "I beg you to open your eyes, as I can tell you the truth about trade unions in Russia. . . . They work for the State and not for their members. . . . By supporting these tools of the Soviet Government, you betray the ordinary Russian working man, the very kind of people you claim to represent."

What was the reaction of the NEA to Mr. Borisov's plea? It attempted to sponsor an official delegation from the Cuban Teachers Union in March 1981, but visas were denied by the State Department. In June 1983, the NEA sent two of its staff members, John DeMars, director of NEA Peace Programs and International Relations, and Sam Pizzigati, associate director of NEA communications, to Nicaragua to interview leaders of the National Association of Nicaraguan Educators (ANDEN), the Sandinista-controlled teachers' union formed after the overthrow of Somoza. The teachers' union supports the Marxist revolution and maintains close relations with its counterpart in El Salvador which supports the guerrilla movement.

According to the NEA staff members' report, an estimated 300 Salvadoran teachers have fled El Salvador and gone to Nicaragua to teach. "These Salvadorans," says the report, "have helped Nicaragua meet the teacher shortage problem, and their presence has contributed to the strong bond between ANDEN and the Salvadoran teachers' union, ANDES."

Apparently the teachers unions in Central America strongly support the revolutionary forces trying to overthrow democratic governments and install pro-Soviet Marxist regimes. The NEA strongly supports these unions and in its resolutions of 1984 said:

> The Association condemns the government of El Salvador for its role in the assassinations and other acts of violence and injustice against the people of El Salvador, especially its teachers and their organization and the children of that country. . . . The National Education Association supports the teachers and students of Guatemala. . . . [and] urges the federal government to deny all military and economic aid to Guatemala. . . . The National Education Association urges the U.S. government to refrain from any U.S. plan for overt or covert action that would destabilize Nicaragua or would adversely affect that government's successful campaign against illiteracy.[13]

It is interesting that the NEA is concerned with protecting the Sandinista campaign against illiteracy in Nicaragua but promotes the very teaching methods that *increase* illiteracy in the United States.

The NEA also passed a rather weak resolution in support of Solidarity, the independent Polish labor union. It said: "The National Education Association supports the aspirations of the people of Poland to achieve an improvement of their living conditions through their own free and independent union, Solidarity." Note that it did not condemn the communist governments of Poland or the Soviet Union for suppressing the rights of Polish workers. Why was the NEA so timid? Who was it afraid of offending? The NEA is not afraid to offend President Reagan or the Moral Majority with its harsh criticism.

But toward communists it offers a cordiality and sympathy it denies its own President.

During World War II when the United States became an ally of the Soviet Union, a sense of euphoria developed over Soviet-American relations which, it was hoped, would endure in the postwar period. A new theme began to take hold of liberals and progressives—the idea of world government which would render war obsolete. In the December 1942 NEA *Journal,* in an editorial entitled "The United Peoples of the World," Joy Elmer Morgan announced the NEA's support of world government. He quoted Tennyson's "Locksley Hall" with its reference to the "Parliament of Man, the Federation of the World." Morgan wrote:

> World organization may well have four branches which in prac-
> tice have proved indispensable: The legislature, the judicial, the
> executive, and the educational. In addition to the framework of gov-
> ernment the world needs certain tools of cooperation: A world system
> of money and credit; a uniform system of weights and measures; a
> revised calendar; and a basic language.
>
> To keep the peace and insure justice and opportunity we need
> certain world agencies of administration such as: A police force; a
> board of education; a board of health; a bureau of statistics; a planning
> board; a labor office; a postal system; agencies to control copyrights
> and patents; a radio-television commission; a board to deal with
> economic matters. . . .

Committed to the idea of world government, the NEA be-
gan its campaign for the metric system and an international educational bureau that would eventually become UNESCO. Meanwhile, the NEA continued to blast away at "Big Business." In March 1944, Morgan editorialized: "Giant corpora-
tions, monopolies, cartels, chain stores, and large-scale farm-
ing are fast destroying personal property and free individual enterprise in America."

For the NEA, the United Nations had become the hope of the world. The NEA *Journal* reported in April 1945: "The

NEA is intensifying its efforts to have provision made for an international office of education in the UNO."

In May 1945 the NEA addressed an open letter to members of the American delegation to the United Nations conference in San Francisco. "We urge . . . that . . . the United Nations agree to explore the desirability and feasibility of including in the overall security organization an international agency to deal with international problems in education." In response, the American delegation named William G. Carr, associate secretary of the NEA, as a consultant. In October, Carr reported what took place on May 22, 1945 at the San Francisco conference: "The climax came when the U.S. Delegation asked that educational cooperation be definitely recognized among the objectives of the United Nations Organization."

In an editorial in the January 1946 NEA *Journal* entitled "The Teacher and World Government," Joy Elmer Morgan wrote:

> In the struggle to establish an adequate world government, the teacher has many parts to play. He must begin with his own attitude and knowledge and purpose. He can do much to prepare the hearts and minds of children for global understanding and cooperation. . . . At the very top of all the agencies which will assure the coming of world government must stand the school, the teacher, and the organized profession.

That same issue of the *Journal* published the constitution of UNESCO—the United Nations Educational, Scientific and Cultural Organization. It was called a "World Charter for Education."

The idea of world government became a constant theme in the NEA *Journal*. In March 1946, Robert M. Hutchins, Chancellor of the University of Chicago, in an article entitled "The Atom Bomb vs. Civilization," wrote: "The United States has the greatest stake in a world state and a world community." In September 1946, Raymond Swing echoed that argument, stating that "the choice before us is either world government or world underground." In December 1946, Morgan ended the year with an editorial entitled "Fundamentals of Abiding Peace." He wrote:

> The organized teaching profession may well take hope and satisfaction from the achievements it has already made toward world government in its support of the United Nations and UNESCO. It is ours to hold ever before the people the ideals and principles of world government until practice can catch up with those ideals.

To help the educators of other nations catch up with the ideals of world government, the NEA sponsored a World Conference of the Teaching Profession in 1946 at Endicott, New York, at which was formed the World Organization of the Teaching Profession (WOTP). William G. Carr of the NEA became its secretary-general. In 1951 the WOTP was expanded to include both elementary and secondary teacher associations and it changed its name to the World Confederation of Organizations of the Teaching Profession (WCOTP). Carr remained as secretary-general.

Articles and reports about the United Nations, UNESCO, the WOTP and later the WCOTP appeared regularly in the NEA *Journal*. But by 1950 the Cold War had ended all illusions about the possibility of a world government with the Soviet Union in it. The January 1950 issue published an article about how the communists took over the schools of Czechoslovakia. In the May 1955 issue appeared a letter from a former Russian school teacher who wrote: "Teachers in this country can't imagine all the horrors of teaching in Russia."

The outbreak of the Korean War in 1950 shattered all dreams that the UN might prevent further wars. Instead of advocating world government, the NEA now advocated the idea of "world citizenship" and the notion that the UN was the only hope of mankind. In 1952, William Carr, who had helped create UNESCO and the WCOTP, became executive secretary of the NEA. Although Carr was probably the most anti-communist executive secretary the NEA ever had, he remained a progressive in matters of curriculum, federal aid to education, psychology, the UN and globalism.

In an editorial entitled "Spiritual Values in Public Education," in the December 1952 *Journal,* Carr left no doubt that he was on the side of the humanists. He wrote:

> I recommend as an operating definition the one suggested by the Educational Policies Commission: "By moral and spiritual values, when applied in human behavior, exalt and refine life and bring it into accord with the standards of conduct that are approved in our democratic culture."

It sounded good, but what it meant in essence is that morals and values are relative in a democracy. Apparently the majority decides what morals and values to approve of at any given time.

Probably the last anti-communist articles to appear in the NEA *Journal* were one on Cuban refugee teachers in December 1962 and one denouncing all forms of totalitarianism in April 1964. With the departure of Carr in 1967 also went the NEA's short-lived anti-communism. In 1971 the new executive secretary, Sam Lambert, visited the Soviet Union and established cordial relations with the government-controlled Soviet teachers union. By then the NEA itself had become a labor union, identifying itself with the working class. It also began to adopt the radical postures of the New Left which had arisen during the political turmoil of the Vietnam War and civil rights movement.

By 1975 the NEA *Journal* was focussing its moral concern on the evils of apartheid in South Africa, while the evils of communism were never mentioned. As far as the NEA was concerned, Solzhenitsyn and the slave labor camps of the Soviet Gulag didn't exist. As for America's bicentennial celebration in 1976, the NEA issued a "Declaration of Interdependence" and advocated "education for a global community," despite the fact that the United Nations was now dominated by the Soviet bloc and third world nations most of which had socialist governments. The idea of a world government dominated by the western democracies was now an unattainable dream. If there was ever to be a world government, it would have to be a communist one, for that was the only kind the communists would ever accept.

While the NEA's resolutions of 1983 contained no call for world government, they called for the NEA's strong support of the World Confederation of Organizations of the Teaching Profession; Multicultural-Global Education to "develop an appreciation of the common humanity shared by all peoples of the earth"; public funding of Chicano-Hispano Self Determination in Education; conversion of the United States to the Metric System; cultural diversity in instructional materials and processes in public schools; world peace by strengthening the United Nations and the creation of a U.S. Academy of Peace.

It is in the NEA's resolution for a nuclear freeze that one finds a hint of a world government to come. It says that the NEA "believes that peoples of the world . . . are evolving toward greater and greater collective consciousness and unity in their recognition that nuclear war is the common enemy of all nations and peoples and is not survivable." Thus, according to the NEA, by uniting with other nations, we can lick the common enemy, which is not communism but nuclear war. The NEA strongly advocates teaching American students about nuclear war. Its resolution states:

> The Association urges its affiliates to work with other organizations to develop age-appropriate materials for all levels. These materials should show the effects of nuclear weaponry and demonstrate strategies for disarmament and appropriate methods to be used to influence national policy to achieve peace.

The wording of the resolution is interesting: "These materials should show . . . appropriate methods to be used to influence national policy to achieve peace." In case the NEA is unaware, we are at peace. The Soviet Union is at war in Afghanistan, but the NEA passed no resolution on Afghanistan. Maybe it hasn't heard from any teachers there. To the communists the word "peace" means total communist victory. Is that the NEA's definition?

The NEA's position on national defense is in harmony with that of the radical left which takes its cue from the Kremlin: nuclear freeze and disarmament, both of which, in the face of the Soviet Union's massive military buildup, can only lead to a western surrender to Soviet world domination.

As for domestic economics, at a time when Americans are rediscovering the virtues and benefits of capitalism, the NEA had this to offer in its resolutions of 1983–84: "The National Education Association believes that a new economic program of 'jobs with peace' for its members, all students, and working people should be a cornerstone of the nation's political structure."

The resolution is sufficiently vague in its wording to make it seem innocuous, but it has several phrases that add up to socialism: "new economic policy," "jobs with peace," "working people," "nation's political structure." Our present economy is a mixed public-private one with an increasing awareness that growth and progress depend on private initiative rather than public planning. What does a "new economic policy" mean in this context? No doubt it means more public planning and spending. What are "jobs with peace"? To the radical left "peace" means unilateral disarmament or, to put it bluntly, surrender to Soviet world domination. Thus, "jobs with peace" would have to mean jobs provided by the government by eliminating defense spending. The singling out of "working people" in the resolution is obviously intended to create working-class consciousness, which is of paramount importance in the class struggle which leads to communism. For all of this to become a "cornerstone of the nation's political structure" means nothing less than a complete change in the American form of government.

In the 1930s the progressives were quite candid and used plain English in telling everyone what they wanted America to become. Today the progressives in the NEA make all sorts of vague, innocuous statements that Marxists understand but that the unwary do not. The NEA is as pro-socialist as was John Dewey. Yet most of its members are obviously not socialists.

All in all, the NEA is everything the communists believe a labor union in America should be: it is creating working-class consciousness among its members; it is forming coalitions with other unions to exert maximum pressure on candidates and legislators; it backs Marxist revolution in Central America; it never criticizes the Soviet Union; no form of anticommunism can be found in its publications; it wages incessant warfare against conservatives, fundamentalist Christians and organizations of the New Right; it is working to bring all teachers and all private schools under government control through certification and accreditation laws; it hates capitalism and loves socialism; it is uncompromisingly atheistic in its adherance to evolution, behavioral psychology, and humanist moral values; it advocates sex education for children, abortion on demand, and passage of the Equal Rights Amendment; it advocates gun control in violation of the Second Amendment; it wants a nuclear freeze and disarmament. In short, for all practical purposes, the NEA might as well be the socialist party of America.

PART FIVE
The Push for Total Power

18. Toward Educational Dictatorship

The idea of a national, centrally controlled public education system in the United States is as old as the public school movement itself. Although the United States Constitution makes no mention of education, leaving that field of activity to the states, the educators have tended to see public education as a national system, regarding the state and local jurisdictions more as inconveniences than prohibitions.

As Charles Brooks, the Unitarian minister who unceasingly promoted the Prussian system in Massachusetts, wrote to the French philosopher, Victor Cousin, in 1837: "You know that in certain respects our liberty hinders us. We cannot put into place an entire education system with the promptness that belongs to the government of a king. We can only begin reform with the people, and it is necessary that the people be enlightened, and then we can have recourse to government."[1]

The first move to organize American educators nationally took place in 1830 with the creation of the American Institute of Instruction. The Institute, which held yearly conventions, was an offshoot of the Lyceum movement founded in 1828 by

Josiah Holbrook. Holbrook had taken it upon himself to organize American educators in support of the public school movement. The underlying goals of the Lyceum movement were uniformity of public instruction, the centralization of educational policy, and control of the teaching profession on a national basis.

In May 1831 the first annual convention of the American Lyceum was held in New York City. Educators from all over the United States attended. All sorts of subjects were discussed. At the 1833 convention, for example, the Lyceum recommended combining manual labor with academic study, an idea that in time would become the vocational school. The Lyceum resolved that the establishment of such schools would be "an important and desirable branch of a system of national education for our country."[2]

Thus, American educators were thinking in terms of a national system of education quite early in the public school movement. In October 1849, a National Convention of the Friends of Education was held in Philadelphia to discuss plans for creating a national education association. In August 1850 an organizing convention took place in Philadelphia, attended by education officers from fifteen states. Horace Mann, president of the convention, told the audience:

> By a National organization of teachers, great and comprehensive plans may be devised, to whose standard each State may be gradually brought into conformity. . . . Now we want uniformity in these matters, so that we may speak a common language; so that the same terms shall express the same ideas all over the country. . . .
> . . . On all school subjects we want: first, the best way; and second, the universal adoption of the best way.[3]

If the educators couldn't have a unified national system like the Prussian because of our division into states, they could leap across state boundaries and form a national organization that would, in effect, create and implement national educational policy. Thus, it ought not to surprise anyone that at the first meeting of the National Teachers Association in 1857, the call was made for a U.S. Department of Education with cabinet status. While Americans as a whole thought of public education in terms of local and state controls, the educators were thinking in terms of national control. Among themselves the system was a national system, and this was confirmed at every annual NEA convention when teachers, superintendents and state education officers from all of the states gathered to discuss the problems of American education and devise "great and comprehensive plans" to solve them. For the publishers and writers of textbooks, uniformity of standards and curricula enhanced the education market. Thus, by creating a national consciousness among educators, the NEA in a sense actually created a national system of public education. And when the progressives took over in the early 1900s they were able to use the NEA to implement their own "great and comprehensive plan."

However, the progressives knew that there would be considerable opposition to their plans to socialize America, and that is why the education mafia came into being. Through the mafia their work could be done without public scrutiny, and they could promote to positions of power and influence those educators who were loyal to the plan and could be counted on to carry it forward. Yet the progressives were willing to take enormous risks, particularly in the conspiracy against literacy. But their network of supporters and their control of educational publications and associations made exposure virtually impossible.

The marriage between Wundtian psychology and education, which led to the creation of graduate schools of education and doctoral degrees in education, made it impossible for conservatives or traditionalists to ever take control of public education. But the socialist-humanist plan could not go forward unless the classroom teachers could be made the willing tools of the progressive mafia. For it was the teachers who would have to implement the curricula and instructional changes at the classroom level despite predictable parental objections. It is important to note that when the progressives decided to change reading instruction from phonics to look-say, they did not ask for parental approval.

Meanwhile, teachers had to be taught to artificially induce dyslexia without even knowing that they were doing it. But it would be impossible to fool all of the teachers all of the time. The mafia learned that the best way to deal with independent teachers was to ignore them, brand them as reactionaries, make sure they never got promoted, or force them out of the profession. But what did you do with professors at the top who went against the mafia? You discredited their work, never invited them to write for your publications or speak at your conventions, you spread unsavory stories about their personal lives. You isolated them and virtually destroyed their influence.

A climate of conformity had to be created to make it difficult if not foolhardy for a teacher to follow any line but the progressive one. The NEA played an important role in creating that climate of conformity. The prestige of progressive educators was constantly bolstered in the pages of the NEA *Journal*. The NEA also performed the tireless task of defending the progressives against attacks from anti-communists and traditionalists. The trick was to make sure that the teachers listened to their professors rather than the critics.

It was also in 1944 that the NEA began its drive for unified membership in order to increase its power and gain greater control over the teachers. But unification proceeded slowly until the NEA made it mandatory by a change in the by-laws in 1972. After that, all teachers who joined local affiliates were forced to become members of both the state and national associations.

But what about teachers who might not want to join the local affiliate? To meet that possibility the NEA resorted to a favorite union checkmate: the "agency shop." Similar to the closed shop, the agency shop forced teachers who did not wish to join the local affiliate to nevertheless pay union fees or lose their jobs—even if they had tenure.

Actually, the agency shop was developed by unions as a device to get around prohibitions against closed shops or forced membership. It is now widely used in the public sector. Compulsory union membership via the closed shop was authorized by the National Labor Relations Act of 1935 (NLRA), passed in the heyday of the New Deal under the sponsorship of Senator Robert F. Wagner of New York. It put government on the side of the unions in their drive to organize American workers. That it trampled on the rights of individuals who did not want to join unions was ignored. But the growth of union power after World War II, the many crippling and violent strikes, the gangsterism of some labor bosses turned public opinion against organized labor.

In 1947 Congress passed the Taft-Hartley Labor Management Act which was designed to curb union excesses. Section 14(b) of the act sanctioned the passage of state Right-to-Work laws forbidding closed shops. President Truman vetoed the bill, but Congress overrode it. Today there are 20 states with Right-to-Work laws: Alabama, Arizona, Arkansas, Florida, Georgia, Iowa, Kansas, Louisiana, Mississippi, Nebraska, Nevada, North Carolina, North Dakota, South Carolina, South Dakota, Tennessee, Texas, Utah, Virginia, and Wyoming. The last state to pass a Right-to-Work law was Louisiana in 1976. In some states Right-to-Work laws have actually been written into the state constitution.

Naturally the unions want Congress to repeal 14(b). The NEA's resolutions for 1983 not only call for a federal collective bargaining law for teachers which would impose agency shops in all school districts, but it also states that "Right-to-Work laws must be opposed and section 14(b) of the Taft-Hartley Act should be repealed."

Because organized labor is determined to wipe out every Right-to-Work law in America and get Congress to repeal 14(b), a group of independent Americans who want to preserve and protect labor freedom created the National Right to Work Committee in 1955. The committee was started after Congress passed the Federal Railway Labor Act, which authorized compulsory unionism for railroad employees, thereby creating the union stranglehold that would eventually lead some of America's greatest railroads into bankruptcy. Five employees of the railroad who opposed forced unionism formed the committee, and since then it has grown into a formidable champion of labor freedom.

In 1975, to meet the threat of forced unionism among teachers, the Right to Work Committee formed Concerned Educators Against Forced Unionism (CEAFU) under the direction of Susan Staub, a former Virginia high school teacher who had refused to join the unified NEA. In terms of size and money the CEAFU is a mere David compared to the NEA Goliath. But the CEAFU's secret weapon is that small body of courageous teachers who refuse to bow down to the NEA's educational dictatorship.

Meanwhile, experienced, tenured teachers have been fired because they have refused to join the union or pay its fees. This is what happened to Kathryn Jackson of Swartz Circle, Michigan, with 19 years of classroom experience; Anne Parks of Detroit, with 40 years experience; and Susan LaVine of Lyons Township, Illinois. In Fremont, California, 11 teachers were fired in April 1982 because they preferred to pay their forced union dues in monthly installments instead of by payroll deduction or in a lump sum as insisted upon by the union. Nine of the teachers caved it and agreed to pay as dictated by the union rather than lose their jobs. However, one teacher resigned rather than work under such conditions. She is Charleen Sciambi, a 13-year veteran of the Fremont school system who had been voted the best foreign language teacher in the state of California by the Foreign Language Teachers Association. Apparently the payment of union dues is more important to the Fremont school board than the quality of teaching. The Fremont *Argus* of July 6, 1983 reported:

> In a letter mailed to her students last Thursday, Ms. Sciambi stated, "My employer is confiscating my wages without my permis-

sion. This is the status of a slave. How can I return to you in September and teach you to stand tall as a free man or woman if I cannot?"

At issue is a $290 fee that must be paid by all non-union teachers to cover collective bargaining costs because of an agency-shop clause in the contract for teachers. . . .

Ms. Sciambi was among 11 teachers fired in April 1982 for failing to pay as specified in the contract. Nine teachers agreed to pay rather than lose their jobs, but Ms. Sciambi and Washington High School teacher Howard Neely successfully appealed the dismissal.

But the ruling became moot with the passage of a law allowing school districts to deduct the fees from teachers' paychecks, which Fremont trustees agreed to do in April. . . .

Ann Halligan, a kindergarten teacher at Hacienda Elementary School, said Ms. Sciambi's resignation "is going to be a tremendous loss for this community. She put 200 percent into teaching." . . .

But Trustee Gloria Carr said, "I support the contract, and part of it is agency shop. If employees change that by vote, fine. But nobody tells (Ms. Sciambi) she has to work."

Apparently the trustee was not concerned about the loss of an exceptionally good teacher. If obedience to the union was more important than the quality of teaching, so be it. Also, the trustees had agreed to become a dues collector for the union, saving the union the clerical expenses of dues collection, courtesy of the taxpayer. Teaching in the Fremont schools is now a privilege which only the union, not the school board, can grant. For all practical purposes, the union has created an educational dictatorship in Fremont with the help of Fremont's own teachers and school board. Is this a pattern that will be repeated in every school district in America? If it is, what will be left of American educational freedom?

The reaction of the executive director of the Fremont teachers association to Ms. Sciambi's resignation was quite interesting: "I think she's a big hypocrite," he told a reporter. "She says we're taking away her freedom, but she wants (association) members to pay her bills. It's been democratically voted on to have a union." The director seemed to have forgotten that the German people also voted democratically—for Adolf Hitler. In addition, no NEA affiliate has ever been willing to open its books so that teachers could see how much of their fees actually went to pay for the costs of collective bargaining.

But who's the hypocrite? According to a poll of educators taken by *Instructor* magazine in 1981, some 82 percent of the nation's teachers oppose forced unionism. In addition, 72 percent of those who were polled identified themselves as members of the NEA or the American Federation of Teachers.

The fight over the agency shop involves much more than merely the forced payment of dues. It involves paying dues to an organization engaged in overt partisan politics, legislative lobbying, the support of ultra-liberal candidates, and the crushing of educational and professional freedom. The NEA favors gun control, decriminalization of marijuana, tax-financed abortion on demand, a nuclear freeze, the drafting of women, the ERA, and a weakened defense. It opposes a balanced federal budget, voluntary school prayer, Right-to-Work laws, and U.S. aid for anti-communists in Central America.

To what extent teacher disagreement with NEA policies is affecting membership is not known. However, NEA membership has declined from a high of 1,886,532 in 1976 to 1,633,205 in 1983, a loss of about 250,000 members. Some of these teachers have created new organizations to represent them. West Virginia Professional Educators (WVPE) was founded in 1980 as an alternative to the state's NEA affiliate. Its executive director is Florena Colvin, 1978 West Virginia Teacher of the Year.

Other new organizations include the Florida Professional Educators, Professional Educators of North Carolina, Professional Association of Georgia Educators, Professional Educators of Iowa, Mississippi Professional Educators, Professional Educators Group of California, Ohio Association of Professional Educators, and Lorain (Ohio) Independent Teachers

Association. Concerning the latter association, the Lorain *Journal* reported in October 1982:

> The chief difference between the two unions will be in affiliation with the Ohio Education Association (OEA), the National Education Association (NEA), and the North East Ohio Teachers Association (NEOTA).
>
> Currently, when teachers join the LEA and pay their $259 annual dues, they automatically join OEA, NEOTA and the NEA. . . .
>
> Fifty dollars goes to the local group, $146 to OEA, $53 to NEA and $10 to NEOTA, said LEA president Jack Yaneris. Clay (president of LITA) and his associates would like to see all of the money used locally.
>
> "I'm concerned about the accountability of the OEA and the NEA. They are reaping millions of dollars in teacher dues money. In 1980 the NEA used dues money to support Jimmy Carter when two polls taken when teachers voted shows 56 percent supported Reagan. The NEA didn't even try to find out what teachers wanted," Clay said.

The president of the Lorain Independent Teachers Association had good reason to be concerned with the NEA's accountability. The courts had already found the NEA guilty of misusing teachers' money. According to the *Advocate* (Victoria, Texas) of August 13, 1980:

> The National Education Association, which brags on itself as "the only union with our own Cabinet department," has finally coughed up the $75,000 fine levied against four of its state affiliate political action committees for using the illegal "reverse (dues) checkoff."
>
> The payment of the fine was the final chapter in one aspect of the unions ripoff of American teachers. It was in addition to a 1978 court order requiring NEA to refund $825,155 the NEA's PAC illegally collected from teachers for use in the 1976 election.
>
> Despite the NEA's obvious violation of federal election campaign laws the Federal Election Commission had refused to act in the case until the National Right to Work Committee took the FEC to court. The FEC looked the other way despite open admission by FEC commissioner Thomas E. Harris, a former AFL-CIO official, that the "reverse checkoff" was illegal.

Tens of thousands of teachers were taken for nearly a million dollars when union officials took the money directly from paychecks without the teachers permission, and often without their knowledge.

"If the National Right to Work Committee hadn't taken the FEC to court, the NEA would still be robbing teachers," said committee president Reed Larson.

Apparently, the NEA will pull any financial trick it thinks it can get away with. What is so appalling is that school boards were making these paycheck deductions for the NEA and thus were accomplices in the ripoffs. Equally appalling was the Federal Election Commission's willingness to look the other way. The FEC had to be dragged into court and forced to do its duty. Clearly, this is the kind of political corruption and favoritism we can expect more of when an NEA candidate occupies the White House.

The simple truth is that most of the money collected from teachers by the NEA goes for union organizing and political action. The NEA now employs 1,172 full-time, highly trained field organizers which the *Reader's Digest* of May 1984 called "the largest grassroots political army ever deployed in the United States." Of the $77.5 million the NEA spent in 1982, only $2.4 million, or a mere 3.1 percent, was spent on "Instruction and Professional Development." The rest went for organizing and training members for political action, bargaining and job action (strike) situations, processing membership lists for political purposes, maintaining legislators' voting records, implementing the NEA's legislative agenda, lobbying Congress, building and maintaining labor and ERA coalitions, operating a clearinghouse on "extremist"—that is, conservative and fundamentalist—groups, operating NEA-PAC, etc. No wonder the teachers have little time to teach. Mary Futrell, president of the NEA, expressed it well in the *Los Angeles Times* of July 4, 1982 when she said: "There's no alternative to political involvement. Instruction and professional development have been on the back burner for us, compared to political action."

Teachers have become so active in politics that in Michigan there are now more teachers or former teachers in the state legislature than there are lawyers. According to the Escanaba, Michigan, *Press* of August 19, 1980:

> At the present time about 21 percent of Michigan's legislators are teachers or former teachers, which is nearly twice the ratio of teacher-lawmakers for the nation. . . .
>
> Nationally, lawyers are the profession with the largest number of state legislature seats—20 percent—but in Michigan they're topped by teachers and comprise less than 10 percent of the State-House and Senate.

None of this political activity has done anything to improve the quality of education. If anything, it has been responsible for its further decline. On the matter of quality, David Broder interviewed Terry Herndon, NEA executive director, at the NEA's convention in July 1980, and asked some pointed questions which got some rather amazing answers. Broder wrote:

> I remarked that the quality of public schools was the issue of greatest concern to parents and voters, but not a major topic at the convention. "Most all the speakers mentioned it," he replied, "but very briefly. They—like the delegates—are concerned about the issue, but they don't know what the answer is."
>
> When I said he seemed less worried about declining consumer confidence in the quality of American public education than his friend Douglas Fraser, the head of the United Auto Workers, did about the same problem in regard to American cars, Herndon naturally disagreed.
>
> "Teachers don't think that schools are worse than they were, but they agree they're not as good as they should be. We don't think we're failing American youth, but we're failing too many of them. But we don't have the answers. Our executive board spent more time talking about the crisis in urban education than any other topic this year, but we have no answer."[4]

What an astonishing admission from the executive director of the nation's leading teachers organization, that *they don't know what the answer is*, that *we don't have the answers*, *we have no answer*. If any industry or profession in America voiced the same helplessness about the quality of its chief product or service, it would be out of business in a very short time. But the National Education Association can get away with its utter professional bankruptcy because it operates within a government-controlled monopoly. This is the organization that wants the power to determine teacher certification for every educator in the country. Yet, it doesn't even know how to teach a child to read!

But the NEA is determined to implement the program outlined by Sam Lambert in 1967: "NEA will have more and more to say about how a teacher is educated, whether he should be admitted to the profession, and depending on his behavior and ability whether he should stay in the profession." Moreover, the NEA rejects any notion that teachers should be tested for academic competency. Why? Is it possible that some of their most active members are lousy teachers?

In Houston in 1983 the school board was shocked to discover that 62 percent of 2,437 teachers tested had failed a standard reading-skills test; 46 percent flunked in math, 26 percent in writing. And of the 3,200 teachers who took the tests, it was found that 763 had cheated!

Yet, it is the goal of the NEA to control all teacher certification in the United States and, through the agency shop, control the hiring and firing of teachers. The agency shop will provide NEA with its own compulsory income tax of the entire teaching profession, and it will bar from the classroom anyone who does not agree with its philosophy. Can the teachers of America save themselves from this sort of dictatorship? What is frightening is that so many teachers want it and so many teachers have been persuaded to accept it. But if the majority of teachers actually oppose forced unionism, and if educational freedom is to be saved in this country, then teachers will have to do more than passively go along with the NEA.

The battles for teacher freedom are not being fought at NEA meetings and conventions, but in the courts. In Indiana, the NEA filed suit against 414 teachers for refusing to pay agency shop fees. In New Jersey, 1,400 state employees filed suit in the U.S. District Court in December 1983 against automatic deduction of agency fees from their paychecks. In Waterbury, Connecticut, 47 teachers filed suit against the teachers' unions, charging that the collection of agency fees violates the constitutional rights of individual teachers. It is obvious that the whole matter of forced unionism and compulsory agency fees will eventually wind up in the U.S. Supreme Court.

Meanwhile, the NEA has tried to prevent teachers from speaking out against its policies by suing them for libel! This is what happened to Suzanne Clark, a teacher in Bristol, Tennessee, who was sued by the NEA for $100,000 because of a letter she had written criticizing the NEA's union policies and ideology which was published in the *Bristol Herald Courier*. However, adverse publicity in the press and strong public criticism forced the NEA to drop the suit.

An NEA affiliate in Worcester, Massachusetts, tried the same tactic by filing a libel suit against Joseph Gustafson, a nonunion teacher who objected to paying the agency fee. Gustafson had written two letters to the local newspaper denouncing the use of the agency fee for any purpose other than teacher negotiations. He also called for a boycott of the payment of these fees and outlined the legal remedies available to teachers who objected to the fees. However, when the National Right to Work Legal Defense Foundation decided to get involved in the case, the Educational Association of Worcester dropped the suit.

It is ironic that the teachers in the world's freest nation should have to struggle to preserve their own freedom against colleagues who would impose a professional dictatorship over them. A profession so dominated by the NEA will be unfit to teach American children how to preserve American freedom, for the first thing they'd have to teach them is how to get rid of the NEA! Indeed, if American teachers can't preserve their own professional freedom, then it doesn't look too good for the rest of us.

19. The Strategy for Monopoly

The last bastions of educational freedom in America are the private schools and the private home. As institutions of learning both are as old as America itself. George Washington was educated by his father and half-brother. Benjamin Franklin was taught to read by his father and attended a private school for writing and arithmetic. Thomas Jefferson studied Latin and Greek under a tutor. Of the 117 men who signed the Declaration of Independence, the Articles of Confederation and the Constitution, one out of three had had only a few months of formal schooling, and only one in four had gone to college. They were educated by parents, church schools, tutors, academies, apprenticeship, and by themselves.

Obviously educational freedom not only contributed to the free spirit of the American people but also made them highly literate. Even in New England, where towns provided tax-supported common schools, children were taught to read in private dames' schools, for literacy was a prerequisite to entering a common school. Teaching reading was not a problem. It only became a problem in the 1930s after America created its graduate schools and doctors of education.

In fact, the private schools did such an excellent job of providing Americans with literacy and academic skills at virtually no cost to the taxpayer that their replacement by the public schools is undoubtedly one of the biggest mistakes this nation ever made. But the forces that generated the public school movement had nothing to do with academics or economics: they were religious and philosophical in kind. The Unitarians wanted public schools in order to secularize education and perfect humanity, the Owenite socialists wanted them in order to create a communist society, the Hegelians wanted them to glorify the state, and the Protestants wanted them to preserve Protestant culture seemingly threatened by large-scale Catholic immigration.

In fact, the Catholic parochial school system was created in the 1850s to offset the anti-religious influences of the secular, nonsectarian common schools. Today the growth of Christian fundamentalist schools is a similar reaction to the anti-religious forces of secular humanism, the philosophy that now dominates American public education.

The private school and home education represent the only escape routes for those parents who do not wish to submit their children to secular humanist indoctrination. But the NEA is doing all in its power to shut off these escape routes by proposing state laws severely regulating private schools and outlawing home education. Some of these regulations are in direct conflict with the First Amendment guarantee of the free exercise of religion, and some of them have actually forced the closing of church schools and the imprisonment of pastors, teachers and parents. They have precipitated a war for religious freedom between fundamentalist Christians and state education officers.

The progressives have always known that violence would have to be used to break the back of the hard-core resistance to their dictatorship. While Dewey expected socialism to come about in America through the use of "organized intelligence," without violent revolution, he nevertheless realized that hard-core resistance would have to be quelled by force. He wrote in *Liberalism and Social Action:*

> The one exception—and that apparent rather than real—to dependence upon organized intelligence as the method for directing social change is found when society through an authorized majority has entered upon the path of social experimentation leading to great social change, and a minority refuses by force to permit the method of intelligent action to go into effect. Then force may be intelligently employed to subdue and disarm the recalcitrant minority.[1]

Dewey realized that while most people would sheepishly permit the chains of socialist control to be placed on them by "organized intelligence," there would always be those stubborn individualists and religious "fanatics" who would fight back. Since 1917, the communists have become very skilled at dealing with resistance to dictatorship. Nowadays, thanks to experimental psychology, they use mental hospitals and psychiatric wards to deal with dissidents. In this country, the communists and their allies have been working hard to cripple the future potential resistance to their takeover by now putting into place, whenever possible, laws which will be used to disarm Americans and regulate their behavior.

Wherever the communists have taken over, private schools have been abolished. As Jonathan Kozol, who toured Cuban schools in 1976, writes in *Children of the Revolution,* "There are no private schools in Cuba." Public education is, in fact, the largest item in the Cuban budget, because, as Castro said in 1959, "each school has become a fortress of the revolution." And as the Cuban minister of education told Kozol: "All education has forever a class bias. No society will foster schools that do not serve its ends. Education is not merely technical instruction, nor the passing-on of information. It is the total training of the human character—its essence and its soul."

The much-heralded Cuban literacy campaign launched by Castro in 1960 was used primarily to indoctrinate the people of Cuba with socialist ideas. What better way to teach Marxism-Leninism than through a campaign for literacy? According to Kozol: "It was the campaign itself which turned a hundred thousand liberal, altruistic, and utopian kids into a rebel vanguard of committed or, at the very least, incipient socialists."[2]

In Nicaragua the same sort of literacy campaign has been launched by the Marxist Sandinista government with the help of Cuban teachers. This is the campaign the NEA wants so much to succeed. Its resolution on Nicaragua states: "The National Education Association urges the U.S. government to refrain from any U.S. plan for overt or covert action that would destabilize Nicaragua or would adversely affect that government's successful campaign against illiteracy."[3]

The NEA knows that the communists use phonics in teaching reading. Must America go communist before the NEA suddenly discovers how to teach reading to Americans?

It is a well-known fact that private schools, in general, do a better job of teaching reading than the public schools. This has been established beyond any doubt by the Coleman report of 1982, *High School Achievement.* That is why the private schools are gaining in popularity. The public school represents so high a risk for the child who passes through it, that signs ought to be posted warning parents that "this school may be harmful to your child's health." The cancer rate for heavy cigarette smokers is far lower than the failure rate for public schoolers. School-induced functional illiteracy is America's biggest educational problem, and the situation would be much worse if it weren't for private schools.

The NEA's opposition to private education goes back to the very beginning of the public school movement. Today, the NEA views private education as its most serious competitor, its barrier to a total monopoly, and it has vowed to bring it under NEA control through teacher certification and state accreditation laws. It's hard to believe that the free public schools, the privileged recipients of billions of federal dollars, should feel threatened by small, frugal private schools that must charge tuition and appeal to private charity in order to exist. The well-heeled prep school of the Northeast is not the typical private school in America. It is the urban Catholic parochial school, or the small church school. But to the NEA, any private school, no matter how small or poor seems to be a threat to its monopolist plans.

The NEA's legislative program for 1983–84 states:

> Nonpublic school instructional personnel must be credentialed according to minimum standards comparable to and comparable with those applied in certifying public educators in the state; nonpublic education institutions with faculty members not in compliance with the standards should be ineligible to participate in federally funded programs.[4]

Few people bother to read the NEA's resolutions adopted at each annual convention by its Representative Assembly. They tend to be dull, repetitive, and self-serving. But the NEA's resolutions of 1984 are nothing less than a blueprint for achieving monopoly power over American education, and anyone seriously concerned with preserving American freedom had better study them very carefully.

It appears that the NEA is using seven concurrent strategies to achieve monopoly control: (1) the professional strategy (teacher certification and teachers college accreditation); (2) the labor union strategy (exclusive representative, agency shop and a federal collective bargaining law); (3) content of education (the secular humanist curriculum); (4) elective politics (NEA-PAC, state affiliate PACs, political party involvement, endorsement of candidates); (5) government agencies (U.S. Department of Education, National Institute of Education, state departments of education); (6) legislation (NEA and state affiliate lobbies, legislative agendas and proposals); (7) federal funding (control of the disbursement of federal funds to schools, research centers, psychological laboratories).

It is obvious that all of these strategies, like the tentacles of an octopus, are coordinated by one central planning group to achieve the NEA's objectives. Here are the objectives the professional strategy is intended to achieve as spelled out in the resolutions. First, the NEA wants complete control of all teachers colleges so that what is taught in them will conform with NEA policies. Control will be concentrated in "a single national nongovernmental agency." The resolution states:

> The National Education Association believes in the importance of national accreditation for all teacher preparation institutions and supports the concept that a single national nongovernmental agency perform this function.
>
> The national agency must be broadly representative of the teaching profession and the preprofession and must include students preparing to teach and equitable representation of K–12 teachers in all matters of policy and function.[5]

The NEA then wants complete monopoly control of the teaching profession in America, as follows:

> The National Education Association believes the profession must govern itself. The Association also believes that each state should have a professional standards board, with a majority of K–12 public school classroom teachers. Professional standards boards should have the legal responsibility for determining policy and procedures for teacher certification, approval of teacher certificaton, approval of teacher preparation programs, recognition of national accreditation of preparation programs and programs designed to improve teacher education.[6]

The NEA also wants to control post-certification teacher development by controlling the use and policies of federally funded Teacher Centers, as follows:

> The National Education Association . . . supports a variety of approaches to required and voluntary professional development, including the concept of Teacher Centers governed by teachers representing their bargaining units and/or local professional organizations. . . .

The Association believes that teachers should strive for complete control of their own professional development. To this end, the Association encourages its affiliates to develop strategies for the implementation of teachers' professional development programs that are fiscally autonomous and teacher governed. . . .

The Association further believes that teachers from the exclusive representative of the bargaining unit and/or the local association should comprise a majority of the membership of Teacher Center policy boards.[7]

As for determining who should be permitted to teach in American schools, the NEA wants the power to screen all candidates for the teaching profession and keep track of them during their training:

The Association urges its affiliates to: Take immediate steps to evalute and improve standards for entrance into the teaching profession by working cooperatively with teacher training institutions and their professional organizations. The selection process shall be continuous and an integral part of the candidate's educational program. The process should include, but not be limited to, early screening, early field experiences, and counseling. . . .

The NEA also wants its affiliates to:

Support inclusion of training in classroom management concerns such as discipline, group processes, the dynamics of intergroup communication, and human relations in requirements for certification, and the provision for professional development workshops in these areas for beginning and experienced teachers and administrators. . . .

Support requirements for specific course work in reading instruction for both elementary and secondary certification. . . .

Recommend Student NEA membership before participation in preprofessional experiences and student teaching.

Recommend that Student NEA advisors be Association members. . . .

Take immediate steps to become involved in college and university committees that control teacher education programs. . . .

Support the inclusion of courses that provide instruction in the changing role of the family.

Support regulations that would place credentialed educators with teaching experience in decision making roles in departments of education and teacher licensing/credentialing agencies.[8]

The NEA also wants substitute teachers to be certified and private schools to be required to hire only certified teachers. The resolution states:

The Association insists that professional positions, including specialized and substitute positions, be filled by an educator who has completed a teacher preparation program in an accredited institution of higher education and holds the appropriate certificate or who holds the appropriate vocational certificate and that there be interstate certification reciprocity for mobile educators. The Association believes that private K–12 educational institutions must employ teachers who hold public educator certificates from their respective states. Private institutions failing to meet this hiring criterion should not be eligible for any federal funds, grants, or tax credits.[9]

The NEA wants all teachers of teachers to be certified, as well as all persons offering remedial instruction:

Teacher educators must be certified and experienced in their instructional areas.[10]

The Association supports any federal legislation and further encourages its state affiliates to seek legislation that would require any person offering services to remediate, correct, or ameliorate reading, speech, language, learning disabilities, or related problems to be certified or licensed under regulations of each state's department of public instruction or appropriate agency.[11]

In other words, if the NEA has its way, it will be illegal for virtually anyone to teach anything in America without a license. Every teacher, public or private, will be licensed, every teacher of teachers will be licensed, every substitute will be licensed, every teacher of remedial reading will be licensed, and schools, public and private, will be required to hire only licensed teachers. And who will control the licensing? Why, the NEA, of course!

As for the criteria to be used to determine who should or should not get a license to teach, the NEA says that a "broad range of factors" will be considered in evaluating candidates. Does anyone believe that the NEA will exclude religious, political and ideological factors in its evaluations? The resolution is conveniently vague:

> The National Education Association believes that no single criterion should be used for determining who should study for or be certified or licensed in the teaching profession. A broad range of factors should be used to evaluate a candidate for professional certification or licensing.
>
> The Association supports rigorous and relevant evaluation in the selection and preparation of teachers and believes that teaching practitioners and student teachers must be fully involved in determining what the criteria should be.[12]

Also, American children attending private schools are to be treated as second-class citizens, ineligible for any of the government's bounty devoted to aiding education, except for basic services. The resolution drips with typical NEA selfishness and greed:

> Public funded services for nonpublic school students must be strictly limited to medical and dental care, public welfare programs, school lunch and milk programs, and public safety services such as fire and police protection, which are budgeted and administered through the appropriate public agencies. . . .
>
> The Association will oppose any provision in federal legislation and/or current laws that include funds, goods, or services related to the instructional process for nonpublic schools or nonpublic school students.[13]

Nor will the NEA permit any private school to purchase or lease a former public school building:

> The National Education Association believes that public school buildings which are closed should be sold or leased only to those organizations that do not provide direct educational services to students and/or are not in direct competition with public schools.[14]

As for vouchers and tuition tax credits, the NEA has long "vehemently" opposed them "at any level" because they "could lead to racial, economic, and social isolation of children and weaken or destroy the public school system." Not only is the NEA opposed to voucher plans but it "urges the enactment of federal and state legislation prohibiting the establishment of voucher plans."[15]

However, in this case, the NEA needn't worry, for many conservatives and libertarians have come to believe that, because of the rules and regulations that would inevitably come with vouchers and tuition tax credits, they would do more harm than good for private schools.

Diane Ravitch, the noted education historian, in an address to the National Association of Independent Schools in March 1984, warned that private schools would in the long run lose their freedom if they accepted vouchers. "No matter how distressed your finances," she said, "you don't need this kind of help, because what will be exacted sooner or later is your independence. Any financial assistance today, well-intentioned though it may be, provides the pretext for state or federal regulation tomorrow. . . . My own child goes to a private school in Manhattan, and the headmaster can hire anyone, with or without state certification." Should a headmaster of a prestigious private school "be thrown in jail for hiring teachers who don't have state certification? . . . For the sake of your continued independence, speak out forcefully against government control and against government subsidy."[16]

As for the NEA's labor union strategy, it is spelled out in these resolutions:

> The NEA will continue to seek federally guaranteed collective bargaining rights. . . .
>
> The NEA will strive to have enacted a law which would attach a state or local obligation to institute collective bargaining rights to receipt of federal funds. . . .

NEA will explore other sources of Congressional power for enacting a federal collective bargaining statute.[17]

Right-to-work laws must be opposed and section 14(b) of the Taft-Hartley Act should be repealed. Any weakening of the minimum wage will be opposed.[18]

The NEA-PAC Council is requested to set as a priority for NEA-PAC endorsements candidate support for the achievement of collective bargaining rights for [public school] employees using the spending power authority or any other appropriate means.[19]

The National Education Association believes in the necessity of a public employees' federal collective bargaining law that will not weaken any state or local bargaining laws currently in effect. The Association also demands that all state and local governing bodies bargain collectively with all public employees. . . .

The Association further believes that local affiliates and governing boards must negotiate written master contracts . . . including a provision for agency shop. . . .

The Association further believes that binding arbitration or the right to strike must be an integral part of any collective bargaining process.[20]

The National Education Association denounces the practice of keeping schools open during a strike. It believes that when a picket line is established by the authorized bargaining unit, crossing it is strikebreaking. This unprofessional act jeopardizes the welfare of teachers and the educational process. . . .

In the event of a strike by professional employees, extracurricular and cocurricular activities must cease. Appropriate teacher training institutions should be notified that a strike is being conducted and urged not to cooperate in emergency certification or placement practices that constitute strikebreaking.

The Association condemns the use of the "*ex parte*" injunction; the jailing of teachers; excessive bail; firing of teachers; fines; decertification of an organization as the bargaining agent; loss of association rights; and the revocation or suspension of tenure, certification, and retirement benefits in school work stoppages. The Association further condemns the denial of credits to students who have honored a teacher work stoppage. The Association urges the state and federal governments to enact, where they do not exist, statutes guaranteeing teachers due process of the law when a work stoppage occurs, including the right to present their case to the state or courts, before back-to-work orders are issued.[21]

In short, the NEA's labor-union strategy is to make use of its political power to acquire national collective bargaining rights in order to dominate the teaching profession and create an educational dictatorship.

20. The Humanist Curriculum

Easily the most important of the NEA's strategies is that concerning the content of education, for the socialist revolution wanted by the progressives will have to be carried out by a younger generation indoctrinated in progressive, humanist values. The road to a humanist curriculum began in 1918 with the NEA's Seven Cardinal Principles which stressed humanist ethical values to replace those of traditional religion. The expulsion of the Bible from the public school did not occur all at once. This writer, who attended the public schools of New York City in the 1930s, remembers hearing the school principal open each weekly assembly with a short passage from the Bible, usually a Psalm. When that practice stopped, is not known.

But the undermining of the Judeo-Christian tradition was well underway when in 1933 John Dewey and 33 other liberal humanists drew up and signed that extraordinary document known as the Humanist Manifesto. It reflected all of the influences of science, evolution, and the new psychology which were reshaping American education. It called for the abandonment of traditional religion and replacing it with a new secular religion better able to accommodate the new moral relativism inherent in a man-centered, godless world. That secular humanism is a religion is easily proven by the Manifesto's own words:

> The time has come for widespread recognition of the radical changes in religious beliefs throughout the modern world. . . . In order that religious humanism may be better understood we, the undersigned, desire to make certain affirmations which we believe the facts of our contemporary life demonstrate.
>
> There is great danger of a final, and we believe fatal, identification of the word *religion* with doctrines and methods which have lost their significance and which are powerless to solve the problem of human living in the Twentieth Century.
>
> . . . While this age does owe a vast debt to traditional religions, it is none the less obvious than any religion that can hope to be a synthesizing and dynamic force for today must be shaped for the needs of this age.[1]

Thus, the purpose of the Manifesto was to announce the creation of a new secular religion to "meet the needs of this age." The Manifesto then goes on to enumerate the tenets or doctrines of this new religion:

> First: Religious humanists regard the universe as self-existing and not created.

Thus, we see in the very first tenet of secular humanism a denial of creationism. And in the NEA's resolutions we find: "The Association . . . believes that legislation and regulations that mandate the teaching of religious doctrines, such as so-called 'creation science,' violate both student and teacher rights. The Association urges its affiliates to seek repeal of such mandates where they exist."[2]

The Manifesto then affirms its faith in the theory of evolution by stating that "Humanism believes that man is a part of nature and that he has emerged as the result of a continuous process." It also denies the existence of the soul: "Holding an organic view of life, humanists find that the traditional dualism of mind and body must be rejected." The Manifesto then affirms its belief in environmentalism: "The individual born into a particular culture is largely molded to that culture."

The rejection of traditional religion is strongly made in the fifth tenet: "Humanism asserts that the nature of the universe depicted by modern science makes unacceptable any supernatural or cosmic guarantees of human values."

Then what is religion? The seventh tenet provides the answer: "Religion consists of those actions, purposes, and experiences which are humanly significant. Nothing human is alien to the religious. . . . The distinction between the sacred and the secular can no longer be maintained."

But if there is no God, then what is the purpose of life? The eighth tenet gives the answer: "Religious humanism considers the complete realization of human personality to be the end of man's life and seeks its development and fulfillment in the here and now. This is the explanation of the humanist's social passion."

Thus, for the humanist, social action is synonymous with religious action. What kind of social action? The Fourteenth tenet addresses that question in unequivocal terms:

> The humanists are firmly convinced that existing acquisitive and profit-motivated society has shown itself to be inadequate and that a radical change in methods, controls, and motives must be instituted. A socialized and cooperative economic order must be established to the end that the equitable distribution of the means of life be possible. The goal of humanism is a free and universal society in which people voluntarily and intelligently cooperate for the common good.

Thus, a socialist society is the goal toward which humanists must strive. The Manifesto ends with this declaration of self-sufficiency for the human race: "Man is at last becoming aware that he alone is responsible for the realization of the world of his dreams, that he has within himself the power for its achievement."

The NEA has remained remarkably faithful to the Humanist Manifesto since 1933. For all practical purposes, the public school has become the parochial school for secular humanism. Its doctrines pervade the curriculum from top to bottom. Among the signers of the Humanist Manifesto in 1933 was R. Lester Mondale, Unitarian minister, a relative of Walter Mondale whom the NEA endorsed as Democratic presidential nominee in 1984.

In 1973, humanists reaffirmed their faith in secular humanism by issuing *Humanist Manifesto II*. It states:

> As in 1933, humanists still believe that traditional theism, especially faith in the prayer-hearing God, assumed to love and care for persons, to hear and understand their prayers, and to be able to do something about them, is an unproved and outmoded faith. Salvationism, based on mere affirmation, still appears as harmful, diverting people with false hopes of heaven hereafter. Reasonable minds look to other means for survival. . . .
>
> The next century can be and should be the humanistic century. . . . Using technology wisely, we can control our environment, conquer poverty, markedly reduce disease, extend our life-span, significantly modify our behavior, alter the course of human evolution and cultural development, unlock vast new powers. . . .
>
> We affirm a set of common principles that can serve as a basis for united action. . . . They are a design for a secular society on a planetary scale.[3]

There it is in a nutshell, the goal of secular humanism: world government based on the humanist worldview. Concerning God, Humanist Manifesto II states: "No deity will save us; we must save ourselves." Concerning ethics, the document states that "Ethics is *autonomous* and *situational,* needing no theological or ideological sanction." Concerning sex, the humanists state: "We believe that intolerant attitudes, often cultivated by orthodox religions and puritanical cultures, unduly repress sexual conduct. The right to birth control, abortion, and divorce should be recognized."

The NEA's resolution on sex education reads:

The Association recognizes that sensitive sex education can be a positive force in promoting physical, mental, and social health and that the public school must assume an increasingly important role in providing the instruction. Teachers must be qualified to teach in this area and must be legally protected from censorship and lawsuits. . . .

The Association urges its affiliates and members to support appropriately establshed sex education programs, including information on birth control and family planning, parenting skills, sexually transmitted diseases, incest and sexual abuse, the effects of substance abuse during pregnancy, and problems associated with and resulting from preteen and teenage pregnancies.[4]

And in order to prevent interference by parents, the NEA passed a resolution on "privileged communications" which reads:

The National Education Association believes that communications between certificated personnel and students must be legally privileged. It urges its affiliates to aid in seeking legislation that provides this privilege and protects both educators and students.[5]

The major difference between *Humanist Manifesto I* and *Humanist Manifesto II* is that the latter puts more stress on individual freedom and democratic rights, and says that economic systems should be judged on their "responsiveness to human needs." Thus, it does not give a blank check to socialism. In this case, the NEA, with its benign attitude toward Marxist revolution in Central America is clearly closer to the radical left than the humanists.

However, the humanists advocate "the development of a system of world law and a world order based upon transnational federal government." The NEA's advocacy of "global education" is in line with this idea. The NEA also echoes the humanist view of the "common humanity of all people."

In general, Humanist Manifesto II is more atheistic than socialistic. It wants the state to "encourage maximum freedom for different moral, political, religious, and social values in society." The state "should not favor any particular religious bodies through the use of public monies, nor espouse a single ideology." Yet, the humanist ideology itself has become the only ideology permitted in the public schools and has thereby become America's "establishment of religion."

The 103 original signers of Humanist Manifesto II assert that "These affirmations are not a final credo or dogma but an expression of a living and growing faith." So while their "faith" is permitted exclusive dominion in the public schools, the "faith" of Christians is excluded because it is "sectarian" and violates the separation of church and state. Is not secular humanism also sectarian?

Among the signers of Humanist Manifesto II are behaviorist psychologist B. F. Skinner; Betty Friedan, founder of N.O.W.; Alan F. Guttmacher, president of Planned Parenthood and advocate of abortion on demand; assorted professors, scientists, writers, and a host of Unitarian ministers and leaders in the Ethical Union, including Lester Mondale, former president of the Fellowship of Religious Humanists.

Progressive education is humanist education, and the NEA *Journal* has promoted progressive education from its earliest days. The most frequent writer on educational philosophy for the *Journal* was William H. Kilpatrick, Dewey's disciple at Teachers College. He was often called upon to answer the critics of progressive education. He was also good at explaining the difference between the old education, which was based on "a psychology that stressed acquisition, even drill, and minimized creative thinking," and the new education based on "the newer psychology which starts with life as the pursuit of ends or purpose."

In 1936 articles by Kilpatrick appeared in the *Journal* virtually every month. His article in April, "Objectives for Curriculum and Method," summed up the progressive philosophy quite neatly: "Let us not think . . . in terms of specific facts or skills," he wrote, "but rather in terms of growing, that present activities shall lead on fruitfully to further, finer, and better activities. . . . The true unit of study is the organism-in-its-interaction-with-the-environment. Learning is the name we give to the twofold fact that the organism facing novelty may devise and create a new way of responding."

In November 1941, Kilpatrick did an article for the *Journal* entitled "The Case for Progressivism in Education." Parents and critics were forever urging educators to get back to the basics, and it was always necessary to answer them.

In 1948, the NEA became a sponsor of the National Training Laboratory in Group Development at Bethel, Maine. The NTL had been founded by Kurt Lewin, a German social psychologist who invented "sensitivity training" and "group dynamics," or the psychology of the collective. Lewin had come to the United States in 1933 as a refugee from Nazi Germany. His work was found to be particularly useful in devising group means to improve worker-management relations. It was only natural that his attention would in time be drawn to education. His biographer writes:

> Students of progressive education also saw the need for studies of group behavior. This was stimulated by the educational philosophy of John Dewey. To carry out Dewey's theory of "learning by doing," teachers organized such group projects as student self-government and hobby-club activities. This called for the development of leadership skills and the collective setting of group goals. . . . The teacher could be seen as a group leader who affected his students' learning . . . by increasing their motivation, encouraging their active participation, and improving their "esprit de corps." Lewin's pioneering research in group behavior thus drew upon the experience of educators in deciding upon and developing topics for research and in establishing a strong interest among social psychologists and teachers.[6]

Lewin's view was that, because of human interdependence, every individual belongs to a group and that "the group to which an individual belongs is the ground for his perceptions, his feelings, and his actions. . . . It is the gound of the social group that gives to the individual his figured character."[7] To Lewin, a person was "a complex energy field in which all behavior could be conceived of as a change in some state of a field during a unit of time."[8]

Gordon Allport, the Harvard psychologist, wrote of Lewin: "There is a striking kinship between the work of Kurt Lewin and the work of John Dewey. Both agree that democracy must be learned anew in each generation, and that it is a far more difficult form of social structure to attain and to maintain than is autocracy.... Dewey, we might say, is the outstanding philosophical exponent of democracy, Lewin its outstanding psychological exponent."[9]

As a liberal humanist, however, Lewin could never understand the religious underpinnings of American individualism. A man's relationship to God was far more important to a Christian than his relationship to any human being or group. In fact, it provided a guide to one's relations with others—family, friends, teachers, employers, colleagues. It was also the basis of the American form of government—government based on laws, not men.

Yet, for Lewin, strong democratic leadership was the key to effective democracy. The weak German republic which had succumbed to Adolf Hitler was the political image that haunted him. He assumed that American democracy was susceptible to the same weaknesses. To him "laissez-faire" individualism was too anarchic and autocratic dictatorship too repressive. His ideal was some sort of secular democratic collectivism.

Lewin died in 1947, but his impact on American educators has been profound. His biographer writes:

> He was one of the few psychologists who could transpose a life problem into controllable experimental form.... The Research Center for Group Dynamics, which Lewin founded at M.I.T., has moved to the University of Michigan, where it continues with many of the same people and remains one of the fountainheads of social research in the United States. The action-research studies, which he initiated, continue to illuminate and shape ongoing community experiments in integrated housing, equalization of opportunity for employment, the cause and cure of prejudice in children, the socialization of street gangs, and the better training of community leaders. Sensitivity

training, which he helped to create, is considered by many people to be the most significant educational innovation of the century.[10]

Lewin was particularly concerned with social change and how to make it happen. He found that it was difficult to change individuals who relied on their own independent judgment. But the group could change the individuals within it. Alfred Marrow, Lewin's associate, writes:

> To effect any sort of change in the goals or outlook of a group, a change in its equilibrium is necessary. To try to do this by appealing to members individually is seldom effective. . . . Thus the behavior of a whole group may be more easily changed than that of a single member. This willingness to stick together (cohesiveness) is an essential characteristic of any group. Indeed, without it, it is doubtful that a group could be said to exist at all. . . .
>
> What renders a group cohesive is . . . how dynamically inter-dependent they are. Out of reciprocal dependence for the achievement of goals there arises a readiness to share chores and challenges, and even to reconcile personality clashes.[11]

It is obvious that the leadership of the NEA took advantage of the sensitivity training sessions held at the National Training Laboratories and applied their knowledge of group dynamics to the problems of the NEA. They learned a great deal from the techniques developed by Lewin. Marrow writes: "Of particular concern were the tasks of introducing change and of overcoming resistance to change. . . . The role of the leader was recognized by Lewin as vital in the process of introducing changes needed to improve group life."[12]

Lewin wrote:

> Acceptance of the new set of values and beliefs cannot usually be brought about item by item.
>
> The individual accepts the new system of values and beliefs by accepting belongingness to a group.
>
> The chances for re-education seem to be increased whenever a strong we-feeling is created.[13]

Thus, the transformation of the NEA itself into a militant

politicized labor organization is a monument to Lewin's group dynamics. Lewin was sensitive to the charge that the purpose of his Research Center was to train experts in "brainwashing" or "group manipulation."[14] But obviously the techniques developed by Lewin and his associates could be used for such purposes. This is particularly true in the application of group pressure. Marrow writes:

> Belonging is signified by adherance to the group code. Those who belong "obey." Thus group pressures regulate the conduct of the would-be deviant member. He stays among those with whom he feels he "belongs" even if their conduct seems unfair and their pressure unfriendly. To change his conduct or point of view independently of the group would get him into trouble with his fellow group members.[15]

In 1948, the NEA *Journal* began publishing articles on group dynamics and group leadership. In February 1949 "Some Skills for Improving Group Dynamics" was published, and in April appeared "Improving the Group Process: Group Dynamics and Local Associations." In January 1950 there was an article describing the purposes of the National Training Laboratory: "To carry on research in . . . group decision-making and action planning, and induction of change, resistance to change, the ethics of leadership in inducing change."

In April 1950 the *Journal* published a case study in group dynamics entitled, "What Makes a Group Tick?" In may 1951 the *Journal* published its first article on "Teenage Drug Addicts." It reported that in New York state, arrests of youths 16–20 years old for violations of the narcotic law had risen from 74 in 1947 to 453 in 1950. In the December 1951 *Journal*, Dr. Lester A. Kirkendall, one of the future signers of Humanist Manifesto II, did an article on sex education for the schools. In the February 1952 issue, Hollis L. Caswell, dean of Teachers College, spoke out against the mounting criticism of progressive education. He wrote: "The disposition of laymen to invade the professional field of selection of instructional materials is a threat to sound curriculum development." A year later, Caswell wrote another article for the *Journal* decrying the fact that "Public education is currently encountering criticism of unusual intensity and scope." The April 1953 issue asserted that "Current attacks on textbooks must be met with calm, constructive, and courageous action."

In April 1954 appeared another article on group dynamics, "More Learning Takes Place When Teacher and Student Understand the Various Roles in the Classroom Group." The next month's *Journal* offered an article on "Group Therapy for Problem Parents," and the October 1955 issue carried an article on human behavior by Ralph W. Tyler, director of the Center for Advanced Study in Behavioral Science. In the following month's issue, the dean of Teachers College once more defended progressive education from its critics.

In the 1950s, the NEA began collecting information on its critics. An article in the December 1955 Journal, entitled "Defense of Teachers," stated:

> A dramatic speech in 1950 by Harold Benjamin, then chairman of the Defense Commission, alerted the profession to a threatening new wave of deceitful and destructive criticism of public education.... His address, "Report on the Enemy," sought to awaken the public and the teaching profession. . . .
>
> The NEA Defense Commission has devoted a major portion of its efforts to helping prevent such organized attacks from having seriously damaging effects. It has collected information concerning the background, nature, and purposes of certain organizations engaged in spreading propaganda.

By 1984, the NEA's "enemies list" had grown into the size of a book and includes virtually every organization in favor of capitalism, fundamental Christianity, and conservatism.

The September 1960 *Journal* published another article promoting humanist psychology, "Behavioral Sciences Can Improve College Teaching," by Professor W. J. McKeachie of the University of Michigan. The February 1961 issue carried an article by Prof. Howard Leavitt of the Department of Secondary Education, Boston University, "Social Force and the Curriculum," in which the professor wrote: "Secondary schools can introduce to students the new, expanding behavioral sciences—psychology, sociology, cultural anthropology and social psychology."

The *Journal* of January 1962 published an article that left no doubt as to how social psychology was already being applied in the classroom. Entitled "The Teacher—Agent of Change," the article explained:

> National Training Laboratories of NEA initiated a program for classroom teachers . . . at Bethel, Maine. . . .
>
> The training lab is an intensive learning experience . . . in which a staff of social scientists help translate research findings into classroom practice. Objectives include greater sensitivity in observing and interpreting social and psychological factors in learning groups. . . .

The May 1963 *Journal* criticized the "Censorship of Textbooks," naming such "censors" as the Daughters of the American Revolution, the John Birch Society and America's Future. The latter organization was described as "one of the nation's principal propagandists against textbooks," when in actuality all it does is simply have the textbooks reviewed by reputable scholars.

In October 1965, after 40 years of progressive education and 15 years of Group Dynamics, the *Journal* reported that teenage syphilis was up 230 percent since 1956! The March 1966 issue carried a revealing article on the impact of psychology on education, entitled "Today's Innovations in Teaching." An article in the same issue by Dr. John I. Goodlad, professor and director of the University Elementary School at U.C.L.A. and director of research and development at the Institute for Development of Educational Activities, was even more explicit. Entitled "Directions of Curriculum Change," Professor Goodlad wrote that the curriculum of the future "will be what one might call the *humanistic curriculum* and that it may become significantly evident by 1990 or 2000." In defining the "humanistic curriculum," Goodlad explained: "Webster defines humanism as 'a way of life centered upon human interests and values.' Only within a humanistic conception of education and a humanistic conception and conduct of the whole of schooling can a humanistic curriculum center upon human interests and values."

The January 1967 issue carried an article, "Sensitivity Training in the Classroom," plus a piece by Dr. Mary S. Calderone, "Planning for Sex Education." The *Journal* also took "A New Look at the Seven Cardinal Principles of Education" and found that American teachers of 1966 "returned an overwhelming verdict in favor of the seven cardinal principles as formulated in 1918."

In October 1967 the *Journal* carried a major article, "Helping Children to Clarify Values," by Louis E. Raths, Merrill Harmen, and Sidney B. Simon. Values clarification is the humanist technique of developing a personal code of morals for one's own personal use, regardless of religious traditions and upbringing. It is the formula for moral relativism. The authors state:

> The old approach seems to be to persuade the child to adopt the "right" values rather than to help him develop a valuing process. . . . Clarifying is an honest attempt to help a student look at his life and to encourage him to think about it in an atmosphere in which positive acceptance exists. . . . The teacher must work to eliminate his own tendencies to moralize.

The November 1967 *Journal* focused its attention on "The 'New' Social Studies." The article explained:

> Probably the most obvious change occurring in the social studies curriculum is a breaking away from the traditional dominance of history, geography, and civics. Materials from the behavioral sciences—economics, anthropology, sociology, social psychology, and political science—are being incorporated into both elementary and secondary school programs. . . .

Recent studies of political socialization suggest that attitudes toward political institutions and processes are formed at an early age. In the new curriculum, therefore, basic political concepts are introduced in the primary grades.

Another assault on the basics was written by Mario D. Fantini of the Ford Foundation and Gerald Weinstein of Teachers College and published in the January 1968 *Journal*. Entitled "Reducing the Behavior Gap," the article explained:

> We are very much aware that what we suggest here is far from simple. To shift content emphasis from cognition to affect means that school people will have to search for new points of departure for subject matter approaches that have been hallowed by time and custom. But our swiftly changing society requires greater flexibility and dynamism of its educational system.

Our "swiftly changing society" is the usual pretext for getting rid of the basics and overthrowing traditional education. Yet the greatest changes in our society took place between 1800 and 1900, when America changed from an agricultural society to a highly industrialized society, all with the help of traditional educational values.

In 1970, Fantini and Weinstein authored a book, *Toward Humanistic Education: A Curriculum of Affect*. To indicate their affinity with John Dewey, the authors wrote:

> Why does the cognitive orientation not affect behavior directly? . . . [Because] cognition is removed from the real and disconnected from the feeling level of learning. Dewey described the experiential level of learning as follows: ". . . Experience is primarily an active-passive affair; it is not primarily cognitive." . . .
>
> The pervasive emphasis on cognition and its separation from affect poses a threat to our society in that our educational institutions may produce cold, detached individuals, uncommitted to humanitarian goals. Certainly, a modern society cannot function without ever increasing orders of cognitive knowledge. Yet knowledge per se does not necessarily lead to desirable behavior. . . . Unless knowledge is related to an affective state in the learner, the likelihood that it will influence behavior is limited.[16]

By now the reader must have gathered that "cognition" refers to traditional academic skills and "affect" refers to the emotions. The humanist shift from cognition to affect in education is in line with Dewey's downgrading of independent intelligence.

The March 1968 *Journal* carried an article, "Behavioral Science in the Classroom," with examples of classroom application. The January 1969 issue published an article on "Role Playing," describing it as "a forceful technique for helping children understand themselves and others and an excellent means of teaching interpersonal and group skills."

By 1969 opposition to the trends in public education began to alarm the NEA. It passed a resolution on "Extremism and the Schools," stating: "The growing opposition to certain curricula and to educational policies is recognized by the Association as a thinly veiled political attack on public education itself. The Association urges its affiliates to take concerted action and, if necessary, legal action, to defend against such irresponsible attacks." So much for freedom of speech!

If the attacks had any influence on the editorial content of the NEA's journal, now called *Today's Education,* they weren't noticeable. The November 1970 issue published an article on homosexuality by Dr. Martin Hoffman, author of *The Gay World.* The same issue discussed "Behavioral Objectives in the Affective Domain."

Was all of this humanistic behavioral psychology doing American children any good? The September–October 1977 issue reported on "The Student Suicide Epidemic." Add to that the devastating increase in student drug use and addiction, declining SAT scores, increased vandalism and violence, the venereal disease epidemic, preteen and teen-age pregnancies—and the picture one gets of American education is one of tragedy, despair, and ruin. Yet the NEA wants more control of education!

The simple truth is that the American classroom has become a place where intense psychological warfare is being waged against all traditional values. A child in an American public school is little more than a guinea pig in a psych lab, manipulated by a trained "change-agent." All of this is being done with billions of federal dollars in the greatest scam in human history. If Americans put up with this much longer, they will deserve the ruin they are paying for.

21. The Point of No Return: Are We There?

In April 1983 the National Commission on Excellence in Education issued its now historic report, *A Nation at Risk,* in which it said: "The educational foundations of our society are presently being eroded by a rising tide of mediocrity that threatens our very future as a nation and as a people." Then it added a comment which must have raised a lot of eyebrows: "If an unfriendly foreign power had attempted to impose on America the mediocre educational performance that exists today, we might well have viewed it as an act of war. As it stands, we have allowed this to happen to ourselves."

In other words, our own educators have done to American education what only our worst enemy would have done if it could! Never were American educators more seriously indicted for their failures, for, as the evidence clearly reveals, what we have today is what the progressives have wanted. They have not failed. They have succeeded in their efforts to rid American schools of independent intelligence. They said exactly what they wanted in their books, articles, speeches, and at conferences and seminars. They prepared the new textbooks and curricula. They designed the new schools. They trained the new teachers. And as comedian Flip Wilson's Geraldine used to say, "What you see is what you get!"

What has been the reaction of the NEA to all of this? They've culled one quotation from the Commission's report which they use quite frequently: "Excellence costs. But in the long run mediocrity costs far more." In other words, more money will give us the quality which has eluded us all these years. Or, as the NEA put it: "The nation can, and *must,* pay the bill."

As far as the NEA is concerned, the Commission's report is a license to plunder the American taxpayer. And if anyone thinks that more money in the hands of the present educational leadership will give us anything but more of what we now have, he is deluding himself. The record speaks for itself. In a booklet entitled *Local, State and Federal Roles* issued by the NEA in December 1983, we are told: "NEA is no newcomer to educational reform movements. Organized teachers have been involved in every reform effort in education in this country—in 1911, 1924, 1934, 1954, and 1974." What the booklet fails to add is that all of these "reforms" deliberately created the "tide of mediocrity" that now threatens our very future, and so the NEA is not about to rescind any one of them. On the contrary, everything the NEA says and does indicates that it intends to carry these reforms to their ultimate goal: a socialist-humanist society controlled by educators and behavioral scientists.

If money were the answer, our problems would have been solved long ago, for no nation in history has pumped more of its wealth into education than this one, and no people has been more generous to and trusting of its educators. But unfortunately that trust has been abused with a cynicism, arrogance, and greed that can only come out of a spirit of pure, unadulterated malevolence.

What are the facts? In 1960 the cost of public elementary and secondary education was $15.6 billion; by 1970 it had risen to $40.6 billion; and in 1983 it was $141 billion, an increase of 800 percent since 1960! In addition, since 1965 Congress has enacted over 100 federal programs aiding education. Title One alone of the Elementary and Secondary Education Act of 1965 has pumped over $42 billion into the schools since its enactment, which is more money than the entire American school budget of 1970. Yet, since 1965, the reading scores have declined alarmingly. Several years ago it was thought that the decline had bottomed out. But on May 16, 1984, *Education Week* reported otherwise:

> Student scores have dropped on standardized reading tests administered to two of the nation's largest public-school populations—in California and in New York City, where scores had previously been climbing.
>
> In New York, school officials announced this month that students' scores in reading had declined by 2.6 percent from last year. . . .
>
> In California, officials reported this month that the reading scores of 12th graders declined by the largest margin in seven years. . . .
>
> In Idaho, state officials reported a decline in the number of 9th grade students who passed the state-administered minimum-competency tests in reading, mathematics, spelling and writing.

Meanwhile, in fiscal year 1982–83, the NEA spent all of $2.4 million of its $77.5 million budget on Instructional and Professional Development, a piddling 3.1 percent of its budget. On the other hand, $14.6 million, or almost 19 percent of the budget, was spent on "Uniserv," the NEA's field army of professional organizers, whose job it is to place a totalitarian straitjacket on the teaching profession. Apparently, the NEA is much more interested in controlling teachers and school boards than in educational quality. Thus, when NEA leaders talk of their devotion to "quality education" they are being nothing short of hypocritical. The truth of the matter is they haven't the faintest idea what quality is. Their goals are political and social, not academic.

Typical of NEA leadership is Mary Hatwood Futrell, president of the NEA in 1983–84. Mrs. Futrell is a fast-talking lady with the reasoning power of a sledgehammer. In the April 1984 *NEA Today,* the association's tabloid written at the intellectual level of the *National Enquirer,* Mrs. Futrell tells the poignant story of how she got involved in political action. It all started twenty years ago when, as a young teacher, she entered her classroom and found a hole in the floor. She also found that she had more students than typewriters. She writes: "I had to accept the grim reality: the quest for educational excellence must of necessity be a political quest. If my students were to be served well, I needed to be able to influence the district budget—and that meant moving the school board and legislators and voters." From that time on, there was no stopping Mrs. Futrell.

There must have been an easier way to repair holes in the floor and get extra typewriters than by controlling Congress, fifty state legislatures, the federal budget, and the President of the United States—which is what the NEA is now trying to do. Mrs. Futrell could have gotten the school custodian to repair the floor, or a student in shop, or she could have gotten a piece of wood and nailed it down herself. Besides, what's a hole in the floor got to do with academic excellence? Abraham Lincoln probably went to a school with no floor at all! As for the typewriters, she could have divided the class into groups and rotated use of the machines.

Mrs. Futrell's logic is typical of today's NEA leadership. If there's a hole in your classroom floor, get Congress to enact a federal program to repair it. If you're short of typewriters, get the lawmakers to cut the defense budget in half and use the money to buy typewriters.

That is the abysmal level of thinking at which today's educators crawl. No wonder the NEA is dead set against testing the cognitive skills of teachers. Where they have been tested, as in Dallas and Houston in 1978, the results have been miserable. Only one state, Arkansas, has dared mandate testing its 24,000 teachers to see how well they can read, write and do math. Teachers who fail will have to improve their skills or face loss of certification. Naturally, Mrs. Futrell is furious at Arkansas' courageous Governor Clinton. "NEA will not stand idly by," she told a news conference, "while the teachers of Arkansas are made the scapegoats in efforts to improve the quality of public education." Obviously Governor Clinton put his political career in jeopardy by opposing NEA policy.

But what better way is there to improve the quality of teaching than by first finding out if your teachers have the skills they are supposed to be imparting to their students? What have the teachers to fear if they know what they're doing? And if they don't, why should taxpayers and parents keep such teachers in the classroom? Is certification a license to engage in educational malpractice with impunity? After all, what can a student do once his life is ruined by such malpractice? In 1977 a student in New York state brought suit against his school district for graduating him despite his being functionally illiterate. In 1979 the Court of Appeals dismissed the case saying:

> To entertain a cause of action for "educational malpractice" would require the courts not merely to make judgments as to the validity of broad educational policies—a course we have unalteringly eschewed in the past—but, more importantly, to sit in review of the day-to-day implementation of these policies.
>
> Recognition in the courts of this cause of action would constitute blatant interference with the responsibility for the administration of the public-school system lodged by Constitution and statute in school administrative agencies.
>
> Not to be overlooked in today's holding is the right of students presently enrolled in public schools, and their parents, to take advantage of the administrative processes provided by statute to enlist the aid of the Commissioner of Education in insuring that they receive a proper education.[1]

In other words, students are at the complete mercy of the educators when it comes to educational malpractice. The educators are accountable to no one but themselves.

In Arkansas, the state NEA affiliate was mortified by the idea that teachers would be tested. Its reaction was typical:

"The governor's unending crusade to test all Arkansas teachers has sent morale plummeting, and as a result some very fine, experienced teachers are leaving the profession. [Of course, no mention of those fine, experienced teachers forced out in California and Michigan by the NEA's agency shop!] We recognize that an opportunity to improve education has been mangled. Arkansas teachers, however, will not give up. We will continue to press for real—not superficial—answers to education's problems." Ask the NEA for the "real answers" and they've got only two: more money and more power.

One local teacher with 12 years experience, in an attempt to gain public sympathy, wrote to the *Arkansas Gazette:* "I would suggest the Communications Skills section of the test include multiple-choice items dealing with how to respond to a 14-year-old who confides in me that she is pregnant, how to help another who wants to commit suicide, and what to say when told, 'I'm sorry but we're having a revenue shortfall and have to cut your pay on your last check.' "[2]

Apparently this teacher's talent is in the "affective domain." She's probably very good at teaching sex education which no doubt led to the pregnancy of the 14-year-old and values clarification which probably contributed to the despair of the youngster who wanted to commit suicide. Perhaps had she concentrated on imparting cognitive—intellectual and academic—skills, she would not have had to play amateur psychiatrist. But, alas, that poor teacher is a product of her training.

All of which brings us to an interesting article which appeared in the *Dallas Morning News* of August 26, 1971. Written by David Hawkins and entitled "Young People Are Getting Dumber," it told of an interview with the director of Human Engineering Laboratory, a vocational research outfit that specializes in aptitude testing. "Do you know," the director told Hawkins, "that the present generation knows less than its parents? All of our laboratories around the country are recording a drop in vocabulary of 1 percent a year. In all our 50 years of testing it's never happened before. Can you imagine what a drop in knowledge of 1 percent a year for 30 years could do to our civilization?"

That was written in 1971, and in 1983 the National Commission on Excellence in Education pronounced us "a nation at risk." The wholesale decline in the cognitive skills of American students is what has brought us to this dangerous state of affairs, and no amount of sex education, values clarification, sensitivity training, role playing, group activities, and other relevant "affective" teachings will ever be able to make up for the deficiency in academic training. That is why teachers who do not know how to train the intellect of their students will never be able to improve the quality of American education. The testing of teachers will merely confirm what everyone already knows: that American teachers are not trained to develop the intellect of their students.

As far as public education is concerned, the situation has gone beyond the point of no return. Public education is firmly and irrevocably controlled by the behavioral scientists, who control the graduate schools, teacher training, curriculum development, textbook writing, professional publications and organizations, federal programs, and the largest private foundations. The thousands of doctoral students who pour out of the psych labs and graduate schools of education are now the professors and social scientists who run the system. It is impossible to truly reform public education without separating it from behavioral science. Without this separation all attempts at reform will fail and all of the new money poured into the system will only enrich those who presently control it.

There is only one way out for the American people. A massive exodus from the public schools into private ones where the freedom still exists to create a curriculum with a strong academic foundation. The public educators know this and that is why the NEA is pressing for the regulation of private schools. Such regulations are already on the books of many states.

However, one very large escape route remains open: the religious school, which is protected from state regulation by Article I of the Bill of Rights: "Congress shall make no law respecting an establishment of religion, or prohibiting the free exercise thereof."

The NEA, the ACLU and the fifty states are quite familiar with this article because they have used it time and again not only to keep religion out of the public schools but to deny parochial schools any public funding. The very reason why the Catholics were forced to create their own parochial system is because of this strong Constitutional prohibition against government regulation of religion, which has been interpreted by the courts as calling for the separation of church and state.

But with the growth of the church-school movement and the increasing dissatisfaction with public schools, the educators are concerned. They are afraid that a massive exodus from the public schools is in the offing if and when Americans become convinced that public school reform is a hopeless cause.

The NEA and the states are using the compulsory attendance laws as the rationale for regulating private schools. All states recognize the right of private schools to exist. That issue was settled in 1925 in a Supreme Court case called *Pierce v. Society of Sisters*. It was the overriding principle of the separation of church and state that decided the case in favor of the private school, in this case a parochial school. Since public schools cannot engage in religious instruction, private schools are indispensable to the free exercise of religion. Therefore religious freedom is closely tied to educational freedom. Abridge one and by necessity you abridge the other.

Thus, although many states have laws regulating private schools, few have been willing to impose them on church schools. But the NEA, the humanists, and their allies in state departments of education are not about to let the Constitution stand in the way of their drive for total control of American education. John Dewey had said that a time would come when force would have to be used, and apparently that time has come.

Which, of course, brings us to the Nebraska case. The NEA affiliate in Nebraska, the Nebraska State Education Association (NSEA), is undoubtedly the most powerful lobby in that state. Its PAC has contributed substantial sums to the campaigns of key state senators. Since Nebraska has a unicameral (one house) legislature with only 49 senators, it can be easily controlled by a lobby as well organized as the NSEA.

In August 1977 the Faith Baptist Church of Louisville, some 15 miles south of Omaha, opened the Faith Christian School with 17 students under the direction of Pastor Everett Sileven. The school, using a curriculum provided by Christian Accelerated Education, had been created at the request of parents who did not want their children to be exposed to the secular humanist curriculum of the local public schools.

Shortly after the opening of the school, two men from the Nebraska State Department of Education visited Rev. Sileven, bringing to his attention Rules 14 and 21 of the Nebraska regulations requiring all private schools to be "approved" by the state and all their teachers to be state-certified. In addition, the school was required to submit reports listing the names and addresses of all its students so that the state could check parents' compliance with the compulsory attendance laws.

Pastor Sileven knew of these regulations. "We tried to get the law changed in 1976 before we opened the school," he told a reporter in May 1984, "but at that time there had already been at least five years of attempts by people in the state to change the law without any success. Our efforts just confirmed the legislature's and the department of education's unwillingness to cooperate."

To Sileven and his church members, the regulations were a clear violation of the Constitutional prohibition against government regulation of religion. They interfered with the free exercise of religion, and they exceeded the competence of the state. On what basis could the state "approve" the school, and how could state-certified teachers, indoctrinated in secular humanism, teach in a Christian school? Also, reporting the names and addresses of the students was tantamount to reporting the names of the church's members. It was none of the state's business. Obviously, if the children were in school, they were in compliance with the compulsory attendance laws.

"At that point we had no choice but to go ahead with the school," says Sileven. "It was not a matter of us trying to challenge the law as much as it was just us having to do what we knew we had to do in the area of training our children."

In March 1978, criminal charges were filed against Sileven and the principal for illegally operating a private school. However, the charges were later dropped when county authorities decided to seek a court injunction to close the school. The injunction was granted, but the school continued to operate pending an appeal. In March 1981 the Nebraska Supreme Court upheld the injunction, but the school remained open pending an appeal to the U.S. Supreme Court.

In September 1981, county authorities decided not to wait for the Supreme Court ruling and the doors of Faith Baptist Church were padlocked to prevent classes from being held. The padlock was removed on Sundays and Wednesday nights for church services. Apparently the state authorities thought they were respecting freedom of religion by merely closing the church school but not the church. But since the school was conducted in the church as part of the church's ministry, and padlocking the church denied its parishoners free access to their place of worship, the state was clearly interfering with the free exercise of religion.

Sileven moved the students to a Christian school in Millard. On October 5, 1981, the U.S. Supreme Court refused to hear the case, citing lack of "a substantial federal question." Apparently, routine violations of the Constitution by state departments of education no longer represent "a substantial federal question," although these state departments are the recipients of billions of federal dollars!

On October 4, 1981, the authorities removed the padlock from the church door on the condition that the school would not be conducted. In January 1982, however, Pastor Sileven decided to resume classes. He could not, in all good conscience, let the state dictate whether or not his church could conduct a school. Religious freedom was at stake. "We had a choice," he said, "obey God and disobey the government or obey the government and disobey God. We chose to obey God."

On February 18, 1982 Rev. Sileven was jailed to serve a four-month sentence for contempt of court. On March 3, 1982 Rev. Sileven was released from jail after church members voted to close the school. When Rev. Sileven decided once more to exercise his God-given, Constitutionally protected freedom of religion by conducting a church school, the county judge ordered Sileven to return to jail beginning September 1, 1982. On that date, Sileven retreated inside the church with about 100 of his supporters and told authorities that if they wanted to take him to jail they'd have to break down the doors and "trample on the flag." Two days later Sileven told the County Sheriff that he would not resist arrest. Sileven was then put in jail. After a brief recess, however, the school continued to operate.

On October 18, 1982, on orders from the judge, 18 law officers and state troopers entered the Faith Baptist Church and physically removed 85 supporters who refused to leave voluntarily. The Sheriff had wanted to use tear gas to force the worshippers out. But cooler heads prevailed. Padlocks were again put on the doors, to be removed only on Sundays and Wednesday nights for church services. Again the state was dictating when religious worship could take place.

Undaunted, members of the church resumed the school in a bus parked outside the padlocked church. By then, news of what had happened at Louisville had spread, and hundreds of visiting preachers came to the town to show their support of the school. On October 20, 1982, about 450 fundamentalist preachers entered the church after the padlocks were removed for church services and vowed not to come out willingly. The judge decided to rescind the padlocking order. Two days later Rev. Sileven was released from jail after promising to close the school until the end of November or the end of a special session of the state legislature.

On November 13, 1982, the legislative session ended with no resolution of the church school issue. On November 30, 1982, Sileven was again arrested, then released from jail on December 3, then rearrested on December 7. On January 31, 1983 Rev. Sileven was finally released after completing his four-month jail term for contempt.

On February 28, 1983, the church reopened its school with 11 students in attendance. Contempt-of-court charges were then filed against 12 parents for operating the school. Rev. Sileven was not in Nebraska at the time, having taken a leave-of-absence. On May 3, 1983 the 12 parents were found guilty of contempt charges by the county judge, but sentencing was postponed until the Nebraska Supreme Court ruled.

With Sileven back at the church, the school reopened on August 30, 1983. Contempt charges were brought in October against Sileven, his daughter, and 16 parents of students. On November 23, 1983, Thanksgiving Eve, seven fathers of Faith Baptist students were jailed for refusing to answer questions at a court hearing. Neither Sileven, his daughter, nor the seven men's wives had shown up for the hearing, and warrants were issued for their arrest. But they had left the state. The seven fathers would remain in jail until they agreed to testify.

On January 6, 1984, after 44 days of imprisonment, one of the fathers decided to answer questions about the school and was released with the understanding that he would take his child out of the school. On February 23, 1984, after 93 days in jail, the remaining six were released on the condition that they would not send their children to the Faith Baptist School until it conformed with state regulations. Their immediate ordeal was over. But the battle to regain full religious freedom in America had really only begun.

In April 1984 Rev. Sileven was again arrested and put in jail to serve an eight-month sentence for refusing to testify about the operation of the school. At about the same time, Gov. Robert Kerrey of Nebraska signed into law a bill that was to supposed to "settle" the issue. According to *Education Week* of April 18, 1984:

> Under the former law, the state could take legal action against schools that failed to comply with rules on teacher certification, attendance reporting, and other standards for state accreditation.
>
> The new law focuses, however, on parents rather than schools themselves. It permits parents who contend that the state's requirements violate "sincerely held religious beliefs" to enroll their children in schools that are not sanctioned by the state education department.
>
> The new law does not require schools to provide any information directly to state officials, but parents . . . must provide the state with certain information about the education their children are receiving.
>
> First, individual parents, or a representative of all the parents at a particular school, must give the state commissioner of education a statement saying that the requirements for approval and accreditation "violate sincerely held religious beliefs."
>
> Next, under reporting procedures to be established by the State Board of Education, the parents must provide education officials with a statement indicating that they are satisfied that teachers in their school are qualified to "monitor instruction in the basic skills."
>
> In addition, the parents must support the statement with the teachers' test scores on "a nationally recognized teacher-competency examination designed [designated?] by the State Board of Education" or arrange an "informal" evaluation of the teachers. That evaluation also would be developed and conducted by the board.
>
> According to the law, if state officials are not satisfied with the test scores or evaluation, the parents may be prosecuted for violating state laws that require children to attend school until they are 16 years old.

That such an incredible law should have been passed in the

legislature of an American state boggles the mind. It not only makes a complete mockery of religious freedom, but it reveals the utter contempt for religion that the Nebraskan legislators have. The law now divides the religious parents of Nebraska into two categories: those who send their children to "approved" schools and those who send them to "disapproved" schools. The latter parents must sign a statement attesting to their "sincerely held religious beliefs." The U.S. Constitution clearly forbids the state from inquiring into the religious convictions of its citizens.

Equally unconstitutional and obnoxious is the requirement that church-school teachers be subjected to a teacher-competency test to be evaluated by state authorities. While the NEA is fighting tooth and nail against teacher-competency testing in Arkansas, does it now approve of such testing to "evaluate" teachers in church schools? If the teachers fail, the parent may go to jail! That's the state of religious freedom in Soviet Nebraska.

It is obvious that the new law is not only as bad as the old one but probably worse. But it has one virtue. It reveals how compulsory education is being used as the means to strip Americans of their fundamental rights and freedoms. According to Larry Scherer, legal counsel for the Nebraska legislature's Education Committee, "The whole intent of the legislation was to deregulate without giving up total control." If that's Nebraska's idea of "deregulation," God help the people there. There must be something terribly deficient in Nebraskan public education that it can turn out so many lawyers and legislators who know nothing about the U.S. Constitution except how to pervert it.

If the state of Nebraska can forbid the slightest hint of religion in its public schools on the grounds that it violates the separation of church and state, how can it then justify its massive intrusion into the life of a church school? And what difference does it make whether the regulation is through the parents or the teachers? The Constitution forbids the regulation of religion, and among virtually all religions the education of children is a fundamental part of religious practice.

Of course the NEA exacted a price for this so-called compromise legislation. According to *Education Week* of May 23, 1984:

> Some legislators also said that they believed the Governor made an agreement with the Nebraska State Education Association to support an education reform proposal introduced in the legislature last session in exchange for a promise that the union would not lobby against compromise legislation, as senators said it has in previous years.

So we have a very clear indication of who runs the state of Nebraska—not the people, not the governor, not even the legislators, but the NSEA and its small army of totalitarians. And Nebraska's commissioner of education, Joe E. Lutjeharms, seems to be in complete agreement with the NSEA. He thinks that Rev. Sileven "has been treated very mildly." If being thrown in jail for exercising one's freedom of religion is "mild," one wonders what other punishment Mr. Lutjeharms thinks would be appropriate. "We have about 33,000 youngsters in church schools that have certificated teachers and are approved, and there are 200 students, at the most, enrolled in the schools involved in this controversy," remarked Mr. Lutjeharms.

So why is the state making all this fuss over 200 children in a few insignificant church schools? Because the authorities want to set an example to keep everyone else in line. For when the Christians of America and others wake up to what is happening to them, they may decide to use the escape route of the church school. So now's the time to shut it.

But what is quite disheartening is that so many Christian schools were willing to surrender their religious freedom without a fight. Like the Jews in Europe who marched like sheep into Hitler's gas chambers, the Christians of Nebraska accepted the shackles of government regulation with hardly a murmur of protest. It took a Rev. Sileven to show them how much of their freedom they had lost, and what it will take in trials and tribulations to regain it. For apparently the majority of the people in Nebraska have been brainwashed to believe that religious freedom is not an inherent right but a privilege bestowed by the state.

It is now quite obvious that the humanists are using public education as the battering ram with which to destroy Christianity in the United States. On every front they are pressing their advantage in the courts and in state legislatures, and they are winning. The Nebraska case simply indicates that the enemies of religious and educational freedom exist in the very heart of America, among the people we generally consider to be freedom loving. Instead, they are willing to destroy every constitutional right to attain their goal. And the humanists are confident that they can succeed because they now control the education of 90 percent of American youth, and they who control the schools control the future. Nebraska State Senator Peter Hoagland inadvertently gave away the humanist strategy when he told a television audience on April 15, 1982: "What we are most interested in, of course, are the children themselves. I don't think any of us in the Legislature have any quarrel with the right of the Reverend or members of his flock to practice their religion. But we don't think they should be entitled to impose decisions or religious philosophies on their children which could seriously undermine those children's ability to deal in this complicated world when they grow up."

Obviously, the next step in the humanist plan is to take the children away from religious parents, educate them with a humanist curriculum, and turn them into pagans. The humanists are also waging constant guerrilla warfare in the courts against religion. For example, in October 1983 the ACLU filed suit against Secretary of Health and Human Services Margaret Heckler because funds allocated under the Adolescent Family Life Act are allegedly being used to teach religious doctrine. One example cited by the ACLU involves a Catholic charity which "uses the money to teach that pre-marital sex and abortion are sins."

Pretty soon we can expect the ACLU to try to get the word "sin" removed from every textbook used in a public school because of its religious connotation. But who knows? Maybe it's already been done!

Education Week of May 16, 1984 reported that in Oregon, the ACLU won a suit to prevent an invocation, benediction, or religious hymn from being included in a high school commencement exercise. The judge ruled that the inclusion of a prayer at graduation is "a violation of the Constitutional prohibition of official sanction of religious beliefs." In other words, the government does not have the right to compose a prayer for use in its own schools, but in Nebraska and elsewhere it claims the right to regulate the curriculum of a church school that doesn't even want government support and would be denied it even if it wanted it on the grounds that such support would violate the establishment clause. Notice how the establishment clause is invoked only when it enhances the government's control of religion. How ridiculous can the courts get. They say that government support of a church school violates the establishment clause, but government regulation of the same school doesn't!

In Michigan, the attorney general ruled in May 1984 that a voluntary Bible-study class, held once a week for 30 minutes for the last 25 years in several public schools in western Michigan, was unconstitutional. According to the school district superintendent: "Until this spring, we never had a complaint about meeting in the school building. However, two parents filed a complaint and sought assistance from the American Civil Liberties Union in late March."[3]

In March 1984, the attorney general of Texas issued an opinion that the State Board of Education's mandate that evolution be taught as only one of several explanations of the origin of man is unconstitutional.[4] This was another humanist victory over creationism. Teaching children that the world might have been created by a sovereign, intelligent force called God instead of by a spontaneous explosion of gas from nowhere is considered an establishment of religion! But it clearly takes more faith to believe that the world arose spontaneously out of nothing than it does to believe in a Creator of superhuman intelligence and powers.

Education Week of March 7, 1984 reported that the Norwin School Board of North Huntingdon, Pennsylvania, decided to prohibit a religious organization from holding its voluntary meetings in a high school auditorium before the start of classes. The school-board members said they feared that the ACLU would sue the district if it allowed the club to meet. Apparently the ACLU now has more power in a school district than the school board! The states are also beginning to bear down on home-schooling. In West Virginia (*Education Week,* December 21, 1981) the state Supreme Court ruled that "sincerely held religious convictions are never a defense to total noncompliance with the compulsory school-attendance law." The case involved parents who withdrew their children from public schools and a private Christian school for religious reasons. The court admitted that the children were probably doing better academically at home than they might have done at school, but the court based its ruling on that section of the law that requires county superintendents to approve home-education proposals not only on academic grounds, but also on the basis of other functions performed by schools such as health, screening and "social development."

In other words, the children are required to attend school so as not to be deprived of the benefits of social contact with delinquents, drug pushers, and the sexually active. Since the state is incapable of protecting children from unwanted pregnancy, venereal disease, drug and alcohol addiction, assault, extortion and other social goodies that thousands of youngsters fall prey to each year in public schools, it ought not to be in the business of fostering "social development."

Yet the judges, completely blind to the social chaos prevalent in American schools, wrote: "We find it inconceivable that in the 20th century the free-exercise clause of the First Amendment implies that children can lawfully be sequestered on a rural homestead during all their formative years to be released upon the world only after their opportunities to acquire basic skills have been foreclosed and their capacity to cope with modern society has been so undermined as to prohibit useful, happy, or productive lives."

So, now, being brought up on a farm and taught at home by one's own loving parents is tantamount to being held in prison during one's formative years, after which one is "released upon the world." The trouble is that many public schools actually deprive their students of the ability to acquire basic skills by turning them into functional illiterates and condemning them to a life on welfare. But the courts and the superintendents blindly operate in a dream world where public schools actually know how to teach and their social environment is safe and healthy. The fact is that the schools are just the opposite, and that is why so many parents want to get their children out!

One can cite case after case of parents being harrassed, imprisoned, and fined for exercising their right to provide their children with a good education and not the sham that passes for education in the public schools. It is obvious that the time has come for the American people to make some hard basic decisions about their educational system. We know where the NEA and their allies want to take us. Do the American people want to go there?

Postscript: What Can Be Done?

The trend is very clear. While the American people want more local control of their affairs, more freedom and flexibility in education, the NEA wants the rigid control of monopoly. At a time when the courts are breaking up such monopolies as the former Bell System, the NEA is busily creating one that will make its private counterpart seem like a model of decentralization. The NEA is a private union that wants the power of a government to crush its private competition. It wants to own American education as its exclusive fief. Why is it immune from the anti-trust laws? And why are American teachers and their students forced to obey its dictates? The NEA wants control but not accountability.

The agency shop in the public sector not only violates the freedom of teachers but makes school boards and taxpayers servants of the unions. Granting public employees the right to strike has made the citizen a hostage to union demands, an intolerable situation. The public servant has become the public's master.

Since the courts and politicians are helping the NEA create its educational dictatorship, the American people must either elect representatives who will defend their freedoms or lose them.

It is also now quite apparent that the humanists do not want freedom of religion but freedom *from* religion. They would like to eradicate Christianity not only from American education but from American life in general. And they are confident that they can do this through indoctrination in the schools. Behind the mask of humanism and behavioral science hide the unrelenting ideological and political pressures of Marxism-Leninism. Even though many humanists oppose communism, their hatred of religion makes them easy targets for communist manipulation, and the communists know how to use others to open the way to power.

The humanist worldview now dominates American public education so completely, that the only escape is the private school or the home school. If Christianity is to survive it must create its own schools, its own colleges and teacher training institutions, its own professional organizations and journals, its own radio and television programs, its own newspapers and magazines. It must also establish a permanent NEA watch, for the NEA has become the most powerful engine of legislation aimed at destroying educational and religious freedom in America.

As for academics, the nation was thrown into shock when Secretary Bell released his report card on U.S. education in January 1983. In the last ten years California dropped 58 points in the SAT scores, Connecticut 49, New York 59, Massachusetts 46, Texas 53. Every state experienced a considerable decline, including New Hampshire which had the highest SAT scores, yet declined 47 points since 1972. What was even more surprising is that the scores showed no correlation with per pupil expenditures. Top-ranking New Hampshire ranked 28th in expenditures, while New York, which ranked second in expenditures, scored 29 points lower than New Hampshire in the 1982 SATs.

What was NEA president Futrell's response to all of this? "I think it's an effort to undermine the fact that we need more money to improve education," she said.

The failure of government education is now so universally recognized by the American people, that most parents would send their children to private schools if they could. What keeps public education going is not public demand but the huge constituency of careerists who have turned the insoluble problems of government schools into a gushing source of economic prosperity for themselves. They have become an army of parasites feeding off the sufferings they have helped create.

America needs schools, but it doesn't need government schools that drain the taxpayer, cripple the children, and destroy our freedoms. The only way to stop being "a nation at risk" is to move education out of government hands. What we need is more educational freedom, more private schools, and more teacher entrepreneurs. They will give us better education at lower cost, and all of the insoluble problems created by government schools will simply vanish.

The question will be asked: but how do we take care of all of those children whose parents cannot afford private schools? The answer is simple: let the communities pay the tuition of poor students either through voluntary scholarship funds or outright grants. Let every child get a good private education with minimum interference from government, and we shall see a "nation at risk" change overnight into a nation of achievement.

Marva Collins did it on a shoestring in Chicago with children who were said to be uneducable. The same can be done in every city and town in the country. That's a vision worth fighting for.

Notes

INTRODUCTION AND CHAPTER ONE
(xiii–18)

1. NEA *Journal*, December 1967, p. 34.
2. *Boston Globe*, March 14, 1982, p. A7.
3. Stanley K. Schultz, *The Culture Factory* (New York: Oxford University Press, 1973), pp. 32–33.
4. Robert Owen, *A New View of Society* (London: 1816, reprinted by Augustus M. Kelley, Clifton, New Jersey, 1972), pp. 168–69.
5. *Ibid*, p. 170.
6. Orestes A. Brownson, *The Convert* in *The Works of Orestes A. Brownson*, collected and arranged by Henry F. Brownson (New York: AMS Press Inc., 1966), Vol. v, p. 56.
7. *The Free Enquirer*, December 5, 1829.
8. Edward A. Newton, *Christian Witness*, May 17, 1844.
9. James G. Carter, "Outline of an Institution for the Education of Teachers," *Essays on Popular Education* (Boston, 1826), pp. 47–51. Reprinted in *Education in the United States, A Documentary History*, Vol. 3, edited by Sol Cohen (New York: Random House, 1974), pp. 1304–05.

CHAPTER TWO (19–30)

1. National Educational Association, *Fiftieth Anniversary Volume* 1857–1906 (Winona: 1907), pp. 517–18.
2. Edward Hitchcock in *The Age of the Academies*, edited by Theodore R. Sizer (New York: Columbia University, 1964).
3. *Ibid.*
4. *Common School Journal*, Vol. 12, No. 5, Boston, March 1850, p. 70.
5. Sizer, *The Age of the Academies*, p. 196.
6. NEA, *Fiftieth Anniversary Volume*, p. 335.
7. *Christian Witness*, May 17, 1844.
8. *Common School Journal*, Vol. 11, No. 14, July 15, 1849, pp. 212–13.
9. The author came across this passage by a Catholic clergyman while searching through a book on common schools for another purpose. He made a Xerox copy of pages 24–25 in which this passage appeared, but failed to record the title and editor of the volume. The title on top of both pages is "Common Schools." The author of the passage was probably Bishop Hughes.
10. Diane Ravitch, *The Great School Wars: New York City 1805–1973* (New York: Basic Books, Inc., 1974), p. 37.
11. *Ibid*, p. 55.

CHAPTER THREE (31–39)

1. William M. Bryant, *Hegel's Educational Ideas* (Chicago: 1896), p. 37.
2. *Ibid*, pp. 187–89, 192.
3. National Education Association, *Proceedings*, 1871, p. 26.
4. NEA, *Proceedings*, 1906, p. 430.
5. NEA, *Fiftieth Anniversary Volume*, pp. 431–33.

CHAPTER FOUR (40–48)

1. G. Stanley Hall, *Life and Confessions of a Psychologist* (New York: 1923), p. 219.
2. *Ibid*, p. 223.
3. Max Eastman, *Great Companions* (New York: Farrar, Straus and Cudahy, 1942, 1959), p. 259.

4. G. Stanley Hall, *Life and Confessions of a Psychologist*, p. 357.
5. *Ibid*, pp. 536–37.

CHAPTER FIVE (49–56)

1. Lawrence A. Cremin, *The Transformation of the School* (New York: Alfred A. Knopf, 1961), pp. 110–112.
2. *Ibid*, p. 114–15.
3. Edward L. Thorndike, *Animal Intelligence* (New York: Macmillan, 1911), p. 294.
4. Katherine Camp Mayhew and Anna Camp Edwards, *The Dewey School* (New York: D. Appleton-Century, 1936; Atherton Press, 1965), p. 436.
5. *Ibid*, p. 428.
6. *Ibid*, p. 429.
7. John Dewey, *A Common Faith* (New Haven: Yale University Press, 1934), p. 87.

CHAPTER SIX (57–62)

1. David Tyack and Elisabeth Hansot, *Managers of Virtue* (New York: Basic Books, 1982), p. 130.
2. *Ibid*, p. 132.
3. *Ibid*, p. 140.
4. *Ibid*, p. 141.
5. *Ibid*, p. 143.

CHAPTER SEVEN (63–71)

1. William T. Harris in "Report on the Committee of Ten on Secondary School Studies," with papers relating thereto in *U.S. Office of Education Report for 1892–93*, Vol. 2, p. 1459.
2. *Atlantic Monthly*, March 1894.
3. John Dewey, *School and Society* (Chicago: University of Chicago Press, 1899), p. 15.
4. National Education Association *Journal*, May 1927, p. 134.

5. Commission on the Reorganization of Secondary Education, *The Cardinal Principles of Secondary Education* (Washington, D.C.: 1918).
6. Tyack, *op. cit.*, pp. 138–39.
7. Cremin, *The Transformation of the School, op. cit.*, p. 216.
8. *Ibid*, p. 217.
9. Jules Abel, *The Rockefeller Billions* (New York: 1967).
10. The American Ethical Union, A Federation of Ethical Culture Societies (New York), brochure, p. 2.
11. *Ibid*, p. 3.

CHAPTER EIGHT (72–80)

1. David Tyack, *Managers of Virtue, op. cit.*, p. 140.
2. *Ibid*, p. 139.
3. David Tyack, *The One Best System* (Cambridge: Harvard University Press, 1974), p. 257.
4. *Ibid*, p. 258.
5. *Ibid*, p. 266.
6. David Tyack, *Managers of Virtue, op. cit.*, pp. 181–82.
7. Lawrence A. Cremin, *A History of Teachers College* (New York: Columbia University Press, 1954), p. 252.
8. John Dewey, *Liberalism and Social Action* (New York: G. P. Putnam's Sons, 1935), p. 84.
9. *Ibid*, p. 54.
10. *Ibid*, p. 61.

CHAPTER NINE (81–91)

1. John B. Watson, *Behaviorism* (New York: W. W. Norton, 1930; Norton Library edition, 1970), pp. 2–3.
2. *Ibid*, p. 6.
3. *Ibid*, p. 11.
4. *Ibid*, p. 20.
5. Rudolf Flesch, *Why Johnny Can't Read* (New York: Harper & Row, 1955; Perennial Library edition, 1966), p. 9.
6. *Ibid*, p. 18.

7. Allan M. West, *The National Education Association: The Power Base for Education* (New York: The Free Press, 1980), p. 179.
8. *Ibid*, p. 180.

CHAPTER TEN (92–101)

1. John Dewey, *School and Society, op. cit.*, p. 26.

CHAPTER ELEVEN (102–111)

1. *School and Society*, Vol. 1, No. 5, January 30, 1915, p. 179.
2. Katherine Camp Mayhew and Anna Camp Edwards, *The Dewey School, op. cit.*, pp. 142–43.
3. "The University School," *University Record*, I (1896), 417–22. Quoted in Mitford M. Mathews, *Teaching to Read* (Chicago: 1966), p. 128.
4. John Dewey, *Democracy and Education* (New York: Macmillan, 1916; Free Press Paperback Edition 1966), p. 297.
5. John Dewey, *The School and Society* (Chicago: 1899; reprinted in John Dewey, *The Middle Works, 1899–1924*, volume 1: 1899–1901, edited by JoAnn Boydston, Southern Illinois University Press, 1976), p. 19.
6. *Ibid*, p. 69.
7. John Dewey, *Liberalism and Social Action, op. cit.*, p. 52.
8. G. Stanley Hall, *Educational Problems* (New York: 1911), II, pp. 443–44. Quoted in Mitford M. Mathews, *Teaching to Read* (Chicago: 1966), pp. 136–37.
9. Mitford M. Mathews, *Teaching to Read* (Chicago: 1966), p. 134.

CHAPTER TWELVE (112–126)

1. John Dewey, *School and Society, op cit.*, p. 144.
2. Samuel L. Blumenfeld, *The New Illiterates* (New Rochelle, N.Y.: Arlington House, 1973), p. 162.
3. Jeanne S. Chall, *Learning to Read: The Great Debate*, updated edition (New York: McGraw-Hill, 1983), p. 21.
4. *Los Angeles Times*, October 4, 1982, Part II, pp. 1, 3 and 4.

CHAPTER THIRTEEN (127–138)

1. *The New York Times Magazine*, November 6, 1983, p. 84.
2. Lewis Albert Alesen, M.D., *Mental Robots* (Caldwell, Idaho: Caxton Printers, 1967), p. 73.
3. "Teaching reading in the Cuban primary schools" by Cecelia Pollack and Victor Martuza, *Journal of Reading*, December 1981, pp. 241–43.
4. N. K. Krupskaya, *Reminiscences of Lenin*, translated by Bernard Isaacs (Moscow: 1959), pp. 515–16.

CHAPTER FOURTEEN (139–151)

1. Allan M. West, *The National Education Association: The Power Base for Education*, op. cit., p. 70.
2. *Ibid*, p. 55.

CHAPTER FIFTEEN (152–162)

1. Lawrence A. Cremin, *A History of Teachers College*, op. cit., p. 252.
2. NEA *Journal*, January 1956, "Education and the 84th Congress."
3. NEA *Journal*, December 1967, p. 34.
4. NEA *Journal*, April 1969.

CHAPTER SIXTEEN (163–180)

1. Allan M. West, *The National Education Association: The Power Base for Education*, op. cit., p. 193.
2. *Today's Education*, Sept.–Oct. 1973.
3. Allan M. West, *The National Education Association: The Power Base for Education*, op. cit., p. 24.
4. *Ibid*, p. 200.

CHAPTER SEVENTEEN (181–199)

1. George S. Counts, *The Soviet Challenge to America* (New York: The John Day Company, 1931), pp. 304–5.

2. *Ibid*, p. 307.
3. *Ibid*, p. 316.
4. *Ibid*, p. 317.
5. *Ibid*, p. 324.
6. *Ibid*, p. 329.
7. *Ibid*, p. 335.
8. *Ibid*, p. 338.
9. George S. Counts and Nucia Lodge, *The Country of the Blind: The Soviet System of Mind Control* (Boston: Houghton Mifflin, 1949), pp. 22–23.
10. *Ibid*, p. 20. Quoted from V. I. Lenin, *Collected Works* (Moscow: 1921), Vol. XV, p. 218.
11. *Ibid*, p. 20–21.
12. *Ibid*, p. 21–22.
13. *Today's Education*, 1983–84 Annual Edition, p. 156. These resolutions were also adopted in 1984.

CHAPTER EIGHTEEN (200–212)

1. J. Barthelemy-Saint Hilaire, *M. Victor Cousin: Sa Vie et Sa Correspondence* (Paris: 1895).
2. "Proceedings of the American Lyceum," *Annals of Education and Instruction, and American Journal of Lyceums and Literary Institutions*, August 1833, p. 358.
3. *Invitation to attend the National Convention of the Friends of Education to assemble in Philadelphia on the Fourth Wednesday in August, A.D. 1850* (Philadelphia: 1850).
4. *The Washington Post*, July 9, 1980.

CHAPTER NINETEEN (213–224)

1. John Dewey, *Liberalism and Social Action* (New York: G. P. Putnam's Sons, 1935), p. 87.
2. Jonathan Kozol, *Children of the Revolution* (New York: Delacorte Press, 1978), pp. XIV, 8, 147.
3. *Today's Education*, 1983–84 Annual Edition, p. 156. These resolutions were also adopted in 1984.
4. *Ibid*, p. 117.

5. *Ibid*, p. 149.
6. *Ibid*.
7. *Ibid*, p. 140.
8. *Ibid*.
9. *Ibid*, p. 139.
10. *Ibid*, p. 140.
11. *Ibid*, p. 130.
12. *Ibid*, p. 141.
13. *Ibid*, p. 138.
14. *Ibid*, p. 128.
15. *Ibid*, p. 116.
16. *Education Daily*, March 6, 1984, pp. 5–6.
17. *Today's Education*, 1983–84 Annual Edition, p. 114.
18. *Ibid*, p. 116.
19. *Ibid*, p. 121.
20. *Ibid*, p. 142.
21. *Ibid*, p. 145.

CHAPTER TWENTY (225–240)

1. *Humanist Manifesto I and II* (Buffalo, N.Y.: Prometheus Books, 1973), p. 7.
2. *Today's Education*, 1983–84 Annual Edition, p. 142.
3. *Humanist Manifesto I and II*, *op. cit.*, pp. 7, 14, 15.
4. *Today's Education*, 1983–84 Annual Edition, p. 133.
5. *Ibid*, p. 145.
6. Alfred J. Marrow, *The Practical Theorist: The Life and Work of Kurt Lewin* (New York: Basic Books, 1969), p. 167.
7. Kurt Lewin, *Resolving Social Conflicts*, edited by Gertrud Weiss Lewin, foreword by Gordon Allport (New York: Harper & Row, 1948), p. VII.
8. Alfred J. Marrow, *The Practical Theorist: the Life and Work of Kurt Lewin*, *op. cit.*, p. 30.
9. Kurt Lewin, *Resolving Social Conflicts*, *op cit.*, p. XI.
10. Alfred J. Marrow, *op. cit.*, pp. IX, XIV.
11. *Ibid*, p. 169.
12. *Ibid*, p. 185.
13. Kurt Lewin, Resolving Social Conflicts, *op. cit.*, p. 66.

14. Alfred J. Marrow, *op. cit.*, p. 178.
15. *Ibid*, p. 170.
16. Gerald Weinstein and Mario D. Fantini, *Toward Humanistic Education: A Curriculum of Affect* (New York: Praeger Publishers, 1970), p. 27.

CHAPTER TWENTY-ONE (241–259)

1. *The New York Times*, June 15, 1979.
2. *NEA Today*, April 1984, p. 3
3. *Education Week*, May 16, 1984.
4. *Ibid*, March 21, 1984.

Appendix

Alternative Organizations for Teachers

National Association of Professional Educators (NAPE)
   900 17th Street, N.W., Suite 300
   Washington, D. C. 20006   (202) 293-2142
NAPE aids professional educators in their efforts to maintain
their individual freedoms, to establish local and state orga-
nizations as viable alternatives to teacher unions, and pro-
vides a professional voice for educators in the nation's capital.
NAPE has allied state organizations in: Alabama, Arizona,
Arkansas, California, Florida, Georgia, Illinois, Kentucky,
Mississippi, North Carolina, Ohio, Tennessee, Washington,
Wisconsin. There are also numerous allied local organizations
around the country.

National Association of Christian Educators (NACE)
   P. O. Box 3200
   Costa Mesa, California 92626   (714) 546-5931
NACE represents Christian educators in public schools who
oppose the one-sided humanistic curriculum being promoted
by the NEA. It publishes a monthly journal, *Christians in
Education.*

Concerned Educators Against Forced Unionism (CEAFU)
  8001 Braddock Road
  Springfield, Virginia 22160   (703) 321-8519
CEAFU, a division of the National Right to Work Committee, is a coalition of educational professionals on all levels — faculty, administrators, and governing officials—dedicated to the principle that no educator should be forced to join or support a labor union as a condition of entering or remaining in the profession.

Reading Reform Foundation (RRF)
  Box 98785
  Tacoma, WA 98498   (206) 572-9966
RRF advocates restoring intensive phonics as the principle means of teaching reading in the primary grades. Provides information about phonics materials, holds conferences and workshops. Publishes *Reading Informer*.

America's Future
  542 Main Street
  New Rochelle, New York 10801   (914) 235-6000
America's Future is a non-profit educational foundation dedicated to producing a better understanding and appreciation of the American constitutional form of government and the free enterprise system. Textbook evaluations are prepared by the Textbook Evaluation Committee, composed of respected educators. These are distributed free of charge upon request. Publishes fortnightly newsletter, *America's Future*.

Institute for Creation Research (ICR)
  10946 Woodside Ave. N.
  Santee, CA 92071   (619) 448-0900
ICR was founded in 1980 as a Graduate School offering degrees in creation studies. The administration and faculty of ICR are committed to the tenets of both scientific creationism and Biblical creationism. Publishes bulletin, *Acts and Facts*. Excellent materials for discussions in biology and geology classes.

The Mel Gablers
    Box 7518
    Longview, Texas 75607   (214) 753-5993
The Gablers have created the largest textbook review clearing house in America. Reviews are furnished on a contribution basis.

Foundation for Economic Education (FEE)
    Irvington-on-Hudson, New York 10533   (914) 591-7230
FEE provides educational materials on the free market, limited government, private property, and individualism. Monthly publication, *The Freeman,* is sent to anyone upon request. Excellent materials for social studies classes.

Index

Important Blumenfeld Education Resources

VIDEO TAPES

☐ **Affective Education.** The dangers of "non directed" education: sex-ed, drug-ed, self-esteeem, — $30.00 post paid
values clarification, etc. Dr. Wm R. Coulson, Samuel L. Blumenfeld. Detroit, September 1990.
2 hours.

☐ **Whatever Happened to Old Fashioned Education?** Samuel L. Blumenfeld. Missoula, MT, — $30.00 post paid
September 1989. Video of Fri. night & all day Saturday Conference on both home-schooling and
general discussion of the current American Educational Scene. Edited to 2 hours. Very
informative.

☐ **May 1988 Speech on American Education.** 2 Hour Color Video. An in-depth talk on problems — $30.00 post paid
of Public Education. The latest information gained from approximately 150 stops in U.S. since
Jan. 88.

☐ **Blumenfeld Explains Difference Between "Look/Say" and Intensive, Systematic** — $10.00 post paid
Phonics. 25 minute color video. Makes difference between the two methods easy to
understand. Short enough to facilitate showing to service club, church and home school groups.

☐ **Two Workshops on Alpha-Phonics: A Primer for Beginning Readers.** 90 minute color — $10.00 post paid
video. Filmed at Teaching Home National Convention, Portland, OR, Oct. 1988. Each
workshop approximately 45 minutes and includes extensive questions and answers. The how,
what, when, where and why of this highly successful, self-explanatory, systematic, intensive
phonics book that works!

AUDIO TAPES

☐ **"Has the NEA Become Politicized? What Affect Has It Had on Education?"** From a — $7.00 post paid
Symposium on Education, St. Paul, Fall 86. Excellent summary of Dr. Blumenfeld's exposé of
NEA and update on his book NEA Trojan Horse in American Education One tape, 60 minutes.

☐ **Blumenfeld's Major Speech on Education in America — Chattanooga, 1985.** Two tapes, — $12.00 post paid
2 hours. Tells it all!

☐ **NEA Trojan Horse in American Education:** entire book on eight audio tapes. Approx. 670 — $40.00 post paid
minutes every word of the book, including footnotes, on tape.

OTHER HELPFUL MATERIALS

☐ **"The Victims of Dick & Jane,"** 22 pages, 3 X 5 size. Explains how the literacy problem
occurred. Excellent for convincing a doubtful friend. You may want a quantity to give
away.   One: $0.50; Four: $2.00; 100: $35.00; 1,000: $300.00 post paid.

☞ ☐ **Free Information Packet.** Send me complimentary information on the many other education ———— **No Charge**
resources Sam offers for concerned parents and taxpayers.

These materials may be ordered by simply filling out the form below and returning to: The Paradigm Co.,
Box 45161, Boise, ID 83711.

Mailing Address (Please Print)

☎ FOR FASTER SERVICE...MASTERCARD OR VISA HOLDERS
CALL (208) 322-4440
24 HOURS — 7 DAYS

Name ——————————————————————————————

Street ——————————————————————————————

City ———————————————————— State ————— Zip —————

Phone No. ————————————————
ORDER NOW!

Checks may be made payable to
The Paradigm Co.
P.O. Box 45161— Boise, Idaho 83711

Enclosed is my check for $_____
Charge my: VISA ☐   Master Card ☐
Credit Card Number (all digits)

Signature ————————————————

Exp. Date ——————

ORDER NOW! — CALL (208) 322-4440

SEND ME BOOKS By Samuel L. Blumenfeld:

☐ **Alpha-Phonics: A Primer for Beginning Readers**... $21.95
(You can easily teach your own children good reading & writing the proper way.
"Alpha-Phonics. . . . we are convinced that you cannnot find an easier to use, more
comprehensive or more reasonably priced reading program than *Alpha-Phonics."*
Ellyn Davis, Knoxville, 7/87).

☐ **Alpha-Phonics Audio Tapes.** (2) 60 minute audio tapes.. $15.00
(Introductory explanation, history of alphabetic system, how to teach reading to
anyone, all 128 lessons verbally explained, all 44 speech sounds clearly
reproduced. Tapes now make *Alpha-Phonics* easier than ever for <u>anyone</u> to
effectively teach reading.)

☐ **The New Illiterates** $11.95
(And how to keep your child from becoming one)
☐ **How to Tutor**.. $11.95
(You need to know how to in today's world)
☐ **Is Public Education Necessary?**... $11.95
(Learn the answer to this vital question)
☐ **NEA: Trojan Horse in American Education**... $11.95
(The first full length exposé of the N.E.A.)

☐ **The Blumenfeld Education Letter** ....
(a monthly newsletter which assists parents in tutoring their children, evaluating their   (3 months) $9.00 ☐
schools, texts, and curricula, and generally assuring that their children actually become   (6 months) $18.00 ☐
educated)   (1 year) $36.00 ☐

Copies of these books may be ordered by simply filling out the form below and returning to:
The Paradigm Co., Box 45161, Boise, ID 83711

Add $2.50 Delivery. Add $.50 each <u>additional</u> book or set of tapes. For larger quantity discounts please inquire
at (208) 322-4440.

Please send me: The books checked above.

Mailing Address (Please Print)

Name _____

Street _____

City _____ State _____ Zip _____

Phone No._____

ORDER NOW!   Enclosed is my check for $ _____
                                                            Charge my: VISA ☐   Master Card ☐
Checks may be made payable to   Credit Card Number (all digits)
The Paradigm Co.
P.O. Box 45161— Boise, Idaho 83711

Exp. Date _____

Signature_____

FOR FASTER SERVICE...
CALL (208) 322-4440
24 HOURS — 7 DAYS

Important Blumenfeld Education Resources

VIDEO TAPES

☐ **Affective Education.** The dangers of "non directed" education: sex-ed, drug-ed, self-esteeem, — $30.00 post paid
values clarification, etc. Dr. Wm R. Coulson, Samuel L. Blumenfeld. Detroit, September 1990.
2 hours.

☐ **Whatever Happened to Old Fashioned Education?** Samuel L. Blumenfeld. Missoula, MT, — $30.00 post paid
September 1989. Video of Fri. night & all day Saturday Conference on both home-schooling and
general discussion of the current American Educational Scene. Edited to 2 hours. Very
informative.

☐ **May 1988 Speech on American Education.** 2 Hour Color Video. An in-depth talk on problems — $30.00 post paid
of Public Education. The latest information gained from approximately 150 stops in U.S. since
Jan. 88.

☐ **Blumenfeld Explains Difference Between "Look/Say" and Intensive, Systematic** — $10.00 post paid
Phonics. 25 minute color video. Makes difference between the two methods easy to
understand. Short enough to facilitate showing to service club, church and home school groups.

☐ **Two Workshops on *Alpha-Phonics: A Primer for Beginning Readers*.** 90 minute color — $10.00 post paid
video. Filmed at Teaching Home National Convention, Portland, OR, Oct. 1988. Each
workshop approximately 45 minutes and includes extensive questions and answers. The how,
what, when, where and why of this highly successful, self-explanatory, systematic, intensive
phonics book that works!

AUDIO TAPES

☐ **"Has the NEA Become Politicized? What Affect Has It Had on Education?"** From a — $7.00 post paid
Symposium on Education, St. Paul, Fall 86. Excellent summary of Dr. Blumenfeld's exposé of
NEA and update on his book *NEA Trojan Horse in American Education* One tape, 60 minutes.

☐ **Blumenfeld's Major Speech on Education in America — Chattanooga, 1985.** Two tapes, — $12.00 post paid
2 hours. Tells it all!

☐ **NEA Trojan Horse in American Education:** entire book on *eight* audio tapes. Approx. 670 — $40.00 post paid
minutes *every word of the book,* including footnotes, on tape.

OTHER HELPFUL MATERIALS

☐ **"The Victims of Dick & Jane,"** 22 pages, 3 X 5 size. Explains how the literacy problem
occurred. Excellent for convincing a doubtful friend. You may want a quantity to give
away.   One: $0.50: Four: $2.00: 100: $35.00: 1,000: $300.00 post paid.

☛ ☐ **Free Information Packet.** Send me complimentary information on the many other education ——— *No Charge*
resources Sam offers for concerned parents and taxpayers.

These materials may be ordered by simply filling out the form below and returning to: The Paradigm Co.,
Box 45161, Boise, ID 83711.

Mailing Address (Please Print)

📞 FOR FASTER SERVICE...MASTERCARD OR VISA HOLDERS
CALL (208) 322-4440
24 HOURS — 7 DAYS

Name ————————————————————————————

Street ————————————————————————————

City ———————————————————— State ————— Zip —————

Phone No. ————————————————

ORDER NOW!

Checks may be made payable to
The Paradigm Co.
P.O. Box 45161— Boise, Idaho 83711

Enclosed is my check for $——————
Charge my: VISA ☐   Master Card ☐
Credit Card Number (all digits)

Signature ————————————————   Exp. Date —————

Important Blumenfeld Education Resources

VIDEO TAPES

☐ **Affective Education.** The dangers of "non directed" education: sex-ed, drug-ed, self-esteeem, — $30.00 post paid
values clarification, etc. Dr. Wm R. Coulson, Samuel L. Blumenfeld. Detroit, September 1990.
2 hours.

☐ **Whatever Happened to Old Fashioned Education?** Samuel L. Blumenfeld. Missoula, MT, — $30.00 post paid
September 1989. Video of Fri. night & all day Saturday Conference on both home-schooling and
general discussion of the current American Educational Scene. Edited to 2 hours. Very
informative.

☐ **May 1988 Speech on American Education.** 2 Hour Color Video. An in-depth talk on problems — $30.00 post paid
of Public Education. The latest information gained from approximately 150 stops in U.S. since
Jan. 88.

☐ **Blumenfeld Explains Difference Between "Look/Say" and Intensive, Systematic** — $10.00 post paid
Phonics. 25 minute color video. Makes difference between the two methods easy to
understand. Short enough to facilitate showing to service club, church and home school groups.

☐ **Two Workshops on Alpha-Phonics: A Primer for Beginning Readers.** 90 minute color — $10.00 post paid
video. Filmed at Teaching Home National Convention, Portland, OR, Oct. 1988. Each
workshop approximately 45 minutes and includes extensive questions and answers. The how,
what, when, where and why of this highly successful, self-explanatory, systematic, intensive
phonics book that works!

AUDIO TAPES

☐ **"Has the NEA Become Politicized? What Affect Has It Had on Education?"** From a — $7.00 post paid
Symposium on Education, St. Paul, Fall 86. Excellent summary of Dr. Blumenfeld's exposé of
NEA and update on his book *NEA Trojan Horse in American Education* One tape, 60 minutes.

☐ **Blumenfeld's Major Speech on Education in America — Chattanooga, 1985.** Two tapes, — $12.00 post paid
2 hours. Tells it all!

☐ **NEA Trojan Horse in American Education:** entire book on *eight* audio tapes. Approx. 670 — $40.00 post paid
minutes *every word of the book,* including footnotes, on tape.

OTHER HELPFUL MATERIALS

☐ **"The Victims of Dick & Jane,"** 22 pages, 3 X 5 size. Explains how the literacy problem
occurred. Excellent for convincing a doubtful friend. You may want a quantity to give
away. One: $0.50; Four: $2.00; 100: $35.00; 1,000: $300.00 post paid.

☛ ☐ **Free Information Packet.** Send me complimentary information on the many other education ——*No Charge*
resources Sam offers for concerned parents and taxpayers.

These materials may be ordered by simply filling out the form below and returning to: The Paradigm Co.,
Box 45161, Boise, ID 83711.

Mailing Address (Please Print)

FOR FASTER SERVICE...MASTERCARD OR VISA HOLDERS
CALL (208) 322-4440
24 HOURS — 7 DAYS

Name _____

Street _____

City _____ State _____ Zip _____

Phone No. _____

ORDER NOW!

Checks may be made payable to
The Paradigm Co.
P.O. Box 45161— Boise, Idaho 83711

Enclosed is my check for $_____
Charge my: VISA ☐   Master Card ☐
Credit Card Number (all digits)

Signature _____ Exp. Date _____